CREATIVE HOMEOWNER PRESS®

MASONRY

CONCRETE ▪ BRICK ▪ STONE

CREATIVE HOMEOWNER PRESS®, Upper Saddle River, New Jersey

Editorial Director: Timothy O. Bakke
Art Director: Annie Jeon

Author: Christine Beall
Editors: David Schiff, Alexander Samuelson
Contributing Editor: Laura Tringali
Copy Editor: Candace Levy, Ph. D.
Editorial Assistant: Georgette Blau

Graphic Designer: Fernando Colon Jr.
Illustrators: Ron Carboni, Craig Franklin

Cover Design: Peter Mills
Photo Researcher: Alexander Samuelson

Manufactured in the United States of America
Electronic Prepress: TBC Color Imaging, Inc.
Printed at: Webcrafters, Inc.

Current Printing (last digit)
10 9 8 7 6 5 4 3 2

Masonry: Concrete, Brick, Stone
Library of Congress Catalog Card Number: 96-084686
ISBN: 1-880029-86-3

CREATIVE HOMEOWNER PRESS®
A Division of Federal Marketing Corp.
24 Park Way, Upper Saddle River, NJ 07458

Photo Credits

p.6: H. Armstrong Roberts
p.11: Elizabeth Whiting Associates
p.12 (top): Portland Cement Association
p.12 (bot l): H. Armstrong Roberts
p.12 (bot r): Phillip H. Ennis
p.13 (top): Phillip H. Ennis
p.13 (bot l): Camerique/H. Armstrong Roberts
p.13 (bot r): Camerique/H. Armstrong Roberts
p.14 (bot): Camerique/H. Armstrong Roberts
p.15 (top): Portland Cement Association
p.15 (bot): Portland Cement Association
p.16 (top): Portland Cement Association
p.69: Keystone Retaining Wall Systems
p.70 (top l): Elizabeth Whiting Associates
p.70 (top r): Creative Homeowner Press
p.70 (bot l): Nancy Hill
p.70 (bot m): Brick Institute of America
p.70 (bot r): Camerique/H. Armstrong Roberts
p.71 (top l): Melabee M Miller
p.71 (top r): Elizabeth Whiting Associates
p.71 (bot): Melabee M Miller
p.72 (top l): Bill Rothschild
p.72 (top r): Keystone Retaining Wall Systems
p.73 (top): Nancy Wolff/Omni-Photo Communications
p.73 (mid l): Jack Parsons/Omni-Photo Communications
p.73 (mid r): Tom Stillo/Omni-Photo Communications
p.73 (bot): Jack Parsons/Omni-Photo Communications
p.141: Melabee M Miller
p.142 (top): John Schwartz
p.142 (bot l): Terry Wild Studio
p.142 (bot r): Melabee M Miller
p.144 (bot): Terry Wild Studio

SAFETY FIRST

Though all the designs and methods in this book have been tested for safety, it is not possible to overstate the importance of using the safest construction methods possible. What follows are reminders; some do's and don'ts of basic carpentry. They are not substitutes for your own common sense.

- *Always* use caution, care, and good judgment when following the procedures described in this book.

- *Always* be sure that the electrical setup is safe; be sure that no circuit is overloaded, and that all power tools and electrical outlets are properly grounded. Do not use power tools in wet locations.

- *Always* read container labels on paints, solvents, and other products; provide ventilation, and observe all other warnings.

- *Always* read the tool manufacturer's instructions for using a tool, especially the warnings.

- *Always* use holders or pushers to work pieces shorter than 3 inches on a table saw or jointer. Avoid working short pieces if you can.

- *Always* remove the key from any drill chuck (portable or press) before starting the drill.

- *Always* pay deliberate attention to how a tool works so that you can avoid being injured.

- *Always* know the limitations of your tools. Do not try to force them to do what they were not designed to do.

- *Always* make sure that any adjustment is locked before proceeding. For example, always check the rip fence on a table saw or the bevel adjustment on a portable saw before starting to work.

- *Always* clamp small pieces firmly to a bench or another work surface when sawing or drilling.

- *Always* wear the appropriate rubber or work gloves when handling chemicals, doing heavy construction, or sanding.

- *Always* wear a disposable mask when working around odors, dust, or mist. Use a special respirator when working with toxic substances.

- *Always* wear eye protection, especially when using power tools or striking metal on metal or concrete; a chip can fly off, for example, when chiseling concrete.

- *Always* be aware that there is seldom enough time for your body's reflexes to save you from injury from a power tool in a dangerous situation; everything happens too fast. Be *alert!*

- *Always* keep your hands away from the business ends of blades, cutters, and bits.

- *Always* hold a portable circular saw with both hands so that you will know where your hands are.

- *Always* use a drill with an auxiliary handle to control the torque when large-size bits are used.

- *Always* check your local building codes when planning new construction. The codes are intended to protect public safety and should be observed to the letter.

- *Never* work with power tools when you are tired or under the influence of alcohol or drugs.

- *Never* cut very small pieces of wood or pipe. Whenever possible, cut small pieces off larger pieces.

- *Never* change a blade or a bit unless the power cord is unplugged. Do not depend on the switch being off; you might accidentally hit it.

- *Never* work in insufficient lighting.

- *Never* work while wearing loose clothing, hanging hair, open cuffs, or jewelry.

- *Never* work with dull tools. Have them sharpened, or learn how to sharpen them yourself.

- *Never* use a power tool on a workpiece that is not firmly supported or clamped.

- *Never* saw a workpiece that spans a large distance between horses without close support on either side of the kerf; the piece can bend, closing the kerf and jamming the blade, causing saw kickback.

- *Never* support a workpiece with your leg or other part of your body when sawing.

- *Never* carry sharp or pointed tools, such as utility knives, awls, or chisels, in your pocket. If you want to carry tools, use a special-purpose tool belt with leather pockets and holders.

C O N T E N T S

How to Use this Book

Brick and stone are among the oldest building materials known to mankind. They are ruggedly beautiful and strong. Concrete offers versatility of form and finish combined with tremendous longevity.

This book will teach you how to work with these materials—even if you have no experience. The step-by-step instructions and techniques are designed to guide you through the planning, estimating, preparation, and construction phases for each project. The work may be slow at first, but as you gain experience you will be able to work faster and more efficiently. A final section on maintenance and repair will tell you how to keep your existing projects in good condition.

Masonry Tools

You'll find that many of the same masonry tools are needed for working with concrete, brick, and stone. Many of these items are easily rented, so check before you buy a tool you may not use often. Many hand tools are available in a range of quality and corresponding price. When you buy, consider how often you will use the tool—no sense buying a top-notch trowel you'll use only once or twice.

Excavating and Groundwork Tools

Most masonry projects start by preparing the ground. This usually involves removing earth from the site. You'll need a spade and a flat shovel for excavating. You may want to rent a small front-end loader to excavate large sites, but be careful when using heavy machinery. It may be better to hire a contractor to do this work. Rakes, hoes, and a hand tamper prepare the

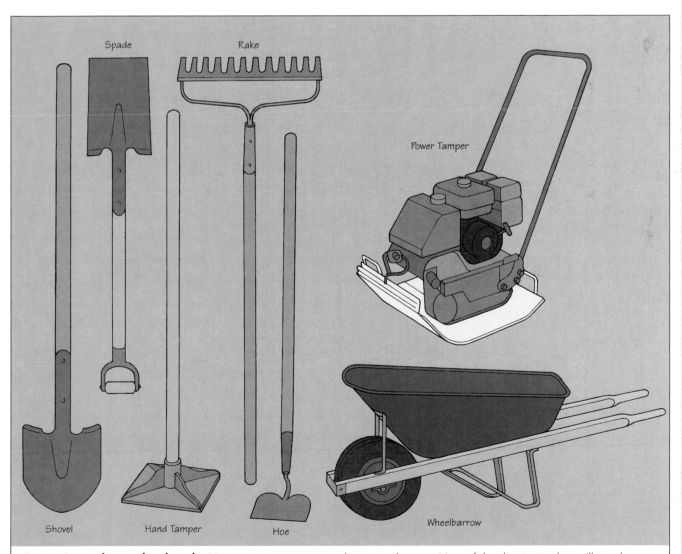

Spade   Rake   Power Tamper

Shovel   Hand Tamper   Hoe   Wheelbarrow

Excavating and groundwork tools. Most masonry projects involve some digging. Most of the digging tools you'll need you may already own. One specialized tool is the tamper, which is used to compact and level the ground and subbase for paving projects.

ground for a masonry project by leveling and compacting it. A rented mechanical tamper makes the work a lot easier and quicker than a hand tamper. Any kind of masonry work will require a wheelbarrow. Masonry loads are heavy, so be sure to buy or rent a heavy-duty wheelbarrow; one with a large capacity and an inflatable rubber tire.

Measuring, Leveling, and Formwork Tools

All construction is an exercise in precision. It is essential that a project be correctly located, measured, leveled, and plumbed. Tools that assist in measuring masonry projects are a 48-inch level, a line level for long spans, a folding rule for brick and block projects, and a 25-foot tape measure. A framing square is needed to check for square in corners. Layout lines are marked with a chalkline. A plumb bob is used for checking that something is plumb or for marking a point directly under another point. Once marked, mason's twine is strung as a guide line to help you keep a structure straight and level, and plumb. Line blocks are used to keep the twine in place.

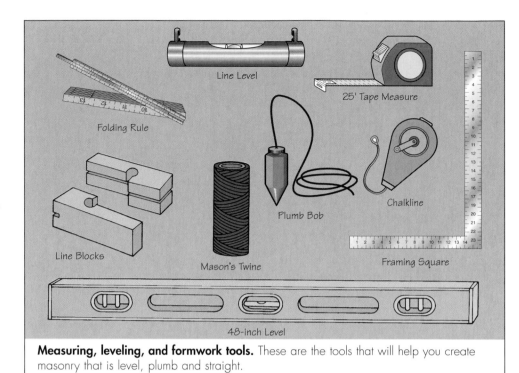

Measuring, leveling, and formwork tools. These are the tools that will help you create masonry that is level, plumb and straight.

Tools for Working with Concrete

These tools are needed for the mixing, placing, and finishing of concrete. You'll need a mason's hoe for mixing and moving concrete. This tool is just like a gardener's hoe except that there are two holes in the blade which help in the mixing of masonry materials.

A mortar box is helpful to mix and hold small amounts of mortar. Concrete is worked smooth with a bull float or darby. Surface-finishing tools include a small pointed trowel to separate concrete from the forms, a wood or magnesium float to apply a smooth finish, and a steel finishing

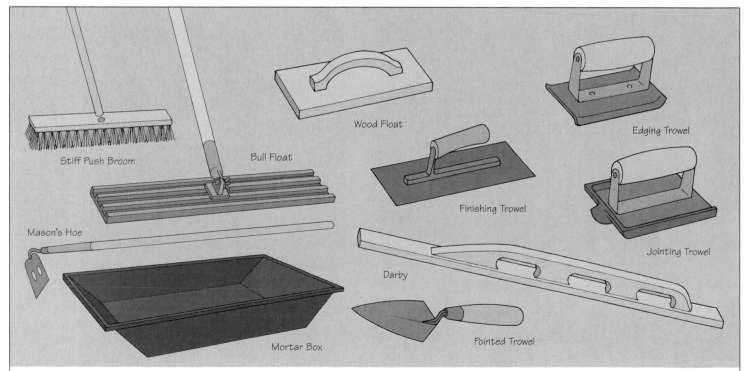

Tools for working with concrete. Building with concrete is mostly a matter of mixing, shaping and creating a surface with the proper texture. Here are the tools you'll need for most jobs.

trowel for a final pass on a concrete surface. An edging trowel creates a rounded edge that is safe and durable. A jointing or grooving trowel with a center blade is used to form control joints. A push broom is required for creating slip-resistant and special finish surfaces.

Tools for Working with Brick and Block

There are a number of specialized tools needed to work with mortar and bricks. A mortar box and mason's hoe (the same tools used for concrete projects) are used for mixing and holding the mortar that binds the bricks together. A hawk (or mortar board) is a flat wood or metal foot-square surface that holds a bit of mortar when laying bricks. A hawk decreases trips to the mortar pile when you're working on a project. A brick hammer is helpful, as it has a curved point that can chip and split bricks. A brickset is a hardened-steel tool that easily splits and cuts bricks and blocks. You need a mason's trowel for spreading mortar. Jointing tools (jointers) are simply metal rods attached to a handle that are shaped to create various mortar joints. Examples are a round jointer or a square jointer. Be sure to have a mason's brush to clean excess mortar off a surface. A mason's brush is just like a dust brush. Brick-carrying tongs are large clamps that hold from 6 to 10 bricks. After a few loads, you'll be glad you bought one of these. You will also need a story pole to measure the correct height for vertical courses. You can make a story pole with a piece of scrap lumber marked in increments equal to the masonry units you're working with. For example, a story pole for standard brick construction is marked every 8 inches to delineate three courses of bricks plus their mortar joints.

Tools for Working with Stone

For stonework, you will need a brick hammer, which has a long curved point for splitting and shaping stones. A small sledge hammer (sometimes

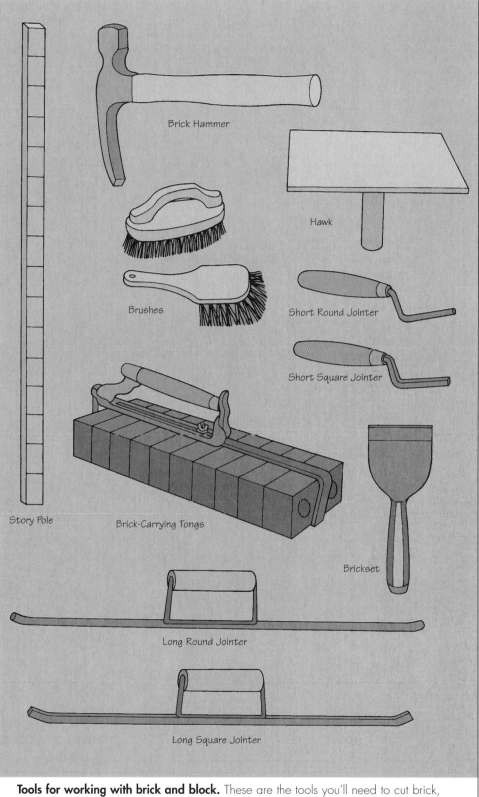

Tools for working with brick and block. These are the tools you'll need to cut brick, build a brick wall that is straight and level and create neat mortar joints.

called a hand drilling hammer) is heavy and is made of steel specifically designed for hitting other metal tools. A rubber mallet is used to seat stones in sand or soil. A point chisel and a pitching chisel shape

stone. Both chisels are made of steel that will not chip when struck with a hammer. A point chisel is slender and is used for precise chipping; a pitching chisel is broad to split stones. If the stone structure

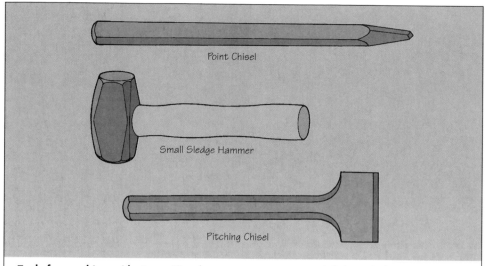

Tools for working with stone. Good stonemasonry requires skill, knowledge and experience, but the techniques are simple and basic. Likewise the tools required are simple, basic, and few.

is held with mortar, you'll need the mortar tools used for brick and block construction.

General Tools and Materials

These are tools you probably already own. To help in masonry construction and to build formwork you need a claw

hammer and a circular saw with a masonry blade for cutting block and for cutting joints in concrete and a carbide blade for cutting wood. (You can cut wood with a crosscut saw if you

don't own a circular saw.) Formwork is held together by either double-headed nails (also called duplex nails), 2-inch drywall screws or common nails. You'll also need a heavy-duty extension cord and carpenter's pencils.

Masonry Safety

Concrete and mortar are caustic and will burn the skin after prolonged contact. Wear sturdy work gloves and clothing with long sleeves to protect your hands and arms when working with mortar. Wear rubber boots when placing and handling concrete, because you may have to stand in the wet mix to spread the fresh concrete. To protect your eyes from cement dust and from splattered mortar or concrete, wear safety glasses or goggles. Since masonry involves heavy lifting, be careful to avoid back strain and injury. Always bend your knees, keep your back straight, and lift with your legs.

General tools and materials. Here are three kinds of fasteners commonly used in masonry work.

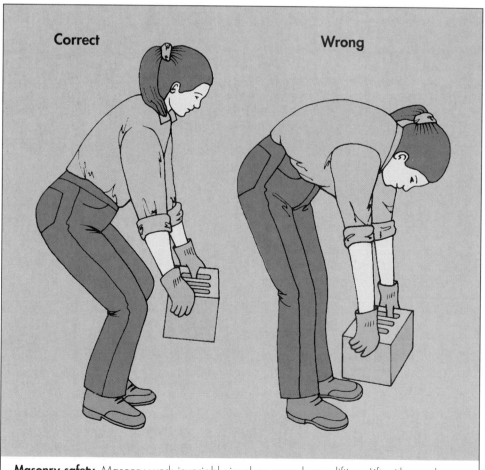

Masonry safety. Masonry work invariably involves some heavy lifting. Lift with your legs, not your back.

Concrete

Concrete is extremely durable and strong. Yet, since it is worked in a liquid form, it can take on virtually any shape. This combination of qualities is the reason why concrete is such a popular outdoor building material. Whether it takes the form of a wide, sweeping driveway into a modern house, a semi-circular drive in front of a stately suburban home, or a modest front stoop, concrete lends substance and permanence to the places we live.

In the form of walks and driveways, concrete leads the way to our homes, providing a safe, comfortable pathway to the door.

In addition to serving our everyday needs for outdoor steps, driveways, and sidewalks, concrete is part of leisure time too, providing the perfect surface for a backyard patio.

Concrete Techniques

Concrete Ingredients

Fresh concrete is a semifluid mixture of portland cement, sand (fine aggregate), gravel or crushed stone (coarse aggregate), and water. As the cement particles chemically react with water, in a process called *hydration*, the concrete hardens into a durable material. When properly mixed, poured, and cured, concrete creates strong structures that will weather the extremes of summer heat and winter cold with little maintenance. The materials used to create the concrete affect how easily it can be poured and finished, how fast it will gain strength, how strong it will be, and how well it will perform in service.

In addition to the ingredients of the concrete mix itself, formwork and steel reinforcement are needed to build concrete structures. Formwork is generally made from wood and may be a simple square or a complex shape, depending on the nature of the project. Reinforcing steel is either heavy or light, depending on size and strength requirements. Concrete is poured into the forms and then the surface is worked smooth and finished in one of a variety of textures.

Portland Cement

Cement is not the same as concrete; cement is one of the ingredients used in concrete. Since the beginning of its use, in the early 1800s, portland cement has become the most widely used cement in the world. Because the cured concrete is the same color as a gray limestone quarried near Portland, England, the term *portland cement* was adopted by the inventor. Portland cement is a mixture of burned lime, iron, silica, and alumina. Typical sources of these materials are clay, limestone, shale, and iron ore. This mixture is put through a kiln and then ground into a fine powder and packaged for sale.

There are five types of portland cement, each with different physical and chemical characteristics.

- Type I is a general-purpose cement that is by far the most commonly used, especially in residential work. This is the type of cement you should use, unless your project has special requirements that would benefit from the characteristics of one of the other types of portland cement.

- Type II cement has moderate resistance to sulfates, which are found in some soils and ground water. If you're not sure about the soil in your area, ask your supplier if local builders typically use this cement.

- Type III cement is a high early-strength cement. This means that it gains strength more quickly than other types, not that it develops greater strength. A cement with a short strength development time can be helpful for winter construction, because fresh concrete must be protected from freezing during the initial strength development stage. If you have to build during the cold winter months, consider Type III cement.

- Type IV cement produces less heat during hydration than other types and is used only in massive structures such as dams and highway pilings. It's not appropriate for residential construction.

- Type V cement has a high resistance to sulfates. This type of cement is usually available only in areas where it is likely to be needed, for example, in the southwestern U.S. Ask your supplier if local builders generally use Type V cement.

Portland cement comes in gray, white, and buff. The white and buff cements are more expensive. Pigments and surface stains can be used to color concrete made with gray or white cement, but they too will add to the overall cost of the project.

Most building centers sell portland cement. Each bag contains about 1 cubic foot of cement and weighs 94 pounds. Don't let the bags get wet during storage—the cement will react with water and harden, making it unusable. Bags of cement must be stored up off the ground; otherwise they can absorb moisture. They also should not be stored on a concrete floor as they can absorb moisture through the concrete. Stack them on wooden skids; then cover the bags with plastic.

Air-Entrained Cement

Type I, II, and III cements are available with an additive that produces evenly distributed microscopic air bubbles in the mix. When manufactured in this way, the cement is said to be "air-entrained," and the letter *A* is appended to the type number (e.g., Type IA). The air bubbles permit enough space for water absorbed by the cured concrete to expand when frozen, keeping the concrete from cracking. Air-entrainment improves the durability of concrete that is exposed to freeze-thaw cycles and to de-icing salts. Be aware that hand mixing is ineffective for air-entrained concrete; you must use a power mixer. If you need air-entrained concrete, use either an air-entrained cement, or use regular cement with an air-entraining admixture.

Aggregates

Cement and water form the paste that binds together gravel or crushed stone (coarse aggregate) and sand (fine aggregate). Since these aggregates are much cheaper than cement, they act as an inexpensive filler to make concrete a practical and economical building material. Aggregates also help reduce shrinkage of concrete.

Coarse aggregate is sold by the cubic foot or cubic yard and can be purchased directly from an aggregate

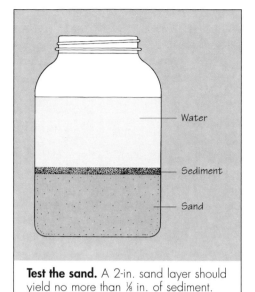

Test the sand. A 2-in. sand layer should yield no more than ⅛ in. of sediment.

company. The mix should include particle sizes ranging from ¼ to 1 inch in diameter—the smaller aggregate particles fill in the spaces between the larger ones. Do not use aggregate that is larger than one-quarter of the concrete's thickness.

The sand particles used as fine aggregate in concrete must measure less than ¼ inch in diameter to fill in the spaces between the pieces of coarse aggregate. Concrete sand should not be the sharp type found in sand made from crushed rock. Instead use "bank-run" sand. The naturally rounded shape of bank-run sand makes the concrete easier to work with and slab surfaces easier to finish. Never use mason's sand or beach sand. You can purchase small amounts of concrete sand at a home

center; get larger amounts from an aggregate supplier.

Test the sand. Although sand is sometimes contaminated with silt, clay, and other materials that can weaken the concrete, most contaminants can be washed away. To test your sand, put about 2 inches of it in a quart jar. Add water until the jar is three-quarters full, shake for one minute; then let the jar stand for one hour. If more than ⅛ inch of sediment settles on top of the sand, clean the sand the day before using by drenching it with water from a garden hose.

Water

The final ingredient in concrete is water, which must be free of foreign materials and impurities. A rule of thumb is to use only water that is fit to drink.

Whether you mix your own or have your concrete delivered to the site, the amount of water used in a concrete mix affects the ultimate strength the concrete will develop. You want a consistency that makes the concrete easy to pour, move around in the forms, consolidate, and finish. Up to a point, a mix with more water is easier to work with than one having less water. But too much water will cause the ingredients to separate during pouring and handling, ruining the concrete. Too much water also lowers strength, increases the porosity and permeability of the cured concrete, and makes the concrete more prone to shrinkage and cracking. The trick is to use enough water to make the concrete workable, but not so much that it creates a weak or porous material. In most instances, professional masons use 4 to 5 gallons of water per bag of cement, depending on the dampness of the sand.

Estimating Concrete Amounts

Before beginning any work involving concrete, you must determine how much you will need. The amount needed dictates whether you should buy bags of prepackaged materials,

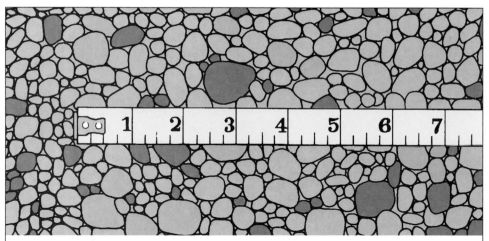

Aggregates. The aggregate in concrete ranges in size from ¼ to 1 in. in diameter. Do not use aggregate larger than one-quarter the thickness of the concrete.

mix your own concrete by hand or machine, or have ready-mix concrete delivered to your site. The estimate of the amount of concrete required is based on the dimensions of a rough layout of the project. You'll do an accurate layout and build the concrete forms later. To allow for slight irregularities in concrete thickness and for some waste, always round up to the next whole or half cubic yard measure, allowing a minimum of 5 to 10 percent extra.

Volume of a Rectangle

For square or rectangular shapes, find the volume by multiplying the width in feet times the length in feet times the height in inches (WxLxH). Divide the final number by 12 to get cubic feet. The figure determined by this calculation is rounded up to the nearest whole number (e.g., 52.7 becomes 53). Then divide this number by 27 to convert to cubic yards (ready-mix suppliers will ask for cubic yard amounts). Don't forget to add 10 percent extra.

Volume of a Cylinder

Although we may think of a rounded driveway or patio as circular, it's really a shallow cylinder because the concrete slab has depth. Note that you would also use this method for estimating the amount of concrete needed for post settings. To find the volume of a cylinder, multiply the square

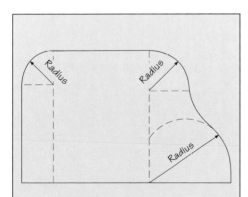

Volume of irregular shapes. To determine the volume of an irregular shape, break it down into rectangles and portions of circles. Then calculate the volumes of each section. Add the volumes together to obtain the total amount of concrete needed.

of the radius in feet times pi (3.14) times the height in inches (R^2x3.14xH). Divide the final number by 12 to get cubic feet. Round the result up to the next whole number and divide by 27 to yield cubic yards.

Volume of Irregular Shapes

Break the irregular shape into rectangles and portions of circles. Using the formulas given earlier, determine the volume of each section in cubic feet. Add the volumes together and divide by 27 to get the total number of cubic yards of concrete needed for your project.

An example driveway. As an example, consider a driveway that leads to a circular turnaround before the garage. The slabs are all 5 inches thick except the driveway apron, which is 7 inches thick.

Start by figuring out the volume of the turnaround. The turnaround is basically a cylinder, so the correct formula is r^2 x 3.14 x H.

$18^2 = 324$
$324 \times 3.14 = 1017$
$1017 \times 5 = 5085$
$5085 \div 12 = 423.7$
$424 \div 27 = 15.7$

The turnaround needs 16 cubic yards of concrete.

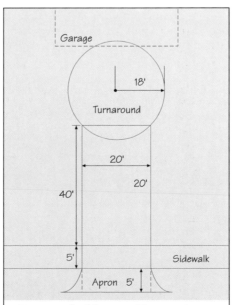

An example driveway. The sample driveway is broken into distinct areas to calculate volume of concrete needed.

The driveway and sidewalk section can be treated as one large rectangle. Use the volume formula given earlier for rectangles (WxLxH).

$20 \times 45 = 900$
$900 \times 5 = 4500$
$4500 \div 12 = 375$
$375 \div 27 = 13.8$

The driveway and sidewalk section needs 14 cubic yards of concrete.

Now calculate the volume of the apron, which can be done by treating the center as a 5-by-20-foot rectangle and the two triangular portions as a single square with 5-foot sides. Remember that the apron is to be 7 inches thick.

Apron rectangle

$20 \times 5 = 100$
$100 \times 7 = 700$
$700 \div 12 = 58.3$
$58 \div 27 = 2.1$

Triangular sections

$5 \times 5 = 25$
$25 \times 7 = 175$
$175 \div 12 = 14.6$
$15 \div 27 = 0.5$

Total apron

$2.1 + 0.5 = 2.6$

The apron needs 3 cubic yards of concrete.

Finally, determine the total cubic yardage of concrete needed for the entire driveway by adding the totals for the parts.

$16 + 14 + 3 = 33$

This project needs about 33 cubic yards of concrete, but order 35 cubic yards instead.

Estimating how much concrete you need for steps may seem difficult, but it's really just a matter of breaking the structure into rectangular parts, calculating the volume of the parts, and then adding up the volumes.

Although the calculations outlined earlier are not difficult, use the chart "How Much Concrete Do You Need?" on page 20, to quickly estimate the volume of concrete needed for your project. To use the chart, first calculate the area of the project in square feet. Use the formulas given above for rectangles and cylinders but do not multiply by the height nor divide anything. Then, locate the square footage at the top of the chart, follow the chart down to the appropriate slab height, then look left for cubic feet or right for cubic yards of concrete needed. If the area of the slab is larger than 300 square feet, first find the volume for 300 square feet, then find the volume for the remainder of the square footage, and add the two volumes together.

Mixing Concrete

Whether you mix it yourself or have it delivered, the cement, sand, coarse aggregate, and water must be present in the correct proportions. The concrete must be workable when it is fresh and strong and durable when it is hardened. The quality of the ingredients, the proportions in which they are mixed, and the mixing method all affect these properties.

Proportions of Ingredients

The amounts of the various ingredients are dictated by the quantity of

How Much Concrete Do You Need?

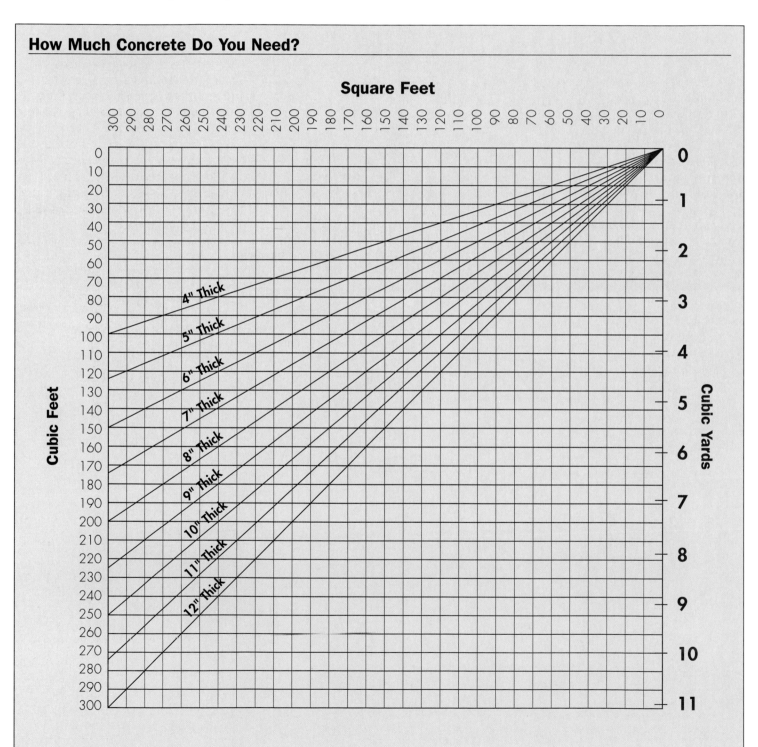

Concrete Proportions by Volume

Maximum Size Coarse Aggregate, Inches	Air-Entrained Concrete				Concrete without Air			
	Cubic Feet of or Number of Buckets of				Cubic Feet of or Number of Buckets of			
	Cement	Sand*	Coarse Aggregates	Water	Cement	Sand*	Coarse Aggregates	Water
⅜	1	2¼	1½	½	1	2½	1½	½
½	1	2¼	2	½	1	2½	2	½
¾	1	2¼	2½	½	1	2½	2½	½
1	1	2¼	2¾	½	1	2½	2¾	½
1½	1	2¼	3	½	1	2½	3	½

Note: 7.48 gallons of water equals one cubic foot. One bag of portland cement equals one cubic foot.
* "wet" sand sold for most construction use.
The combined volume is approximately ⅔ the sum of the original bulk volumes.

concrete needed. Use the table "Concrete Proportions by Volume" above to determine the proportions of cement, sand, gravel, and water required. For estimating purposes, you can make about 1 cubic yard of concrete with five 94-pound bags of cement, 14 cubic feet of sand, and 21 cubic feet of gravel. (It takes about forty 80-pound bags of prepackaged materials to make 1 cubic yard of concrete.)

Note that the volume of the combined ingredients is about one-third less than the sum of the volumes of the individual ingredients. For example, if you use 1 cubic foot of cement, 2¼ cubic feet of sand, 1½ cubic feet of gravel or crushed stone, and ½ cubic foot of water, you get a combined total volume of 5¼ cubic feet. But the mix will actually produce 3½ cubic feet of concrete (or two-thirds of the combined total).

If you do not need this much concrete or you want to work with smaller batches, use the same proportions, but with smaller quantities, substituting buckets for cubic feet. (For the mix proportions given previously, you'd use 1 bucket of cement, 2¼ buckets of sand, 1½ buckets of gravel and ½ bucket of water.) For any batch size, the most important thing is to keep the proportions of the ingredients the same. You can double or triple the batch size simply by doubling or tripling the number of buckets of each ingredient you add to the mix.

Ready-mix concrete. Small quantities of concrete can be mixed at the project site, but for quantities of 1 cubic yard or more (the minimum sold by most suppliers), it is most convenient to order ready-mix delivered to your site. The cost will vary according to the distance the concrete must be hauled, the size of the order, the day of delivery (weekday or weekend), the unloading time, and the type of mix. Ready-mix can be ordered infused with polypropylene fibers for reinforcement. This reinforcement helps reduce shrinkage cracking. Be aware that fiber-infused concrete is not a substitute for rebar or steel mesh applications (see "Steel Reinforcement," on page 26).

If the project is accessible, the wet concrete can be poured directly into your forms from the truck, saving hours of back-breaking labor. If the truck can't get to within about 20 feet of the forms, the concrete can be pumped from the truck through a hose, but this method usually costs extra. A cheaper but more difficult method is to cart the concrete to the forms using a few wheelbarrows and some strong backs.

Recommended Concrete Mixes

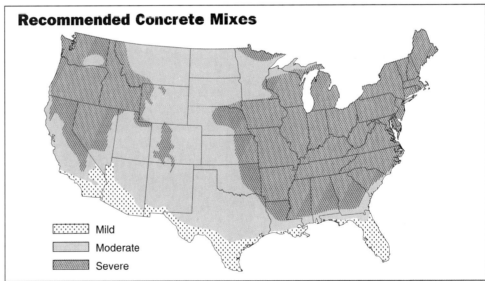

Mild
Moderate
Severe

Element	Exposure Condition (map)	Minimum Compressive Strength, psi	Normal Maximum Coarse Aggregate Size, inches	Minimum Cement Content, lb./cu. yd. of concrete	Slump, in.
Foundations, basement walls, and slabs not exposed to weather	Severe	2500*	1	564	5-7
	Moderate				
	Mild			520	
Foundations, basement walls, exterior walls & other concrete work exposed to weather	Severe	3000*	1	564	5-7
	Moderate	3000			
	Mild	2500		520	
Driveways, garage floors, walks, porches, patios & stairs exposed to weather	Severe	3500*	1	564	4-6
	Moderate	3000*			
	Mild	2500		520	

* Use air-entrained concrete for exterior construction.
Note: All of Canada is in the severe region.

When ordering ready-mixed concrete, you will have to provide the supplier with some other information in addition to the volume of concrete needed. Use the table "Recommended Concrete Mixes," on page 21, to determine the recommended compressive strength, minimum cement content, maximum aggregate size, and slump needed for various types of projects and climates. Give this information to the supplier when you place your order. (See also "Measuring Slump.") Your ready-mix supplier will have standard mixes suited to residential work or to specific projects such as driveways.

Mixing Concrete On Site

If you need less than 1 cubic yard of concrete or if ready-mix delivery is not available, you can mix your own concrete on site either by hand or with a power mixer. When mixing concrete by any method, make sure to protect yourself by wearing long sleeves, long pants, and heavy waterproof gloves. If concrete accidentally spatters on your skin, wash it off immediately, as it causes burning irritation.

Prepackaged concrete mixes. For very small projects, such as setting a mailbox post or doing repairs, you may want to purchase a packaged concrete mix. Such a mix combines cement, sand, and gravel in the correct proportions and requires only the addition of water to create fresh concrete. The most commonly available sizes are 40-, 60-, and 80-pound bags. The 40-pound bag makes about ⅓ cubic foot of concrete. A 60-pound bag makes about ½ cubic foot, and an 80-pound bag about ⅔ cubic foot. While convenient, prepackaged mixes are too expensive to use for all but the smallest projects. If you use pre-mixed bags, you can pick them up yourself from the supplier or spend a little extra and have them delivered. If you pick them up yourself, make sure none of the bags has already hardened. However you get the concrete to your house, be sure to store it up off the ground (such as on a pallet) in a dry location. If the bags are stored outdoors, cover them with plastic

Measuring Slump

It's easiest to gauge the amount of water in a concrete mix by measuring "slump." To do this you need a special mold called a slump cone—you should be able to buy one from a building supply yard. Perform the test on a nonabsorbent surface such as a scrap of sheet metal or a sheet of plywood that has been sprayed with water.

Place the concrete into the cone in three layers while standing on the cone projections. Tamp each layer with a metal rod 25 times to completely consolidate the concrete and to eliminate any air pockets. When the cone is full, scrape off any excess concrete, leaving a level top. Then remove the cone by lifting upward and measure the amount of settlement (slump) with a rod and ruler.

The wetter the mix, the higher the slump measurement; the drier the mix, the lower the slump measurement. For residential concrete, a 5- to 7-inch slump is recommended to ensure the proper ratio of water to cement. Slump tests can also be used to check that your batches are consistent.

Slump Cone

sheeting or a waterproof tarp. If you live in a humid climate, buy the concrete no more than one or two days before you intend to use it.

Mixing concrete by hand. If your project uses air-entrained concrete or an air-entraining admixture, you cannot hand mix the concrete, because you won't be able to stir vigorously enough to produce the proper air entrainment. Hand-mixing concrete involves using a square-point shovel or a mason's hoe to combine the ingredients. Hand-mixing is hard work. While you can mix the ingredients in a wheelbarrow, it's usually easier to mix them on a clean, flat surface, such as an old sheet of plywood, or in a mortar box (also called a concrete barge).

Test water content. Note that the sand used to make the concrete should be wet, but not too wet. Proper sand will hold a ball shape without wetting your hand. Very wet sand will make a ball and "leak" water, while dry sand crumbles and will not hold a shape. If the sand is too dry, wet it thoroughly with a garden hose the day

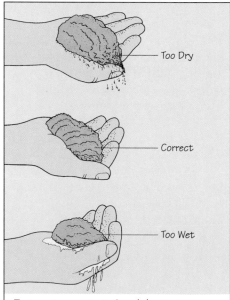

Too Dry

Correct

Too Wet

Test water content. Sand that is too dry will not hold a ball shape (top). Sand with the correct amount of water holds its shape without "leaking" (middle). If water runs out of the sand, it is too wet (bottom).

before beginning work. Always cover your sand pile with a sheet of plastic when you're not working, to prevent the sand from drying out.

Here's how to mix concrete ingredients by hand:

1 Measure the ingredients. For mixing purposes, you can measure proportions by the bucket, by the shovelful, or with a measuring box, like the one shown in the illustration. A measuring box is built to hold exactly 1 cubic foot of dry ingredients, as opposed to a concrete barge, mortar box, or other container in which wet and dry ingredients are combined. Use the same amount of each ingredient for each batch. Careful measuring ensures correct proportions. Place the materials in layers on top of each other, beginning with the gravel, then the sand, and finally the cement.

2 Mix the dry ingredients. If you're working on a flat surface or mixing the ingredients in a wheelbarrow, use a mason's hoe to combine the dry ingredients thoroughly before adding the water. When using a mortar box, you can either premix the dry ingredients or mix them together as you add the water.

3 Add the water. Whether you use a premix bag or a combination of separate ingredients, the water used to make the concrete must be clean enough to drink. Start with a gallon of water and keep track of the amount you use so that you can add the same amount to subsequent batches. Make sure to mix all ingredients thoroughly, scraping any unmixed cement and aggregates from the sides and bottom of the box or pile. The concrete mix should be an even color and have the same consistency throughout.

If mixing on a flat surface, make a shallow depression in the center of the dry mix with your hoe; then pour in a little water. Mix thoroughly by pulling dry material from the edges into the depression. If using a mortar box, place the dry materials so they fill about two-thirds of the box (from one end), leaving the rest of the box empty (on the side nearest the forms). Add water to the empty end, then pull the dry materials into the water, mixing them together as you go. Continue adding water in small amounts while turning over the mix until it reaches the proper consistency: not crumbly, not sloppy.

4 Test the mix. You can tell if the concrete has too little or too much water by using the blade of your hoe or shovel to make ridges in the concrete. If the mix is too dry, you won't be able to make distinct ridges; if the mix is too soupy, the ridges won't hold their shape (you'll also notice water seeping out around the edges of the pile). In a proper mix, the ridges will hold most of their shape.

Using a power mixer. If you don't want to mix your concrete by hand, you can rent a small concrete mixer with a capacity ranging from ½ to 6 cubic feet. Electric mixers are quieter and simpler to operate than gasoline-powered mixers, but you must have access to an electrical outlet. If an extension cord is required, make sure the wire gauge is heavy enough to handle the ampere draw of the motor. The size of the concrete batch is usually only about 60 percent of the total capacity of the mixer to allow room for proper mixing without spilling. Never load a mixer beyond its maximum batch size.

1 A measuring box holds exactly 1 cu. ft. of dry ingredients. Use it to proportion the ingredients.

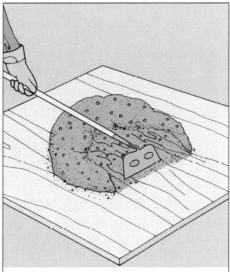

2 Use a mason's hoe to thoroughly mix the dry ingredients.

3 Make a depression in the middle of the dry ingredients. Add water slowly and pull the dry mix into the water. Continue to add water until the mix reaches proper consistency.

4 In a proper mix, ridges made with a mason's hoe will hold their shape.

Using a power mixer. Electric (top) and gasoline powered (bottom) mixers are available from rental equipment dealers. Power mixers speed up a concrete job.

As previously stated, be sure to use the correct proportions of concrete ingredients. For best results, follow this procedure: With the mixer stopped, add all the coarse aggregate and half the water. Start the mixer; then add the sand, cement, and remaining water. After all ingredients are in the drum, continue mixing for at least three minutes or until the ingredients are thoroughly mixed and the concrete has a uniform color.

Thoroughly clean the mixer as soon as you have finished using it. Place water and a few shovelsful of coarse aggregate into the drum while it is turning, to scour the inside of the mixer. Then dump out the water and gravel, and hose out the drum.

Making Square Corners

For most of the concrete projects in this book, including the driveway, stairs, and sidewalk, it is essential that the corners be square. You can easily check a project for square using the 3-4-5 layout method. Simply remember that if one side of a right triangle measures 3 feet and the other measures 4 feet, the hypotenuse must measure 5 feet. If any of these measurements are off, the corner is not a true right angle. The same rule holds true for multiples of these dimensions. A right triangle with sides measuring 6 and 8 feet will have a hypotenuse of 10 feet. Here's how to check for square corners.

1 **Rough out the dimensions.**
Use a tape measure to rough out the perimeter dimensions of the project. Drive in temporary stakes at each corner.

Erect batter boards at right angles to each other about 2 feet outside the rough corner locations of the concrete slab. These batter boards provide support for guide strings and a location to mark out key dimensions. The batter boards can be any scrap stock as long as they are about 2 feet long. Support each batter board with two short stakes. Use a line level to set the batter board crosspieces at the same height.

2 **String the lines.** Set up guide lines to outline the entire slab.

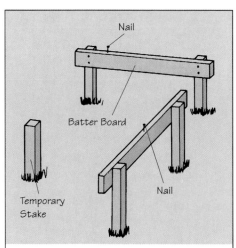

1 Drive in temporary stakes at the corners of the project and set up level batter boards.

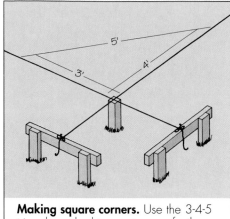

Making square corners. Use the 3-4-5 triangle method to create a perfectly square layout.

Check that the line is level and secure it to the batter boards. Use mason's twine for the guides, as it is specifically made to resist sagging.

Make right angles at each corner by using the 3-4-5 triangle method. Measure from point A on the first stake along the line 3 feet and mark point B. Run a second line perpendicular to the first across point A. Mark point C 4 feet from point A. Move line AC so that the distance BC is exactly 5 feet. Angle BAC is now a 90-degree angle.

With all four string lines in place, double-check squareness by measuring the diagonals between opposing corners. The measurements should be equal. If they are not, recheck your layout.

3 **Reposition the corner stakes.**
Accurately reposition the tempo-

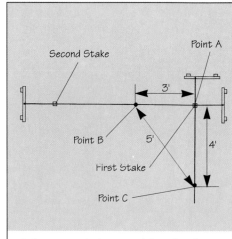

2 Set up guide lines to define the shape of the project. Test for square by using the 3-4-5 triangle method.

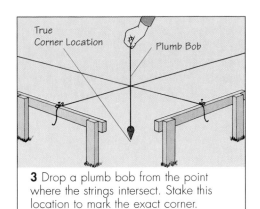

3 Drop a plumb bob from the point where the strings intersect. Stake this location to mark the exact corner.

rary corner stakes using a plumb bob to transfer the point of intersection to the ground.

Excavation

Concrete slabs must be supported on soil that is hard, uniformly graded, and well drained. A poorly or improperly prepared subgrade can cause uneven settlement and cracking. The excavation phase of a concrete project is labor intensive and, depending on the size of the layout, may be just plain impractical for a homeowner to consider doing. A 4-inch-thick concrete sidewalk, 5 feet wide and 25 feet long, supported by a 4-inch layer of gravel, requires an excavation of more than 3 cubic yards of dirt. This amount of excavation can be backbreaking—it hurts just to think about a driveway excavation. It is best to hire a contractor with heavy machinery to excavate large sites.

If the project is not too large, and you will do the excavation yourself,

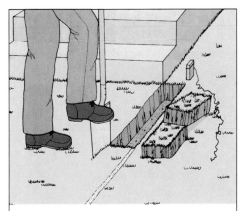

Excavation. Excavate to a depth that will accommodate the slab plus any base materials. Excavate about 8 to 10 in. wider than the layout lines to provide room for constructing the formwork.

first contact your utility company to inspect your site. They will mark any utility lines that you need to avoid. When you start excavation, begin by temporarily untying the layout strings and excavate 8 to 10 inches wider than the layout line to allow room for building the formwork. Remove all grass, sod, roots, and large rocks from the area. Dig out any soft or spongy areas and fill them with good soil or with gravel, crushed stone, or sand. Loosen and tamp hard spots to provide uniform support. Remove enough soil to accommodate the thickness of the slab and any base materials. If necessary, shape the surrounding grade to make sure that runoff drains around rather than over the slab.

Leave the subgrade undisturbed wherever possible as the natural soil will be better packed than any fill material you place and tamp. Smooth the loose surface soil with a rake, and fill in holes left by stones or roots with sand or gravel. Level the subgrade surface with the edge of a 2x4, and then compact the soil with a hand tamper. Large areas are best tamped with mechanical rollers or vibratory compactors.

Drainage problems. In areas with poor drainage, you must excavate deeply enough to place a 4-inch layer of gravel under the concrete and plan to finish the slab 2 to 3 inches above the adjacent ground. Your local building department can advise you on the depth of gravel bases typical for your region. The gravel is poured, leveled, and tamped into the formwork in layers. The type of gravel to use is called compactable because you can tamp it to form a well-drained, firm subbase. Crushed limestone, with stones sized ¾ inch or less, is ideal for this application; avoid smooth river-run, or pea gravel.

Formwork

The forms, or molds, that contain and shape the wet concrete are built from lumber, and for curved sections, from plywood. Formwork must be strong to support the considerable weight of the concrete pushing against it. Depending on the thickness of the slab, 2x4, 2x6, or 2x8 lumber is used for the

forms, and 1x2s, 1x4s, or 2x4s are used for stakes and braces. Cut the stakes to a point with a circular saw to make it easier to drive them into the soil. Metal landscape edging or ¼-inch plywood or hardboard is used to form curves. (Plywood used to form curves will bend more easily if it is cut perpendicular to the face grain rather than along the grain.) Form boards should be free of holes, cracks, loose knots, and other defects that might reduce their strength or mar the finished surface of the concrete.

Any type of straight, smooth lumber can be used for temporary forms (those that will be removed when the concrete is cured). Some formwork stays in place permanently. Use redwood, cedar, cypress, or pressure-treated lumber for permanent formwork.

Specific techniques for building the formwork are explained in each of the projects in this book, but there are some general points to remember. Always set form boards on a true perpendicular to the subgrade and set all stakes deep enough to hold the form boards securely. Be sure the stakes are plumb. Remember to use double-headed nails when attaching form boards and stakes—they make the forms easy to remove. Screws are another option. Use stakes at 3-foot intervals, and stake both boards where they meet at corners. Wherever two form boards join together, you must use a stake at the butt joint. Butt the ends up tight, and nail both.

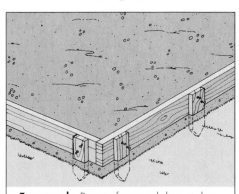

Formwork. Proper formwork has stakes positioned every 3 to 4 ft., is perpendicular to the subgrade, and is held together with double-headed nails. Make tight corners and joints.

boards to the stake. If the ends of the boards are angled or uneven, square them off with a circular saw before attaching them to the stake.

Isolation joints. Isolation joints are an important element in the form-work. These strips separate new concrete from existing adjacent construction and other concrete slabs that might expand and contract differently or experience different soil settlement or other movement. If the fresh concrete were not separated from these elements by an isolation joint, a crack could form where the two meet. Isolation joints are ¼- to ½-inch-wide molded fiber, cork, or rubber strip dividers that are set ¼ inch below the surface of the concrete. Do not use caulking or asphalt fillers. These could be squeezed out of the joint when it contracts, creating an unsightly hump that could cause someone to trip and fall.

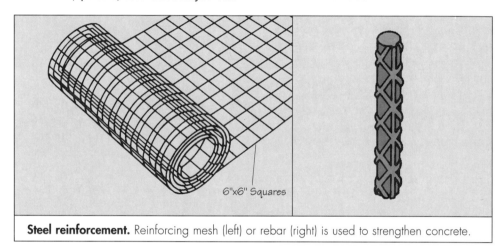

Isolation joints. These joints prevent cracks by separating concrete structures that may settle and move differently.

Steel Reinforcement

Steel reinforcement helps control the cracking associated with the natural shrinkage of concrete as it dries. Reinforcement is installed in the form-work before any concrete is placed. Two basic types of reinforcing steel are bars and wire mesh.

Rebar. Reinforcing bar (called rebar for short) used in residential construction ranges in size from ¼ to 1 inch in diameter and has ridges on its surface to provide a better bond with the concrete. Rebar is numbered according to its diameter in eighths of an inch. A #3 bar, for example, has a ⅜-inch diameter, and a #4 bar has a ⅝-inch (½-inch) diameter. Reinforcing bars are stronger than reinforcing mesh and are used for concrete that will carry a heavy load, such as footings, foundation walls, columns, and piers. In applications calling for rebar, do not substitute reinforcing mesh or a ready-mix with fibers.

Reinforcing mesh. This mesh is made from steel wires woven or welded into a grid of 6-inch squares. The wires are usually 6, 8, or 10 gauge and have smooth surfaces. Reinforcing

mesh comes in rolls and mats and is used primarily in flatwork such as sidewalks, patios, and driveways. The

rolls are generally 5 by 150 feet. The mesh can be cut with large fencing pliers or electrical wire cutters. You must flatten the mesh thoroughly to prevent it from moving to the top or bottom of the pour. Flat sheets of mesh may be easier to work with than the rolls. Where the form is wider than the mesh, overlap sections by at least 6 inches and bind them together with wire. Reinforcing mesh is laid on small rocks, bricks or broken concrete and is placed 2 inches from the boards on all sides. Place the mesh in the middle of the slab. Do not allow the mesh to come into contact with the sides of the forms, because the metal may end up sticking out of the concrete. This metal will eventually discolor and rust.

Steel reinforcement. Reinforcing mesh (left) or rebar (right) is used to strengthen concrete.

Reinforcing mesh. This mesh is laid on bricks or small rocks. Place the mesh in the middle of the slab, about 2 in. away from the formwork boards on all sides.

Pouring and Placing Concrete

Regardless of whether you mix your own or have ready-mix delivered to your site, you must work quickly when placing concrete in formwork. If your project is large enough to require a delivery of ready-mix concrete, you will probably need to enlist some friends to help with the pour. Be sure to wear rubber boots, gloves, and protective clothing, because prolonged contact with fresh concrete mixtures will burn your skin.

Mix your concrete as near to the job site as you can, or have the ready-mix truck park as close as possible. Before placing concrete, check the formwork for proper grade and correct depth. Once you're sure that everything is in order, spray the inside surfaces of the forms and the soil or gravel base with water from a garden hose. This will prevent water from being drawn out of the concrete, which can result in a soft or crumbly surface. Moistening the forms and soil is especially important on a warm and windy day.

Use wheelbarrows. For large projects such as driveways, have at least two wheelbarrows for transporting the

Use wheelbarrows. When using wheelbarrows to transport concrete over a lawn, protect the lawn with 2x12s.

concrete to the forms. Lay 2x12s across lawn areas to protect them from the weight of the wheelbarrow, and build ramps over the forms so you don't bump them out of place.

1 Place the concrete. Begin placing the concrete in the farthest corner of the forms, making piles that are slightly higher than the formwork. Fill the forms completely. Move the concrete with hoes or shovels—a hoe is best because you can pull

the concrete into place then lift the hoe out. A shovel is used to fill low areas. Concrete is very heavy; therefore, when lifting the shovel out of the concrete, turn it sideways to slide it out. As the concrete is placed, use a hook or a hammer claw to lift up the wire mesh to ensure that it stays in the middle of the pour.

2 Tamp out air bubbles. During the pour, you must repeatedly consolidate the concrete by moving a

1 Start by placing concrete in the far corners of the forms. Use a hoe to spread the concrete evenly.

2 Tamp the fresh concrete to eliminate air bubbles. Tap the outside of the forms to further settle the concrete.

shovel, hoe, or 2x4 up and down vertically to remove all air bubbles. This is especially important near the edges and in corners. Do not overdo it though! If you overwork the concrete, the water will separate and rise to the top, a condition called *segregation*. Further settle the concrete against the perimeter by tapping the outside of the form boards with a hammer.

3 **Screed the concrete level.** Once the form is filled and tamped, begin striking off, or screeding, the surface level with the top of the forms. Use a length of 2x4 that is slightly wider than the forms. Try to use a straight piece of lumber, but if there is a bow to the wood, screed with the convex side up. Move the screed back and forth as you slide it along the top of the forms. Keep both

3 Once the concrete is poured and tamped, pull a 2x4 across the forms to screed the slab.

ends pressed down on top of the forms to force all the aggregate into the concrete. Fill hollow areas with a shovelful of concrete, and strike them off level. For a large pour, two people can begin screeding as concrete is placed ahead of them.

4 **Float the surface smooth.** Floating is the first step in the finishing of concrete and is done immediately after screeding. The initial floating depresses large aggregates and knocks down small ridges. Do this with either a bull float or a darby, depending on the size of the pour.

To use a bull float, push it across the surface with the front edge raised a bit; when pulling it back, lay the blade flat to cut off bumps and fill any tiny holes. At the end of each stroke, lift the float and move it over to make a parallel stroke.

A darby is smaller and easier to control. A darby should reach across half the pour; if it doesn't, use a bull float. Use two hands to move the darby in sweeping arcs across the concrete surface. Do not allow the edges or end of the tool to dig into the concrete.

CAUTION: After the first floating, do not do anything else until the water sheen is gone from the surface of the concrete. The time this takes will vary, depending on the temperature, wind, humidity, and type of concrete mix. If you begin edging and further finishing while there is water on the surface, the concrete quality, especially at the surface, may be lessened. Of course,

if you wait too long, the concrete will be unworkable.

Types of Joints

Construction joints. Construction joints are installed wherever a concrete pour is interrupted for more than 30 minutes or stopped at the end of the day. Within the formwork, the section being poured is closed off with a temporary stop board. The section is poured, screeded, and floated. Construction joints can act as control joints when placed accordingly. For slabs that are only 4 inches thick, a straight-edged butt joint is adequate, but for thicker slabs, a keyed tongue-and-groove joint may be used to help transfer loads between adjoining sections of concrete. The tongue-and-groove construction allows the slab surface to remain level, but the sections can expand and contract independently. A tongue-and-groove joint is shaped by attaching a wood, metal, or molded plastic beveled form along the middle of the temporary stop board. The edge of the pour takes this beveled shape. The subsequent pour takes an inverse shape. The oil

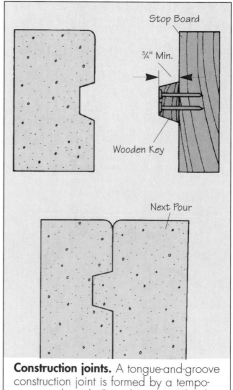

Construction joints. A tongue-and-groove construction joint is formed by a temporary stop board. Coat the joint with oil to prevent a bond.

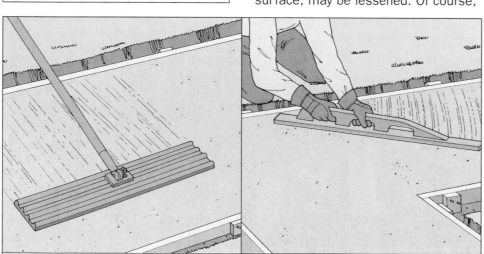

4 A large pour is smoothed with a bull float (left) while smaller ones are done with a wooden darby (right).

coating prevents a bond between the pours. After the second pour has set, tool a control joint above the construction joint.

Edging joints. When the water sheen is gone from the first floating, it's time to run an edger along the forms. Edging gives the pour rounded edges that are resistant to cracking. But first use the point of a small trowel to cut the top inch or so of concrete away from the face of the form, so that the form will pull away from the concrete easily when it is removed, without breaking the edge. Then run an edging trowel around the entire slab perimeter to form an attractive finished edge. Run the edger back and forth to smooth the surface, being careful not to gouge the concrete. Raise the front edge slightly when moving the edger forward, and raise the back edge when moving the tool backwards.

Control joints. Shrinkage cracks in concrete are controlled by special joints called control (or contraction) joints, which are tooled into the surface. Control joints make the concrete crack in straight lines at planned locations. They can be hand-tooled into fresh concrete with a special jointing tool; cut into partially cured concrete with a circular saw fitted with a masonry blade; or formed with fixed divider strips of wood or of specially molded fiber, cork, or sponge rubber. (When the divider strips are used at full slab depth, the control joint is also an isolation joint.) Tooled and saw-cut control joints must be at least one-quarter the thickness of the concrete. This weakens the section, causing cracks to occur at the bottom of the joints where they will be inconspicuous.

The table "Control Joint Spacing," shows the recommended maximum control joint spacing for concrete slabs based on the thickness of the pour, the slump, and the maximum aggregate size. Remember that concrete slump is an indication of how much water is in the mix. Low-slump mixes have less water and will shrink less, so control joints can be spaced farther apart, but these mixes are stiff and can be hard to work. With

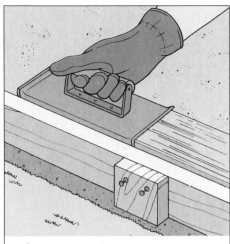

Edging joints. Edging gives a pour a rounded edge, which is attractive and resists cracking.

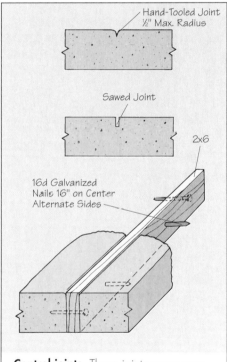

Control joints. These joints cause concrete to crack at specific locations. They are either hand-tooled (top), cut with a circular saw (middle), or created with a fixed divider strip (bottom).

the maximum spacing recommendations from the table in mind, it is best to subdivide concrete into panels that are square rather than elongated. Rectangular areas that are more than one and a half times as long as they are wide are prone to cracking in the middle across the width. For a slab that is 4 inches thick and is constructed with concrete that has a 5-inch slump and 1-inch maximum aggregate size, the table recommends control joints spaced every 10 feet. For a 10-foot-wide driveway, these control joints would create square panels; but for a 3-foot-wide sidewalk, these control joints would create elongated rectangular panels. Thus the spacing of the joints in a sidewalk should be much closer; the concrete will be less likely to crack if the joints are spaced 3 feet apart to form square panels.

Final Floating, Troweling & Brooming

Floating. Floating after jointing and edging will drive the large aggregate below the surface and further smooth the concrete. Floats are made of wood.

Hold the float nearly flat, keeping the leading edge slightly raised so you don't gouge the surface. Move it in wide sweeping motions. Be sure to smooth over any marks or gouges left from edging or jointing. If water comes to the surface when you begin the floating, stop and wait a while before trying again. Go back over the edges and control joints with the edger and jointing tool to touch up after floating. In some exterior applications, the concrete should not be made any smoother after this floating.

Control Joint Spacing

Recommended Maximum Spacing of Control Joints (in feet)			
	Slump 4 in. to 5 in.		
Slab Thickness, in.	Maximum-Size Aggregate Less Than ¾ in.	Maximum-Size Aggregate ¾ in. And Larger	Slump Less Than 4 in.
4	8	10	12
5	10	13	15
6	12	15	18

Floating. Hold the float nearly flat, keeping the leading edge slightly raised to prevent gouging the surface. Move it in wide sweeping motions.

Troweling. This finishing step is for interior concrete applications and concrete without air-entrainment. Do not trowel air-entrained concrete in any situation. Troweling can impair the frost resistance by removing entrained air near the surface.

If you are troweling, follow the float with a steel finishing trowel. Hold the blade flat against the surface. Sweep it back and forth in wide arcs, overlapping each pass by one-half the trowel blade length. This in effect trowels the surface twice in one operation. For an even smoother finish, go back over the surface after you have finished the initial troweling. Let the concrete set a while before retroweling. Touch up the control joints and edges with the edger and jointing tool after troweling.

Brooming. A lightly broomed finish creates a slip-resistant surface that is important for sloping driveways and sidewalks. Brooming is done after floating and troweling. It may be done with almost any broom, but a stiff bristled, push-pull shop broom works best. You can purchase concrete brooms made specifically for this purpose.

The biggest problem with brooming is working the bristles into the concrete without marring the surface. It is best to pull the broom across the surface, lifting it up after each stroke. To create the most effective surface, pull the broom across the concrete in a direction that is perpendicular to the general direction of foot or vehicular traffic.

Special Finishes for Concrete

There are several types of finishes that can be applied to concrete to dress up its otherwise utilitarian look. The particular finish to use depends on the structure and its ultimate purpose.

Exposed Aggregate

One way to add color and texture to your concrete project is to use an exposed aggregate finish. You will need to divide the pour into small, manageable areas so that the aggregate can be seeded into the surface before the concrete becomes too hard. This is also important because the seeding method of creating an exposed aggregate finish takes about three times longer than normal finishing. For large slabs, you may need to add a retarder to the concrete to allow you enough time to work in the stones. Consult a concrete supplier about types of retarding admixtures.

You will get a more uniform texture if the stones are similar in size, so choose an aggregate that has a fairly narrow range of size variation, such as ¼ to ½ inch in diameter, ⅜ to ⅝ inch, or ½ to ¾ inch. For best results, select rounded river gravel; avoid crushed stone that is sharp or angular.

1 **Place the aggregate.** After the concrete has been floated in the usual way, spread the aggregate over the slab by hand or with a shovel —the surface should be completely and uniformly covered with a single layer of stones.

2 **Set the stones.** Embed the aggregate in the fresh concrete with a shovel, wooden float, or flat board until it is almost completely covered by the concrete.

3 **Brush away surface concrete.** When the concrete has cured enough to bear the weight of a person kneeling on a flat board without leaving marks in the surface (from one to three hours, depending on condi-

1 After floating the surface, spread aggregate uniformly and completely with a shovel.

2 Push down the aggregate with a board until it is almost completely covered by concrete (left). Use a float near the edges (right).

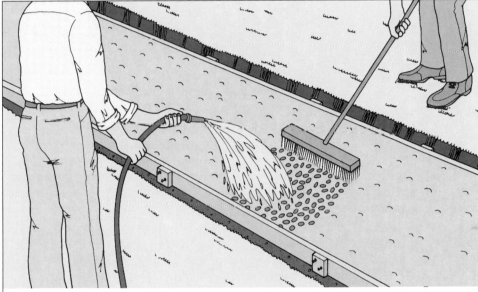

3 Brush away concrete until the stones are uniformly exposed. Lightly spray the concrete with water from a hose.

the aggregate is uniformly exposed. Edge and joint the concrete as needed for any slab.

Flagstone Pattern

You can "carve" a design into concrete to create a flagstone pattern. To do this, use a length of ½- or ¾-inch copper pipe bent into a gentle S shape. After smoothing the concrete surface with a darby, use the pipe to cut a random stone pattern into the surface, making grooves that are about ½ inch deep. When the surface water has evaporated, float and trowel the surface as usual, retooling the grooves after each operation. When you are finished, brush out the grooves carefully with a dry paintbrush to remove any remaining small particles of concrete.

Pitted Surface

In warm climates that are not subject to winter freezing, you can easily create a pitted texture that resembles travertine marble. After troweling or brooming the concrete, scatter ordinary rock salt evenly over the surface at a rate of 3 to 6 pounds of salt per 100 square feet of concrete. Use a section of plastic pipe to roll the salt crystals into the surface until only the tops of the grains are exposed. After seven days of curing the concrete as usual, wash and brush the surface

tions), begin brushing away the top surface of the concrete to expose the aggregate. First, lightly brush the surface with a stiff-bristled nylon broom. Work carefully so that you do not dislodge the stones; if some do dislodge, reset them, and wait a little longer before continuing.

Brush the surface again while simultaneously washing away the loosened cement paste with water from a garden hose. The water spray should be strong enough to remove the loosened concrete but not to blast the aggregate loose or gouge the surface. Continue washing and brushing the surface until the runoff water is clear and the top one-third to one-half of

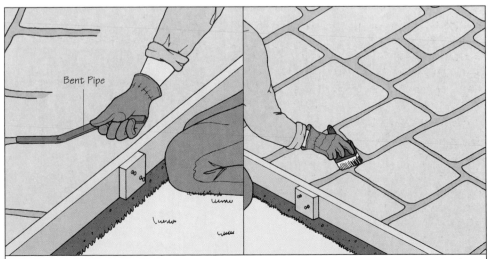

Flagstone pattern. Create a flagstone pattern by carving a design into wet concrete (left). Gently brush the design to remove the loose concrete particles (right).

to dissolve the salt, which will leave a pattern of holes. Rock salt finishes can be used only where winter freezing is not a regular occurrence; any water that freezes in these holes will expand and may damage the surface.

Colored Concrete

You can add color to concrete to create interesting patterns that demand attention, or you can add color to blend structures unobtrusively into the surrounding landscape.

Using coloring agents. Coloring agents for concrete consist of natural and synthetic oxides, which are added in one of two ways. The first and easiest method is to add coloring agents to the wet concrete when mixing. Read the instructions on the color additive package to determine the correct amount per volume of concrete. This method of coloring permeates the whole pour.

The second method, a much less costly technique, is to make a two-layer pour. First pour a layer of uncolored concrete to within ¾-inch of the top of the forms. Tamp to level. Leave this layer rough. Allow the concrete to set just until the surface water has evaporated. Then pour a second, colored layer, which will bond to the first. The top layer is colored mortar; it contains no coarse aggregate—just pigment, sand, cement, and water. Again, read the instructions on the color additive package to determine the correct amount per volume of mortar mix. Float and trowel the pour as usual.

Using dry powders. It is also possible to color concrete with a dry powder that is made up of pigment, portland cement, and graded sand or another fine aggregate. To use it, sprinkle two-thirds of the material over a freshly floated surface after the excess surface moisture has evaporated. Spread the powder by hand or with a garden pesticide duster. Get an even coating over the whole surface. Allow the pigment to absorb some moisture from the

Colored concrete. Concrete can be colored with pigmented powder. Sprinkle it on; then trowel it into the surface.

slab, then use a steel trowel to blend it evenly into the concrete. Finally, cast the remaining third of the material onto the surface at right angles to the first application. Wait for any moisture to absorb and float the surface for a second time.

Staining and painting concrete. Concrete must be dry before it can be stained or painted—usually six months of curing is right. The paint or dyeing agent must be applied according to the manufacturer's directions. In most cases, old paint or dye must be removed before you can recolor a concrete surface. The key to painting concrete is surface preparation. The surface must be free of dirt, dust, grime, and efflorescence. All concrete paint comes with instructions for proper surface preparation.

Curing Concrete

Concrete worked to its normal texture or enhanced with a special finish must be kept moist for several days to allow the portland cement in the mix to cure and harden properly. When moisture is pulled from the concrete too quickly, the surface can

develop many hairline cracks or have a chalky residue. Concrete should be kept moist for seven days. Hot, dry, or windy weather increases evaporation, making it more difficult to keep the slab moist. Cold weather requires special precautions for curing.

There are many different ways to cure concrete properly. Here are some of the more practical methods.

■ Cover the surface completely with large sheets of plastic. Be sure to keep the plastic flat on the surface of the concrete, or it will cause uneven coloring. Weigh down the edges and joints with bricks or lumber.

■ Cover the surface with roofing felt. Tape the joints and edges with duct tape or weigh them down with bricks or pieces of lumber to help seal in moisture and slow evaporation.

■ Cover the surface with burlap. Spray the burlap with a garden hose twice daily to keep it wet. Use lumber or bricks to hold down the burlap.

■ Set a sprinkler to continually pool water on the surface of the concrete—this method uses a good deal of water, however. Be sure the surface has hardened enough to resist being marred by the sprinkler.

Temperature extremes. Cold weather creates problems for uncured concrete. Concrete hardens best between 50 degrees and 70 degrees F, but sometimes you must pour when the temperature is lower. Concrete that freezes before two days of proper curing will be flaky, weak, and in effect, ruined. If you expect cold weather, a heavy layer of straw or blankets covered with plastic sheeting is required. If there will be a long period of cold, keep the straw or blankets on the concrete, and prohibit use of the slab for at least two weeks.

Very hot weather can also be a problem for curing concrete. Simply keep the concrete moist (a prerequisite for curing anyway), and you'll be fine. When sprinkling, do not use ice-cold water that can "shock" the concrete into cracking.

Curing colored concrete. It is more difficult to cure colored concrete than normal concrete. Curing requires water. However, water may splotch colored surfaces. Be careful of the force with which water is sprayed onto colored surfaces. Also, do not use burlap or other water-laden materials to aid in curing—they cause splotching.

Removing the Forms

After the concrete has cured for one day, carefully remove the forms. Forms left on for longer periods are more difficult to remove, but after only a day, the concrete can be easily damaged. Do not pry or hammer against the concrete itself when disassembling the formwork. The concrete will continue to cure to full strength after about a month, but it is safe to use after the first week.

Curing concrete. Cure the concrete by covering the slab with roofing felt. Hold down the felt with lumber or bricks.

Temperature extremes. In cold weather, protect curing concrete with straw covered by plastic sheeting. Prohibit use of the slab for at least two weeks.

Concrete Projects

Now that you understand how to mix concrete and the fundamentals of working with it, it's time to start building. Here you will find specific concrete projects. Some jobs, such as building a sidewalk, are easy for the beginning mason; other projects are more challenging, such as pouring an entire driveway slab. Follow the step-by-step instructions given for each project, and refer back to the previous technique sections for details.

Concrete Sidewalk

Though sidewalks can be made of many different materials, one of the most popular is concrete. Concrete sidewalks are long lasting, require little maintenance, and can be made slip-resistant by brooming the wet surface. Special finishes such as exposed aggregate or a flagstone pattern look terrific on sidewalks. The relatively small surface area of a sidewalk makes it easy to create special finishes.

Planning the Project

A concrete walk is a great beginner's project because the concrete is easily split into sections. Before embarking on a sidewalk project, talk to your building department about any ordinances, particularly in regard to work near street curbs. Also contact your utility company before excavating. Usually, the company will come to your site and paint the locations of any utilities or it will contact you if there are none present.

Using a piece of grid paper, draw a plan of the sidewalk to scale. If there are no stairs (such as a patio door entrance), the top of the sidewalk slab should be 1 inch below the door sill (to prevent water from flowing into the house) and about 2 inches above the adjacent ground. Sidewalks are generally a minimum of 3 feet wide. A narrower 2-foot width can be used for a garden path or for service access, but primary entrance walks look better at 4 feet or even 6 feet, depending on the size, style, and design of the house.

Sidewalks usually are 4 inches thick. If they lead from a house, sidewalks are sloped ¼ inch per foot

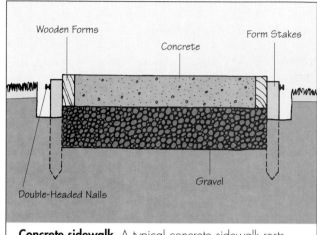

Concrete sidewalk. A typical concrete sidewalk rests on a bed of gravel and is held in wooden forms until properly cured.

to carry off surface water. Some sidewalks are supported by a bed of gravel for drainage; consult your building department for appropriate thickness of the gravel base.

Plan the control joints to prevent cracking (see "Control Joints," on page 29). Set an isolation joint wherever the sidewalk will join the house, steps, or other existing construction.

Excavating

As with any concrete project, the first step is excavating and preparing the subgrade. Concrete slabs must be supported on a soil subgrade that is reasonably hard, uniformly level, and drained with gravel if necessary. A poorly or improperly prepared subgrade can cause uneven settlement and cracking.

1 **Lay out the sidewalk.** Lay out rectangular shapes with marker stakes and string. Set stakes adjacent to the house, porch, or steps to mark where the edge of the concrete will be, allowing 1½ inches for the thickness of the form boards. Set stakes for the outside corners a little beyond the proposed concrete edge so they will not be in the way of the excavation. Use the 3-4-5 layout method for squaring the corners as described in "Making Square Corners," page 24. Outline the size and shape of a curved sidewalk with garden

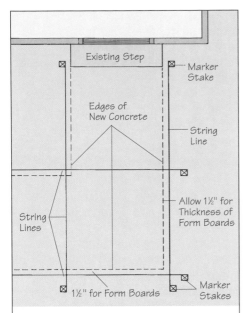

1 Set string to outline the shape of the walk. Set the strings back 1½ in. to allow for the thickness of the form boards.

2 Temporarily untie the strings and excavate for the slab and any base materials.

3 Level the subgrade with a hand tamper.

hoses. Remember that the form boards for curved shapes are only ¼ inch thick, so do not set the hoses back 1½ inches as you did when setting the string for two-by lumber. Then sprinkle sand along the entire outline to mark the shape of the concrete on the ground to guide the excavation.

2 **Excavate the soil.** Temporarily untie the string, and excavate several inches wider than the sand marking lines to allow room for building the formwork. Remove all grass, sod, roots, and large rocks. Dig out any soft or spongy areas and fill them

with good soil or with gravel, crushed stone, or sand. Loosen and tamp hard spots to provide uniform support. Remove enough soil to accommodate the thickness of the slab and any base material. In areas with poor drainage, excavate deeply enough to place a 4-inch layer of gravel under the concrete, and plan to finish the concrete slab 2 inches above the adjacent ground. In areas with better drainage, excavate deeply enough to allow a 2-inch layer of sand.

3 **Smooth and tamp surface.** Leave the subgrade undisturbed wherever possible—it is packed firmer than any fill you add and tamp. Smooth the loose surface soil with a rake, and fill in holes left by stones or roots with sand or gravel. Level the surface with the edge of a 2x4, then compact the soil with a hand tamper or vibratory compactor.

Building the Formwork

1 **Set the elevation.** Once the subgrade is prepared, you're ready to begin the formwork. Start at the stakes placed adjacent to the house. If they have been loosened or moved during the excavation, reset them firmly in the ground. Use a board and a mason's level or a string and line level to set the grade. This is the

elevation for the top of the new concrete. The elevation is set equal to the height of the bottom step, or if the door is flush to the ground, the elevation is 1 inch below the door sill. Mark the stakes with a pencil and tie your string at the correct height.

2 **Set the string lines.** Stretch string lines to the stake at the outer corners of the sidewalk or to where it turns. Be sure the corners are square. It's best to use mason's twine because it sags less than other

1 Mark the elevation of the slab. Mark both stakes adjacent to the house and tie the strings at these marks.

string. If necessary, drive intermediate stakes about 10 to 15 feet apart along the way to keep the string from sagging. (Stakes for the string are 10 to 15 feet apart; stakes to hold the form boards will be placed 4 feet apart.) Using a line level, mark each stake and tie the string so that it is level or follows the slope of the ground. Set both sides of the walk level to the height of the finished slab.

A sidewalk must slope for proper drainage. To set the slope across the width of a sidewalk, calculate the amount of slope needed for the slab width; ¼ inch per foot is the standard recommendation. For example,

a 3-foot-wide sidewalk sloped ¼ inch per foot should be ¾ inch lower on one side than the other. To set the strings for the correct slope, simply measure down on the stakes on the lower side the required distance, and retie the string to the lower height. Mark all the stakes holding the string on the lower side. Be sure to set the slope on the same side throughout— especially if your walk turns or curves.

3 Drive stakes to support the forms. Drive additional stakes along the string line, spacing them 3 to 4 feet on center. Make sure the tops of the stakes are slightly below the string line so they will not inter-

fere with leveling and finishing the top of the concrete, but leave enough height to drive nails into the forms. At the corners, drive a stake near the end on each side to hold the form boards. When in doubt, use an extra stake or two to help ensure that the forms won't bulge or bow during the pour.

4 Make any curved formwork. If you need to make curved forms, use ¼-inch plywood forms for short-radius curves. Orient the grain of the plywood face vertically so it will bend more easily. Space supports 1 to 2 feet apart. Use 1x4 or 1x6 lumber for long-radius curves. Wet the wood first to make bending easier, and space the stakes at 2- to 3-foot intervals. Nail curved formwork from the inside outward to the stake to hold it securely. Use regular nails here, not double-headed nails, so the heads will not be embedded in the concrete when the stakes and forms are removed.

5 Attach boards to the stakes. Once all the stakes are driven into the ground, align the tops of the forms with the string. Hold the boards tightly against the stakes; nail through the outside into the form. Use double-headed nails to make it easier to remove the forms.

Butt the form boards tightly together to prevent the wet concrete from leaking out. Where the ends of two boards

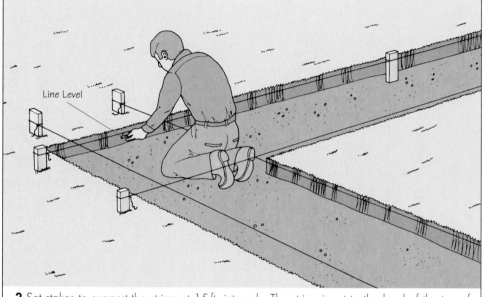

2 Set stakes to support the string at 15-ft. intervals. The string is set to the level of the top of the slab.

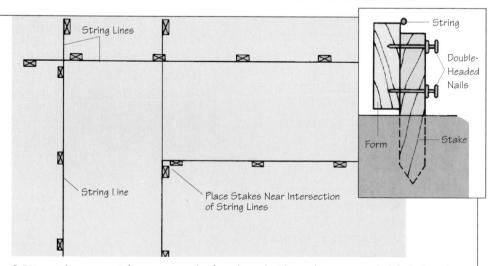

3 Drive stakes every 4 ft. to support the form boards. The stakes are set slightly below the string lines.

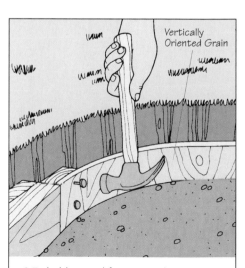

4 To hold curved forms to stakes, use single-headed nails, and drive them from the inside of the forms into the stake.

adjoin, drive a stake so that it supports the ends of both boards.

6 **Mark the control joint locations.** After you have built your forms, mark the locations of control joints, which will be tooled or saw-cut later. Mark the top of the forms, using a wax crayon or other marker that will show up easily when the forms are wet and splattered with concrete.

7 **Add the base.** Depending on local conditions, add the appropriate sand or gravel base inside the forms. Add half the amount of gravel and level and tamp it into the forms. Then add the remaining gravel, and tamp again. Sand can be poured all at once, then tamped. Use a 2x4 to level the sand or gravel to a height that will allow the concrete slab to reach the top of the form boards.

8 **Lay the wire mesh.** Concrete is reinforced with steel to add strength and reduce cracking. Sidewalks are reinforced with steel wire mesh. See "Steel Reinforcement," on page 26 for details on using reinforcing mesh. Place the mesh so it's in the middle of the concrete pour; use stones, bricks, or pieces of concrete to support it. When reinforcing mesh must be spliced, lap one full row of squares and tie the laps (as you would twist a twist tie) with a soft steel wire. If you are having your concrete delivered, you can order a mix that contains fiber reinforcement that provides additional cracking resistance to the concrete.

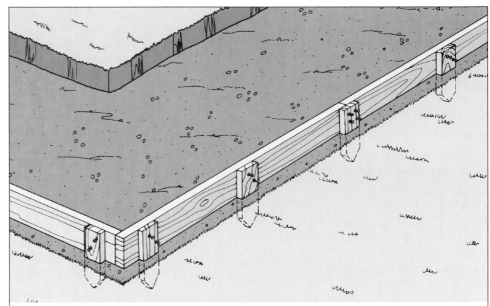

5 Proper formwork has stakes positioned every 3 to 4 ft., is perpendicular to the subgrade, and is held together with double-headed nails. Make tight corners and joints.

6 Mark the locations of the control joints with a marker or wax crayon.

7 If required, add a gravel base. Add half the amount, and then tamp and level. Add the rest of the gravel, and tamp again.

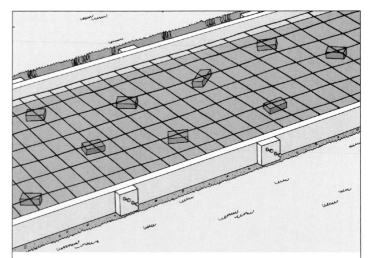

8 Place the mesh so it is 2 in. below the top of the form boards. When reinforcing mesh must be spliced, lap one full row of squares and tie the overlap with wire.

Handling and Placing the Concrete

Detailed instructions for placing concrete in a form are given in "Pouring and Placing Concrete," on page 27. A brief summary is provided here with specifics for sidewalks.

Before you start mixing or pouring concrete, check all the formwork for proper grade, the markings for the control joints, and the correct depth. Remember that a sidewalk is sloped at a rate of ¼ inch per foot to allow for drainage. Once you're sure that everything is in its proper place, lightly spray the inside surfaces of the forms and the gravel or sand base with water from a garden hose. This will keep them from drawing too much water from the concrete mix, which would result in soft, crumbly, partially cured concrete. Moistening the forms and soil is especially important on a warm, windy day.

Whenever you are working with concrete, be sure to wear rubber boots, protective clothing, and gloves, because prolonged contact with fresh concrete will burn your skin.

Always mix your concrete as near to the job site as you can, or have the delivery truck park as close as possible. Use a wheelbarrow to move the concrete to the project site. Lay 2x12s across lawn areas to protect them from the weight of the wheelbarrow, and build ramps over the forms to keep from bumping them out of place.

Start dumping the concrete in the farthest corner of the forms, making piles that are slightly taller than the formwork. Be sure to fill the forms completely. Fill low areas with a shovel, and spade the concrete with a hoe or shovel to fill in corners and eliminate large air voids. Settle concrete against the perimeter forms by tapping the outside of the form boards with a hammer. Then use a hook or hammer claw to lift up the wire reinforcing mesh, making sure that it is fully embedded. Continue transporting and dumping the concrete until the forms are full.

Handling and placing the concrete. Dump concrete in the farthest corner of the forms. Use a hoe to spread the concrete evenly and tamp to eliminate air bubbles.

Finishing the Concrete

Once the concrete is in the formwork, you are ready to level and smooth the pour then give the surface the texture of your choice.

1 **Strike the concrete level.** As soon as the first few feet of the formwork or the first complete section is poured, begin striking off, or screeding, the surface level with the top of the forms. Use a straight length of 2x4 that is slightly wider than the form. Drag it along the top of the forms to level the surface of the concrete. Keep both ends

1 Use a sawing motion to drag a 2x4 across the top of the form boards.

pressed down on top of the forms. Fill hollow areas with a shovel, and strike them off level.

2 **Smooth the surface with a darby.** Smooth the surface of the concrete with a large wooden darby. Make large sweeping arcs, keeping the front edge raised slightly so you don't gouge the surface.

Do not continue the finishing process until the water sheen is gone from the surface and the concrete will hold your weight without your foot sinking more than ¼ inch. The time that this takes varies with the temperature, wind, and humidity as well as with the type of cement you used.

3 **Edge the slab.** First, use the point of a small trowel to cut the top inch or so of concrete away from the face of the form, so that the form will pull away from the concrete easily when it is removed. Then edge the slab with an edging trowel to form an attractive, finished edge. Run the edger back and forth to smooth the surface, being careful not to gouge the concrete.

4 **Form the control joints.** Use a jointing or grooving trowel to form control joints at the locations you marked on the top of the forms. Use a straight piece of 2x4 as a guide for cutting the joints. Lay a 2x12 support-

ed by concrete blocks or bricks across the tops of the forms to kneel on while you work. You can also cut joints with a circular saw equipped with a masonry blade. A saw will produce a clean cut that is narrower than a hand-tooled cut but equally effective.

5 **Float the surface.** Hold the float nearly flat, and move it in wide, sweeping motions. Be sure to smooth over any marks or gouges left by the edging or jointing process. If water comes to the surface when you begin the floating, stop and wait for it all to evaporate. Go back over the edges and control joints with the edger and jointing tool to touch up after floating.

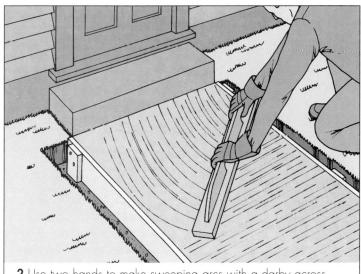

2 Use two hands to make sweeping arcs with a darby across the entire surface of the sidewalk.

3 Edging gives a pour a rounded edge, which is attractive and resists cracking.

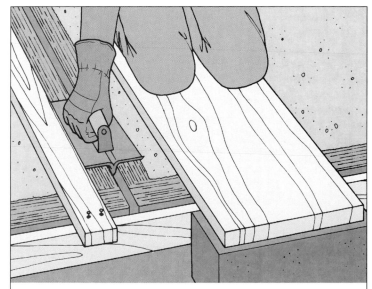

4 Tack a 2x4 to the top of the forms as a guide for tooling the control joints. Kneel on a 2x12 as you progress across the walk.

5 Use a wooden float to smooth the walk. If water rises to the top, do not continue until it all evaporates.

If the walk will be a base for brick pavers, leave the surface with the floated finish. This is the time for a special finish if one is being applied (see "Special Finishes for Concrete," on page 30).

After the floating, you can produce a nonskid finish by pulling a damp broom across the surface perpendicular to the direction of traffic. For a fine texture, use a soft-bristled brush. For a coarser texture, use a broom with stiffer bristles. You will get best results if you buy a broom made especially for concrete finishing.

Cure the concrete. Correctly curing concrete is essential to a successful pour. Specifics about this very important process are given in "Curing Concrete," on page 32. After the concrete has cured for one day, carefully remove the forms. Do not pry or hammer against the concrete itself. The concrete will continue to cure slowly for another month until it reaches full strength; however, it can be walked on after the first day. Keep vehicles off for a week.

Patio Slab

A concrete patio slab can provide durable and low maintenance outdoor living space in any climate. Large or small, geometric or free-form, the design is dictated by available area, personal taste, and landscape style.

A patio most often is located near a kitchen area, a family room, or a dining room. A less common site, but an especially appealing one, is a small patio off a bathroom. Accessed by sliding glass doors and fenced in for privacy, a bathroom patio can be a lovely addition to your home. When designing a patio, consider the views, climate protection, and privacy. Also determine if the traffic flow between the house and the outside area can be modified without drastically changing the everyday operations of the household. Also, be aware that the addition of a patio may change the traffic pattern inside the house. For example, will more people be tromping through the kitchen, getting in the cook's way?

Planning the Project

Individual needs vary, but as a general guideline your patio should provide about 20 square feet of space for each person who will occupy it at the same time. This guideline is based on the premise that each person needs a 4- by 5-foot space for a chair and space to move around comfortably.

As with other concrete slabs, the top of the patio should be 1 inch below the door sills to prevent water from flowing into the house and about 2 inches above the adjacent ground. Patio slabs should be at least 4 inches thick and sloped ¼ inch per foot away from the house to drain off surface water. Support the slab with a gravel base if site drainage is poor. If not, 2 inches of tamped sand is a good base.

Patios are often laid with a permanent formwork that divides the space into sections. The forms break up the slab to make concrete placement easier, and the patio is visually more appealing than a monolithic concrete slab. When placed at the right distances, permanent forms eliminate the need for control joints. If you're not using permanent forms, minimize cracking in patios by incorporating control joints as discussed in "Control Joints," on page 29.

Install an isolation joint everywhere the patio comes into contact with the house, steps, driveway, or other existing construction. Isolation joints separate new concrete from existing adjacent construction that might expand and contract differently or experience different soil settlement or other

movement. You can also embellish a patio with a border of a different material, such as brick.

Patios on uneven ground. A patio may be built with a slight slope in the grade, but when the slope is more than about 5 or 6 percent, the patio must be designed accordingly. For a patio built on ground that rises away from the house, one possibility is to excavate into the higher portions of the lot so that the patio nestles into the rise. In this case, the sides will require retaining walls, rock gardens, or ground cover plantings.

If the patio is on a downward slope, you may thicken the lower edge of the slab to follow the grade, while the top of the slab stays level. This is only feasible with a slight slope or a slope that is only at the end of the slab. Another option for downward slopes is to divide the patio into high and low areas connected by ramps or steps. These steps can be brick, lumber, or railroad ties. This design will require a lot of excavation in order to create level slabs and may need a retaining wall.

Permanent formwork. Patios are formed and built in much the same way as a driveway or any other large concrete slab. For the following project, permanent formwork, broken into isolated sections, has been chosen to illustrate a design specific to a patio. For permanent forms use redwood, cypress, or cedar. Coat the wood with a sealer to protect it from the alkalis in fresh concrete and to retard decay. You may also use cheaper pressure-treated lumber, which needs no coating. If you choose a simpler design with tempo-

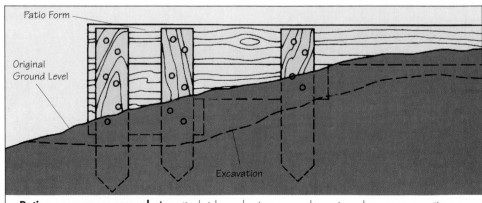

Patios on uneven ground. A patio laid on sloping ground requires deeper excavation and forms at the lower edge to maintain the basic level of the slab.

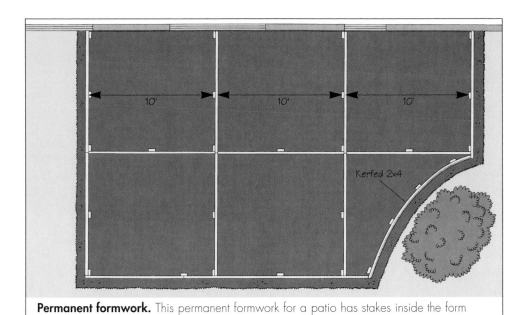

Permanent formwork. This permanent formwork for a patio has stakes inside the form boards and is divided into equal sections. An isolation joint is located against the house.

rary forms, excavate as directed here, and then follow the formwork techniques for a driveway as explained in "Building the Formwork," on page 42.

Excavating

Before digging, consider the size of the excavation. You may want to contract the excavation and tamping to a professional with heavy equipment. It's important to do the excavation well because a slab needs a firm, level subgrade. Depending on the site conditions, you may need a gravel base over the subgrade for proper drainage.

1 **Lay out shapes with string.** First lay out the shape of the patio using marker stakes and string. It's best to use mason's twine, which will sag less than other string. Unlike the sidewalk or driveway projects, the forms are permanent, and the stakes will be inside the forms. For this reason the stakes will be placed at the exact dimensions of the slab, not 1½ inches back from the string.

Set the stakes at the corners adjacent to the house first, then set stakes at the outer corners. Attach string to these stakes. Run the string to define the far edge of the patio.

Use the 3-4-5 layout method for squaring the corners, as explained in "Making Square Corners," on page 24. Outline the patio curve with a

garden hose. Then sprinkle sand along the entire patio outline to mark the shape on the ground.

2 **Excavate and tamp the soil.** Temporarily untie the string, and excavate several inches wider than the sand marking lines to allow room for building the formwork. Remove the stakes if they are in the way. Remove all grass, sod, roots, and large rocks. Dig out any soft or spongy areas and fill them with good soil or with gravel, crushed stone, or sand. Fill any holes in the subgrade. Loosen and tamp hard spots to provide uniform support. Leave the subgrade undisturbed wherever possible.

Remove enough soil to accommodate the slab plus a 2-inch-thick sand leveling bed or gravel base if needed. The finished concrete surface should be 2 inches above the adjacent ground and 1 inch below door sills. (If there is more than 7 inches of rise from the patio to a doorway you'll need to build steps: see "Concrete

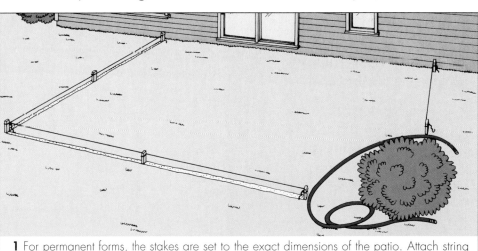

1 For permanent forms, the stakes are set to the exact dimensions of the patio. Attach string to the stakes to mark the layout. A garden hose marks the location of the curved section.

2 Tamp the subgrade with a mechanical tamper. A hand tamper works well at the edges.

Steps," page 54). When excavation is complete, tamp with a mechanical vibratory tamper and a hand tamper at the edges.

Building the Formwork

1 Set the patio elevation. After excavating, reset the perimeter stakes and retie the marker strings. Run a line level across the string adjacent to the house. This string is tied to the stakes at the elevation of the slab and checked for level. Then set stakes and tie string for forms running perpendicular to the house. You may need stakes every 15 feet to keep the string from sagging. When you've determined that everything is level or follows the grade, you can then adjust for slope.

2 Adjust the slope for drainage. To set the slope for proper drainage, calculate a ¼-inch-per-foot drop away from the house. If the patio is 12 feet long, for example, the total slope is 3 inches from house to far end. Mark the outer stakes 3 inches down from level and retie the strings at this lower mark.

3 Attach the form boards. To secure the form boards, drive stakes below the string line at a spacing of 3 to 4 feet. All the stakes must be 2 inches below the top of the forms to allow for screeding and, in this case, to be hidden by the concrete. Stakes for permanent forms remain in position; for this reason, do not use double-headed nails. Instead use regular 10d galvanized nails and drive the head flush to the stake or to the 2x4s on the outside of the form.

For permanent forms, make neat butt or miter joints at intersections and corners. Use 16d galvanized finishing nails to attach butt joints and corners

1 After excavating, set temporary stakes for string. Tie string to the stakes at the elevation of the slab and use a line level to check for level.

2 Calculate a ¼-in.-per ft. drop away from the house for drainage. Mark the outer stakes down from level and retie the strings at this lower mark.

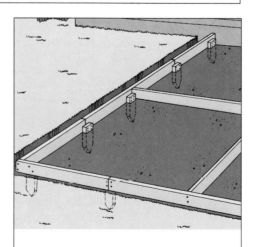

3 Drive stakes below the string line at a spacing of 3 to 4 ft. Permanent formwork has stakes inside the slab perimeter. Use a stake where two boards meet.

Making Permanent Curved Forms

Use ¼-inch plywood for short-radius curves and 1x4 or 1x6 lumber for long-radius curves. These materials work well to shape concrete into curves but do not match the thickness of 2x4 lumber when used as permanent formwork. For this reason, curves in permanent formwork are made by kerfing and bending straight 2x4s. To do this, set a circular saw to make cuts (kerfs) about two-thirds of the way through the wood; cut kerfs about every inch along the board. These cuts will create voids, allowing you to bend the 2x4 and close the voids. Attach the curved form board to stakes, and be careful not to drive nails into the kerfs.

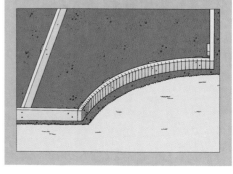

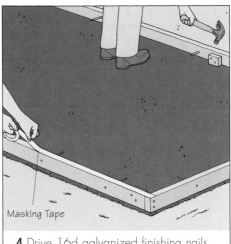

4 Drive 16d galvanized finishing nails through the wood at 16 in. on-center to anchor the slab in the forms.

outside the forms. Butt the form boards tightly together to prevent the wet concrete from leaking out. Where the ends of two boards adjoin, drive a stake so that it supports the ends of both boards.

Drive anchoring nails. To anchor the concrete slab to the form boards, drive 16d galvanized finishing nails through the wood every 16 inches. On interior forms, alternate the direction of these nails. On the outside of the form boards, use a nailset to drive the heads slightly below the surface of the wood so that they will not show in the finished construction. Use masking tape to protect the tops of permanent forms from damage or staining during the concrete pour.

Note: If you have chosen to use temporary forms for your patio, now is the time to mark the locations of the control joints. Use a wax crayon or other marker that will show up easily when the forms are wet and splattered with concrete.

Making the Final Preparations

Add base materials and isolation joints. Once the forms are set, add either the sand or the gravel base. Add sand inside the forms and level it off to a 2-inch thickness. Use a screed made of two 2x4s nailed together so that one will slide along the top of the form boards while the other drags the sand surface. If using

gravel, add half the amount; then level and tamp it into the forms. Add the remaining gravel and tamp again. From the top of the gravel to the top of the forms should equal the thickness of the slab. Isolation joint material is attached between the slab and the house.

Place the wire mesh. Use welded wire mesh to minimize shrinkage cracks that may form in the patio slab. Roll out the mesh, keeping it about 2 inches away from the edges of the form. Fibers added to a ready-mix pro-

vide additional resistance to shrinkage cracks, but do not replace mesh or rebar.

Reinforcing steel must be completely embedded in the concrete to develop full strength. It should be located in the middle of the concrete slab. Small stones, bricks, or pieces of concrete block can be used to support the wire mesh. When reinforcing mesh must be spliced, lap one full row of squares and tie the laps with a soft steel wire, the way you would secure a twist tie on the bag of a loaf of bread.

1 Whether sand or gravel is used as a base over the subgrade, it must be tamped and leveled.

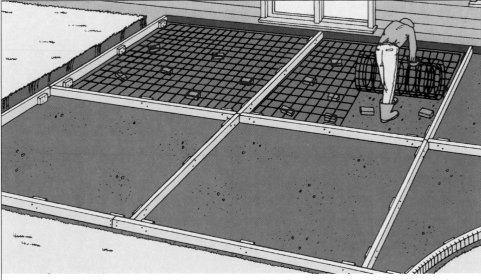

2 Locate reinforcing mesh 2 in. from the edges of the form and 2 in. below the top of the form boards.

Pouring and Finishing the Concrete

Detailed instructions for pouring concrete are contained in the section "Pouring and Placing Concrete," on page 27, but there are some specifics to bear in mind for a large pour. Before you begin placing the concrete, check the formwork for proper grade and correct depth. Once you're sure that everything is in its proper place, spray the inside surfaces of the forms and the subgrade or base with water. This will prevent water from being drawn out of the concrete, which can result in a poor-quality surface and diminished strength. Moistening the forms and soil is especially important on a warm, windy day. Be sure to wear rubber boots, protective clothing, and gloves, because prolonged contact with fresh concrete will burn your skin.

1 **Place the concrete.** With large pours in particular, mix your concrete as near the job site as you can, or have the ready-mix truck park as close as possible. Use a wheelbarrow to move the concrete from the mixing area, or from the truck, to the site. Lay 2x12s across lawn areas to protect them from the weight of the wheelbarrow. Build ramps over the forms to keep from bumping them out of place.

Start dumping the concrete in the farthest corners of the forms, making piles that are slightly taller than the forms. Fill the forms completely. Fill low areas with a shovel and tamp the concrete to fill in corners. Settle the concrete against the perimeter forms by tapping the outside of the form boards with a hammer.

As the concrete is placed, use a hook or hammer claw to lift up the wire reinforcing mesh and make sure that it is completely embedded. For this patio, which has individual sections, it is acceptable to pour the concrete in one section, immediately screed and darby it, then move on to the next square. If you have helpers, pour more than one section at a time.

2 **Smooth the concrete.** As soon as you've poured an area, screed the surface level with the top of the forms. Use a straight 2x4 that is slightly wider than the forms. Drag it along the top, pressing both ends down on the forms. Fill hollow areas with a shovel, and make them level.

After screeding, smooth the surface of the concrete with a large wooden darby. Make large, sweeping arcs, keeping the front edge raised slightly so you don't gouge the surface.

Note: Do not do anything else until the water sheen is gone from the surface of the slab.

1 Pour concrete in the farthest corner of the forms. Spread concrete to the corners with a shovel or hoe.

2 Working in sections, sweep a darby across the patio surface after it is screeded.

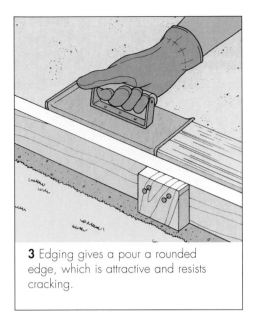

3 Edging gives a pour a rounded edge, which is attractive and resists cracking.

4 Pull a broom across the troweled concrete to create a slip-resistant surface. You can purchase brooms made specifically for this purpose.

3 **Edge the slab.** Run the edger back and forth to form a rounded, smooth edge against the permanent forms. Be careful not to gouge the concrete.

If you are not using permanent forms (which serve as control joints), now is the time to tool control joints at the locations you marked on top of the form boards. Lay a 2x12 across the tops of the forms to kneel on; use its edge as a guide for the jointing tool.

4 **Float and trowel the surface.** Hold the float nearly flat and move it in wide, sweeping motions. Be sure to smooth over any marks or gouges left by the edging or jointing process. If water comes to the surface when you begin the floating, stop and wait for it all to evaporate. Go back over the edges and control joints with the edger and jointing tool to touch up after floating. A specialty finish is applied now, if desired (see "Special Finishes for Concrete," page 30).

For a smooth, dense finish, work the surface with a steel finishing trowel. Hold the blade nearly flat against the surface. Sweep it back and forth in wide arcs, overlapping each pass by one-half the trowel blade length. This in effect trowels the surface twice in one operation. For an even smoother finish, go back over the surface again after you have finished the initial troweling. The edges and control joints may need to be touched up after troweling.

Note: In regions with freeze-thaw cycles, do not trowel air-entrained concrete.

After the floating or troweling, you can produce a nonskid finish by pulling a damp broom across the surface perpendicular to the direction of traffic. For a fine texture, use a soft bristled brush. For a coarser texture, use a broom with stiffer bristles. You will get best results if you buy a broom made especially for concrete finishing.

Cure the concrete. Correctly curing concrete is essential to a successful pour. Specifics about this very important process are given in "Curing Concrete," on page 32. After the concrete has cured for a day, carefully remove the forms. Do not pry or hammer against the concrete itself. The concrete will continue to cure for another month until it reaches full strength, but it is safe to walk on it after the first day.

Concrete Driveway

A concrete driveway that is properly designed and built will provide many years of service. Size and shape is dictated by your site and its physical restrictions, but there are some general rules to follow in determining width, slope, and turning radius. Make sure to consult your building department before beginning a driveway project; a permit may be required. In addition, you want to know where utility lines are before excavating, especially near the street. Usually, your utility company will come to the site and mark the location of lines and pipes. Schedule an appointment before excavating.

Planning the Project

On a piece of grid paper, draw a plan of the driveway to scale. Straight driveways for single car garages and carports are 10 to 14 feet wide. Curved driveways are a minimum of 14 feet wide. A driveway leading into a two-car garage or carport is between 16 and 24 feet wide. If your city or subdivision does not dictate requirements for an apron where the driveway meets the street, follow the guidelines explained in this project. The top of the driveway slab is 1 inch below the garage slab, to prevent water from backing into the garage; the street end of the drive is 1 inch above the street elevation, to keep off water from the road. If your driveway site runs downhill to the garage, you must install a storm drain in front of the garage doors to prevent flooding.

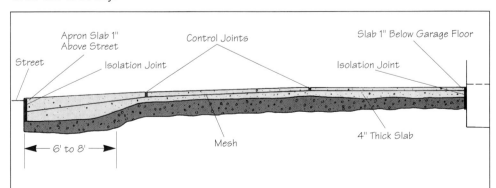

Concrete driveway. Cross-section of a typical driveway, showing a gravel base, a 4-in.-thick slab, steel reinforcing mesh, and control joints. Notice the thicker apron.

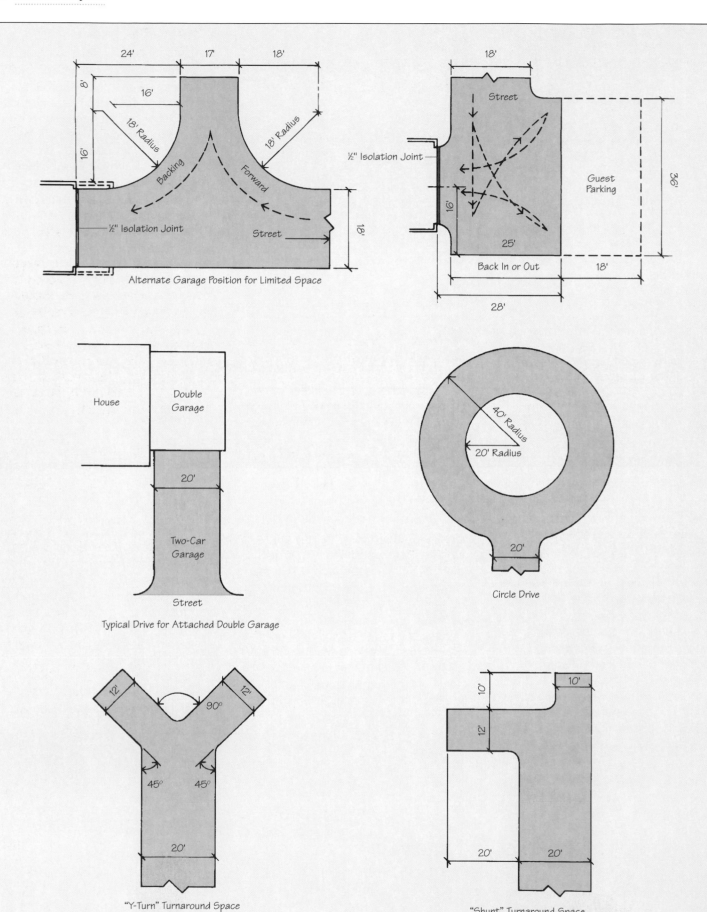

24' 17' 18'

8'

16'

18' Radius

16'

Backing

Forward

18' Radius

½" Isolation Joint

Street

18'

Alternate Garage Position for Limited Space

18'

Street

½" Isolation Joint

16'

Guest Parking

36'

25'

Back In or Out

18'

28'

House

Double Garage

20'

Two-Car Garage

Street

Typical Drive for Attached Double Garage

40' Radius

20' Radius

20'

Circle Drive

12' 90° 12'

45° 45°

20'

"Y-Turn" Turnaround Space

10' 10'

12'

20' 20'

"Shunt" Turnaround Space

Concrete driveways should be at least 4 inches thick. If there will regularly be heavier vehicles, such as delivery trucks, increase the thickness to 6 inches to support the extra weight without cracking. All aprons are 5 to 6 inches thick. If site drainage is poor, you may need a gravel as a base for drainage under the slab, usually to a depth of 4 inches.

Drainage. If your house is on a hill, the driveway should not slope more than 1¾ inches per foot of length, or a car's undercarriage and back bumper will scrape the ground at the top and bottom of the slope. If there is no slope to or from the street, flat driveways must be crowned or cross-sloped a minimum of ¼ inch per foot for water drainage.

When building a driveway, you need an isolation joint wherever the garage, a sidewalk, or the street meets the driveway. Set a control joint down the center of the drive and elsewhere,

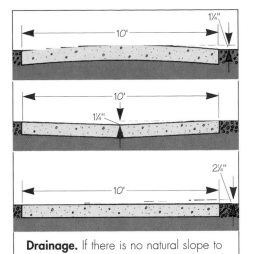

Drainage. If there is no natural slope to your driveway, the slab must be shaped to allow for water drainage. Three possibilities are the crown (top), concave (middle), and cross-slope (bottom).

as needed. Remember that for a pour as large as a driveway you may need to include some construction joints if the project cannot be completed in one day. Refer back to "Types of Joints," on page 28 for details about these joints.

Excavating

The first part of the project consists of laying out the driveway and then excavating and preparing the subgrade. Concrete driveways must be supported on firm soil that is hard, uniformly graded, and well drained. A poorly or improperly prepared subgrade will cause uneven settlement and cracking.

1 Lay out the shapes with string. First lay out the size and shape of the pour using marker stakes and string. Set stakes adjacent to the house or garage to mark the edge of the slab, allowing 1½ inches for the thickness of the form boards. Set the stakes for the outside corners a little beyond the proposed concrete edge so they will not be in the way when excavating. Tie mason's string to the stakes. Use the 3-4-5 layout method for square corners. (See page 24.)

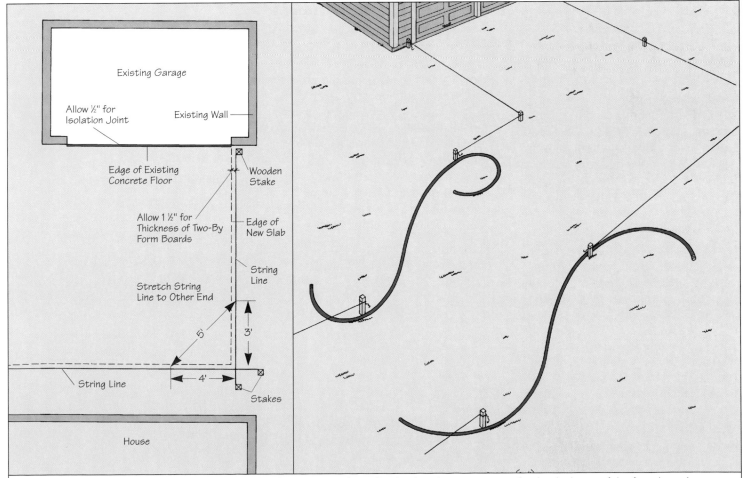

1 (Left) Set marker stakes and string to lay out the driveway. Set the stakes back 1½ in. to account for the thickness of the form boards. (Right) Curved shapes are defined with garden hoses. Mark the entire driveway location with sand.

2 For a project as large as a driveway, hire a professional to do the excavation.

3 A mechanical tamper is used to compact a large area of subgrade.

If your drive is curved, outline the shape with garden hoses. The form boards for curved shapes are only ¼ inch thick, so set the hoses back accordingly—not 1½ inches back as you had set the string for two-by lumber.

After the shape is all laid out, sprinkle sand along the entire outline to mark the shape of the pour on the ground. This will aid your excavation.

2 Excavate the soil. Temporarily untie the strings, and excavate several inches wider than the sand marking lines to allow room for building the formwork. For a large driveway project, it's best to hire an excavating contractor or rent a small backhoe for this stage of the work.

If you do the excavation yourself, remove all grass, sod, roots, and large rocks from the area. Dig out any soft or spongy areas and fill them with good soil, gravel, crushed stone, or sand. Loosen and tamp hard spots to provide uniform support. Remove enough soil to accommodate the thickness of the slab and any base. The finished concrete surface is usually 2 inches above the adjacent ground, and 1 inch below the garage or carport slab.

If site drainage is poor, excavate deeply enough to place a 4-inch layer of gravel under the concrete, and plan to finish the concrete slab 2 inches

above the adjacent ground. If necessary, shape the surrounding grade to make sure that runoff drains around, rather than over the slab. Ask your local building department how deep the gravel base should be in your area.

3 Tamp the soil. It is very important that the soil be well tamped at this point. In warm, arid areas of the country this may well be the base for the concrete, but even if a layer of gravel is being added, the excavated surface must be flat and have no gaps or holes. If you've hired an excavating contractor, they will tamp the soil. If you do it yourself, rent a mechanical tamper or roller for large areas. Small areas and the edges of the pour can be done with a hand tamper.

Building the Formwork

1 Set the elevation. Once the subgrade is prepared, you're ready to begin the formwork. Start at the stakes that are adjacent to the garage. If they have been loosened or moved during excavation, reset them firmly in the ground. Use a string and a line level to set the grade. (Mason's twine will sag less than other string.) This is the elevation for the top of the new concrete. Remember to stay at least 1 inch below the garage or carport slab. Mark the stakes with a pencil and retie your string at the correct height above the subgrade.

2 Set the string lines. Stretch the string to the stake at the far end of the apron or to the nearest corner

1 Place stakes adjacent to the garage and use twine with a line level to set the elevation of the driveway. Stay 1 in. below the garage slab.

where it turns. If necessary, drive intermediate stakes about 10 to 15 feet apart along the way to keep the string from sagging. (Stakes for the string should be placed 10 to 15 feet apart; stakes to hold the form boards will be placed 4 feet apart.) Using a line level, mark each stake and tie the string so that it is level or follows the slope of the ground. Driveways should slope away from the garage at a rate of ¼ inch per foot. Mark the lowest elevation near the street.

3 **Mark the apron curves.** The apron formwork is similar to the formwork for the rest of the driveway: Boards held by stakes contain the concrete. If the top of the apron meets a sidewalk, put an isolation joint between them. If the top of the apron meets the last section of the driveway, use a control joint where they are placed together. You also need an isolation joint at the bottom of the apron—anywhere that new concrete meets hardened concrete or asphalt.

Build the same slope into the apron that you have in the concrete driveway. The apron follows the slope elevation started at the last section of concrete (or the sidewalk) and runs down to the street normally at ¼ inch per foot for drainage. Do not make the apron grade steeper than 1¾ inches per foot or a car's undercarriage will scrape against it.

The sides of the apron are curved to make turning onto the driveway from the street easier. If the driveway is more than 15 feet wide, you needn't curve out the sides. Simply shape the edges of the apron to meet the curb. If you do need a curve, the amount depends on the length of the apron. If the apron is 10 to 15 feet long (from the sidewalk or last section of driveway to the street), use a radius measurement equal to that length to determine the side curves of the apron. For example, if your apron is going to be 11 feet long, mark a point 11 feet straight out to the side from the top edge of the apron. (If a sidewalk exists, measure along the sidewalk.) Drive a pivot stake at that point (11 feet in this case). Attach a string to the stake and mark the string's

2 Set stakes at a distance of every 15 ft. to support the marker string. Set the string with a slope of at least ¼ in.-per-ft. for drainage.

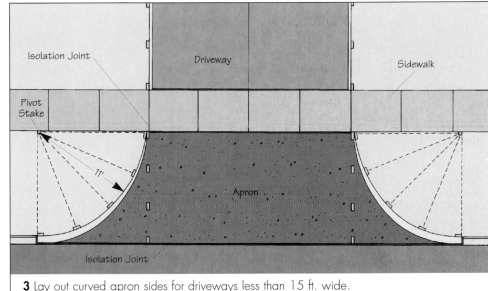

3 Lay out curved apron sides for driveways less than 15 ft. wide.

length at 11 feet. Use the string as a compass, with its center as the pivot stake, to lay out the apron's curve. Drive a stake into the ground every one to two feet along the arc's path. These stakes will support the plywood form board. Repeat the process for the other side of the apron.

If the apron is to be less than 10 feet long, use a radius of 10 feet to mark the curve. If the apron length is more than 15 feet, follow the procedure for setting straight forms along the side of the apron until you are within 10 feet of the street, and then use a corresponding radius to mark the curve.

4 **Drive the stakes and set the form boards.** For the straight forms, drive stakes along the string

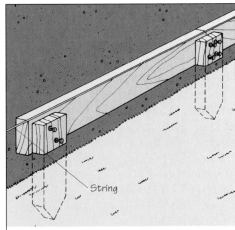

4 Drive stakes along the string line at a spacing of 3 to 4 ft. on-center. Set the tops of the stakes slightly below the string line. The boards are set to the height of the string.

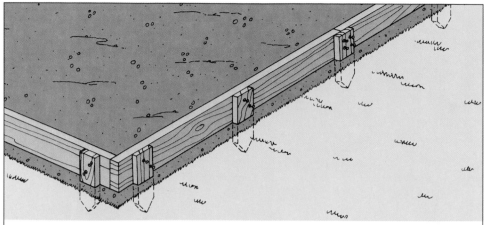

5 Proper formwork has stakes positioned every 3 to 4 ft., is perpendicular to the sub-grade, and is held together with double-headed nails. Make tight corners and joints.

6 Mark the locations of the control joints with a marker or wax crayon.

line at a spacing of 3 to 4 feet on center. Make sure the tops of the stakes are slightly below the string line so they will not interfere with leveling and finishing the top of the concrete, but leave enough height to drive two nails into the forms. When in doubt as to the number of stakes, use an extra stake or two to ensure that the forms won't bulge or bow during the pour.

When the stakes are set, attach the form boards. Use double-headed nails to make it easier to remove the forms. Set the boards so the tops are aligned with the string. Place your foot against the form board inside the form when driving nails through the stakes to prevent movement. For a large driveway pour, you may want to install a temporary construction joint form down the middle to split the pour into more manageable halves.

If your drive has curves, the forms must follow the shape. For short-radius curves, use ¼-inch plywood forms. Orient the grain of the plywood veneer vertically so the board will bend more easily. Space supports 1 to 2 feet apart. For long-radius curves, use clear 1x4 or 1x6 lumber. Wet the wood first to make bending easier and space the stakes at 2- to 3-foot intervals. Nail curved formwork from the inside outward to the stake to hold it securely. Use regular nails here, not double-headed nails, so the heads will not be embedded in the concrete, making it impossible to remove the stakes and forms later.

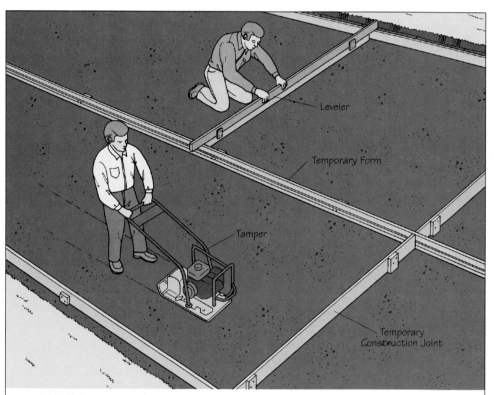

7 Add half the amount of gravel, level it, and tamp it into the forms. Then add the remaining gravel and tamp.

5 Support the joints and corners. Butt the form boards tightly together to prevent the wet concrete from leaking out. Where the ends of two boards adjoin, drive a stake to support the ends of both boards. At the corners, drive a stake on each side near the end. Hold the forms tightly against the stake and nail through the outside into the form.

6 Mark the locations of the control joints. After you have built your formwork, mark on the tops of

the forms the locations of the control joints that must be tooled or saw cut later. Use a wax crayon or other marker that will show up easily when the forms are wet and splattered with concrete. Remember to install any isolation joints (e.g., where the drive meets the garage floor slab).

7 Add the gravel drainage base. If your site has poor drainage and severe weather conditions, you may need to add a gravel base over the soil subgrade. If you will be adding gravel, first add half the amount of gravel; then level and tamp it into the forms. Then add the remaining gravel and tamp. If gravel is not needed, a 2-inch layer of sand can be laid and tamped to provide a level surface for the slab.

Placing the Reinforcement

Place the wire mesh. Use welded wire mesh to minimize any cracks that may form in the driveway. Roll out the mesh, keeping it about 2 inches away from the edges of the slab. Fibers added to a ready-mix control shrinkage cracking, but do not replace mesh or rebar.

Reinforcing steel must be completely embedded in the concrete to develop full strength and corrosion protection. It should be located just below the middle of the concrete slab. Small stones, bricks, or pieces of concrete block can be used to support the wire mesh. When reinforcing mesh must be spliced, lap one full row of squares and tie the laps with a soft steel wire, the way you would secure a twist tie on a garbage bag.

Pouring the Concrete

Before pouring the concrete, spray the inside surfaces of the forms and the soil subgrade or base with water from a garden hose. This will prevent water from being drawn out of the concrete, which would result in a

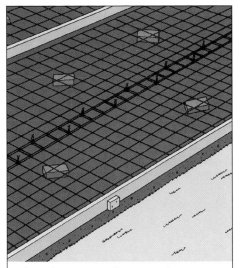

Place the wire mesh. Lay reinforcing mesh in the forms. When reinforcing mesh isn't wide enough, lap one full row of squares (6 in.) and tie the laps with steel wire.

poor quality surface with reduced strength. Moistening the forms and soil is especially important on a warm and windy day.

Detailed instructions for pouring concrete are contained in the section "Pouring and Placing Concrete," on page 27. Here we will discuss specifics to bear in mind for a large driveway project.

1 **Place the concrete.** With large pours in particular, mix your concrete as near the job site as you can, or have the ready-mix truck park as close as possible. Use a wheelbarrow

to move the concrete from the mixing area or from the truck to the site and lay 2x12s across lawn areas to protect them from the weight of the wheelbarrow. Build ramps over the forms to keep from bumping them out of place.

Start dumping the concrete in the farthest corner of the forms, making piles that are slightly taller than the forms. Fill the forms completely. Fill low areas with a shovel and tamp the concrete to fill in corners. Settle the concrete against the perimeter of the forms by tapping the outside of the form boards with a hammer.

2 **Lift the reinforcing mesh.** Use the claw of a hammer to lift up the wire mesh. Make sure it is completely embedded and in the middle of the slab. Continue transporting and dumping the concrete until the forms are full.

3 **Level the concrete.** As soon as the first few feet or the first section of the driveway is poured, begin screeding the surface level with the top of the forms. Use a length of 2x4 that is slightly wider than the forms. Drag it along the top of the forms to level the concrete, keeping both ends pressed down on top of the forms. Fill any hollow areas with a shovel; then strike the concrete off level.

If you want your driveway to be higher in the middle than the edges so that

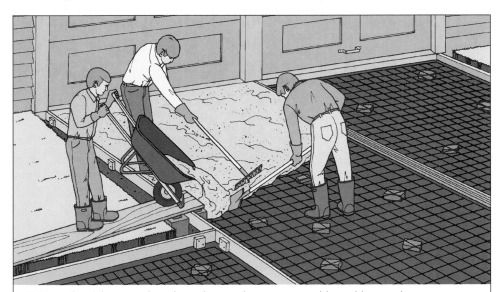

1 Have the delivery truck park as close to the site as possible and begin placing concrete into the far corner of the forms.

2 Use the claw of a hammer to lift the mesh. It must be in the middle of the pour.

water will drain to the sides, or if you want it lower in the middle to channel water away, you will need to make a curved screed. The lumber used for the strike-off board must be longer than the width of the driveway to be able to rest on the sides of the form-work while screeding. For a crowned driveway, lay two 2x4s edge to edge and nail them together in the middle by overlaying a piece of scrap wood. Insert small wooden blocks or wedges at the ends to hold the boards, creating a ¼-inch-per-foot slope. Nail a piece of scrap wood near each end to hold this bow shape. For a concave driveway, nail scraps of wood at the ends first, and then drive a wedge or block in the middle before nailing the boards together.

4 **Bull float the surface.** Since driveways are so wide, a bull float, not a darby, is used to smooth the screeded concrete. You can make one by attaching a 4-foot-long 1x12 to a 12-foot-long 2x2 handle. Simply cut one end of the handle to a 30-degree angle and screw it into the 1x12 base. Use a scrap of 2x2 as a brace under the handle, as shown in the illustration. Do not allow screws to penetrate the 1x12 or you'll mar the surface of the concrete. Bull floats can also be rented.

When using a bull float, push it across the surface with the front edge raised a bit; when pulling it back, lay the blade flat to cut off bumps and fill any tiny holes. At the end of each stroke, lift the float and move it over for a parallel stroke. Repeat this process from the opposite side when finished.

5 **Form the curb transition.** At the street curb you need to form a slight transition from the flat driveway up to the curb height. Most curbs are an integral part of a gutter that runs across the bottom of the apron, separating the apron from the street. Remember to put an isolation joint between the apron and the street.

To form the curb transition, first screed the middle area of the slab with a flat 2x4, and push the excess concrete toward the sides of the form

Making a Screed

By inserting scraps of wood between 2x4s, you can make a crowned (top) or concave (bottom) screeding board.

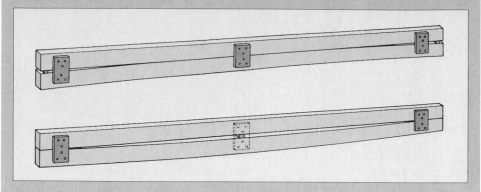

3 As soon as a section is poured, begin screeding the surface level with the top of the forms.

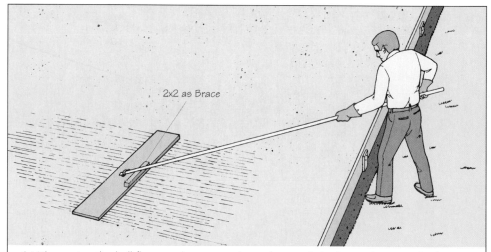

4 When using the bull float, push it across the surface with the front edge raised a bit; when pulling it back, lay the blade flat to cut off bumps and fill any tiny holes. At the end of each stroke, lift the float and move it over for a parallel stroke.

5 Use a wooden float to form the sides of the curb transition.

Isolation Joint

Existing Curb

6 Run an edger at the perimeter of the pour to create rounded edges.

7 Use a circular saw with a masonry blade to cut control joints as needed.

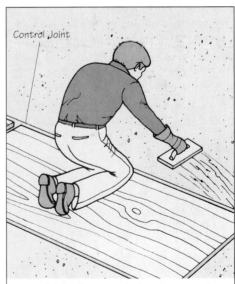

Control Joint

8 Hold the float nearly flat, keeping the leading edge slightly raised to avoid gouging the surface. Move it in wide sweeping motions.

into the curved sections. Remove the straight form boards and quickly fill the holes made by the stakes. Begin to smooth the rest of the concrete in the apron edges. As you meet the edge next to the curb, use a float to move the concrete into a gentle curve that moves from the apron up to the curb height.

Note: Do not do anything else until the water sheen is gone from the surface. The time that this will take depends on the temperature, wind, and humidity as well as the type of cement you used.

6 Edge the slab. First, use the point of a small trowel to cut the top inch or so of concrete away from the face of the form, so that the form will pull away from the concrete easily when it is removed. Then edge the slab with an edging trowel to form an attractive, finished edge. Run the edger back and forth to smooth the surface, being careful not to gouge the concrete.

7 Create the control joints. Use a jointing or grooving trowel to form control joints at the locations you have marked on top of the form (see "Control Joints," on page 29). Use a straight piece of 2x4 as a guide

for cutting the joints. Lay a 2x12 supported by concrete blocks or bricks across the tops of the forms to kneel on while you work.

If the curve of the apron creates a tightly angled strip of concrete (45 degrees or less) at the bottom of the apron where it meets the street, cut a control joint on either side of the bottom of the apron. Cut the joint at an angle (not perpendicular to the street) by making the inside two angles of the triangle formed by the cut roughly equal.

If you have a circular saw, you may want to saw rather than tool your control joints. A saw will produce a clean cut that is narrower than, but as effective as, a hand-tooled cut. You must wait until the concrete has hardened for about three hours before sawing control joints. Continue your finishing operations; then use the circular saw with a masonry-cutting blade to saw grooves to a depth of about one-fourth the slab thickness. Use a straight 2x4 as a cutting guide.

8 Float the surface. Use a wooden float to smooth the surface and bring the cement paste to the top of the slab. Hold the float nearly flat, keeping the leading edge slightly

raised to avoid gouging the surface, and move it in wide sweeping motions. If water comes to the surface when you begin the floating, stop and wait a while before trying again. Go back over the edges and control joints with the edger and jointing tool to touch up after floating. (If the driveway slab is to be a base for masonry pavers, leave the concrete with this float finish.)

9 Pull brooms across the driveway to create a slip-resistant surface.

10 Cover the drive with burlap secured with bricks. Leave the covering on until the concrete has cured.

9 **Broom the surface.** To produce a finish that will not be slippery when wet, pull a damp broom across the surface in a direction that is perpendicular to the direction of traffic. For a fine texture, use a soft-bristled push broom. For a coarser texture, use a broom with stiffer bristles. You will get best results if you buy a broom made especially for concrete finishing.

10 **Curing the concrete.** Review the section "Curing Concrete," on page 32, for specific information

about curing concrete. Cover the surface of the driveway with burlap roofing felt, or plastic sheeting. If you use burlap, spray it with a garden hose twice daily to keep it wet. Use lumber or bricks to hold down the burlap. After the concrete has cured for a day, carefully remove the forms. Do not pry against the concrete or you may crack or break the edges. Your project will gain its full strength in about 28 days, but you can use the drive after about a week.

Concrete Steps

Concrete steps are most commonly found at entrances to homes. These durable, low-maintenance steps can also work very well as garden steps to traverse slopes in the landscape. This project provides instructions for building and designing both types of concrete steps.

Planning the Project

Any stairs, indoor or out, must be designed to be comfortable and safe to use. One of the most important aspects of creating a proper stair is to size the horizontal treads and the vertical risers to accommodate the average person's normal stride. This means that the taller the risers, the more shallow the treads, because the higher you have to raise your leg, the less far out you can extend it. As a rule of thumb, twice the height of the riser plus the depth of the tread should equal between 25 and 27 inches. Another universal rule for stairs is that all the risers must be identical in height and all the treads must be identical in depth. Once we begin a flight of stairs, we usually stop looking at our feet. We expect all the steps to be identical; and if one is off, we'll probably trip.

One more design criterion to shoot for: For flights of stairs less than 30 inches high, try to make each riser 7½ inches or less and each tread at least 11 inches. For flights of stairs higher than 30 inches, risers should be 6 inches or less and treads, at least 12 inches. These are goals rather than rules. They're intended to help design stairs that are as comfortable as possible.

Local building codes require a minimum stair width of 30 to 36 inches. In general, make your stairs as wide as possible or, at the very least, as wide as the doorway or walkway they will serve.

The way you apply these guides depends on where the steps will be located. For example, if you are building a front stoop, you may have exactly 8 feet 2 inches from the front door to the sidewalk. This horizontal distance is called the total run of the stairs, and in this case, you'll have to design your steps around this unchangeable measurement. We view steps leading into a building as part of that building, and as such, we expect the stoop stairs to be similar in rise and run to interior stairs. Like interior stairs, the ideal riser height for a stoop is 7 inches; the ideal tread depth is 12 inches.

Building garden stairs is an entirely different situation from stairs built to enter a building. If you are building steps to traverse a slope, you usually have some leeway in deciding exactly where you want to locate both ends of the stairs, as there is generally no house or walk defining the space. Gradual steps with short risers and deep treads blend better into the landscape than do steep stairs. As a result, the ideal riser height for garden steps is 6 inches, and the ideal tread depth is 15 inches.

Because the design criteria for a front stoop and a garden step differ, the methods for calculating their rise and run and for building their forms differ. However, the procedures for pouring and finishing the concrete are exactly the same for both types of steps. So, if you are building a stoop, read "Calculating a Stoop" and "Excavating and Building the Stoop Forms,"

below. If you are building garden steps, read "Calculating Garden Steps" and "Excavating and Building the Garden Step Forms," below. Then, regardless of which type of stair you are building, follow the steps under "Pouring and Finishing the Concrete," on page 44.

Calculating a Stoop

1 **Determine the total rise.** If the ground between the door and the location of the bottom of the last step were perfectly level, you could determine the total rise simply by measuring from the bottom of the door sill to the ground and then subtracting 4 inches. The landing is lower than the door sill to keep snow and rain from being blown under the door and into the house. Unfortunately, you don't know the ground is level. Here's a method for determining total rise that incorporates any change in grade, either across the width of the steps or from the sill to the bottom step.

If possible, plan your steps to be wider than the doorway by at least 1 foot on each side. Measure down 4 inches from the bottom of the door sill and use a 4-foot level to draw a level line under the sill across the foundation wall. Make the line a little longer than the planned stairway width and make two vertical marks on the line to define the step width.

Drive long stakes into the ground, locating them so that their inside edges define the outside corners of the bottom step, as shown in the illustration. In the example shown, the bottom step ends at a sidewalk; this is the total run of the steps. Use string and the 3-4-5 method (see page 24, "Making Square Corners") to make sure the stakes are aligned to the marks on the wall. Check that the stakes are plumb.

Put a line level on the string and hold one end against one of the marks on the foundation wall. Have a helper hold the other end against the inside of one of the stakes and adjust the height until the string is level. Then have the helper mark the stake where the line crosses it. Repeat this process at the other stake.

Measure from the ground up to the mark on each stake. If one measurement is longer than the other, use the longer measurement as your total rise. For this example, let's say that the total rise is 32 inches.

2 **Determine the unit rise.** Start by dividing the total rise of 32 inches by the ideal riser height of 7 inches. The result is 4.57 risers. Since it's impossible to have 4.57 risers, just use the whole number, or 4 risers in this case. Now, divide the total rise by the number of risers to get the unit rise: 32 ÷ 4 = 8. Indoors, you might

1 Use stakes, string, and a line level to determine the total rise of the stairway.

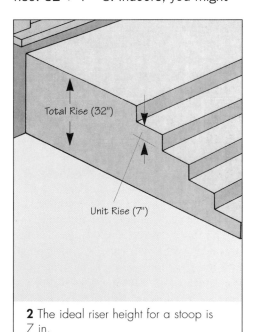

2 The ideal riser height for a stoop is 7 in.

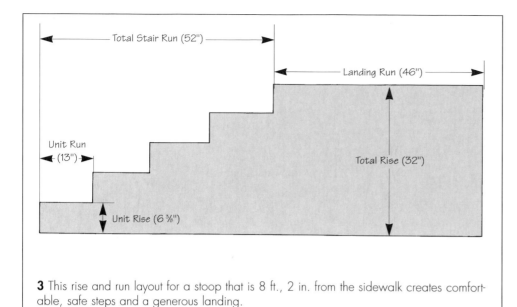

3 This rise and run layout for a stoop that is 8 ft., 2 in. from the sidewalk creates comfortable, safe steps and a generous landing.

be able to get away with 8-inch high risers, but it's a bit steep for outdoor stairs that could become icy. With five steps each riser would be 6 ⅜ inches, which is better. Although it exceeds the 6-inch maximum rise for stairways more than 30 inches high, this unit rise is close enough to ensure a comfortable step.

3 **Determine the unit run.** In the example shown, the total run of the stoop is determined by the fact that the distance from the foundation wall to the sidewalk is 98 inches. Now you must calculate the run of all the stairs and the landing run. In our example, the stoop has four treads, not counting the landing. The ideal tread depth (called the unit run) is 12 inches. The first stair-building rule of thumb says that twice the unit rise plus the unit run should equal between 25 and 27 inches. In the example: Two times the rise of 6 ⅜ inches equals 12 ¾ inches. Add a unit run of 12 inches and you get 24 ¾ inches—a little shy of our requirement. These stairs would still work fine, but again, outdoors it is better to be generous. So let's make the treads 13 inches deep. Multiply 13 inches by four treads to get a total run of 52 inches for the steps. Since the total run of the stoop is 98 inches, that leaves 46 inches of landing run, which is plenty. In fact, one design option would be to locate the bottom step a foot or so closer to the

house, reduce the landing run by an equal amount, and pour a concrete pad at the level of the sidewalk. The smaller the landing, the less concrete you will need.

Excavating and Building the Stoop Forms

1 **Level the ground.** In Step 1, you drew a level line on the foundation wall and made two marks to define the width of the stairs. Measure from the marks you made on the foundation wall to the ground. Let's say in

our example we find that measurement to be 33 inches at the left mark and 34 inches on the right mark. When you measured at the stakes earlier, you found the distance from the left level mark to be 32 inches and the distance from the right level mark to be 31 inches. Your excavation should be at least 6 inches deep. The illustration shows how the excavation depths can vary at the corners to create level stairs.

Remove all grass, sod, roots, and large rocks from the excavation. Dig out any soft or spongy areas and fill them with good soil, or with gravel, crushed stone, or sand.

In areas with cold winters, flights of three steps or more need a footing that extends below the frost line (see "Concrete Footings," page 63). If you need a footing, dig it now and pour it before you form and pour the steps. Leave several steel reinforcing bars sticking out of the top of the footing to tie the steps and footing together.

2 **Lay out the side forms.** Make the side forms from ¾-inch-thick exterior- or exposure-grade plywood. A standard sheet of plywood measures 4x8 feet, although you can purchase sheets that are 10 or 12 feet long. In the example, the

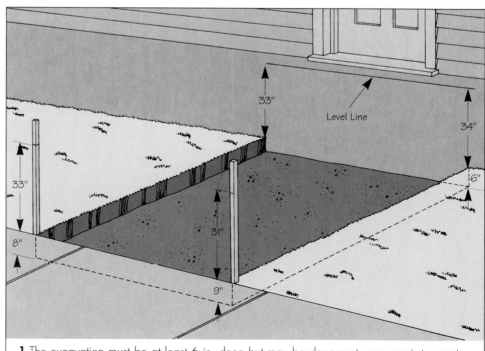

1 The excavation must be at least 6 in. deep but may be deeper at some spots to create a level bottom.

combined run of the landing and steps is 98 inches, just 2 inches longer than a standard plywood sheet. You can solve the problem by buying 10-foot-long sheets, or you can save money by easily adding small pieces for the bottom step, as shown here.

Place a full sheet of plywood on a pair of sawhorses and lay out the treads, risers, and landing full-scale. In the illustration, this layout is shown with dotted lines. Lay out your lines lightly, they won't be your final cutting lines. Allow 6 inches of plywood on the bottom for the portion of the form that will be below grade.

For drainage, the landing and treads should slope away from the house about ¼ inch per foot. In the example, the landing has a run of 46 inches—close enough to 4 feet to add 1 inch for slope, as shown in the illustration.

The steps should slope for drainage too—the 13-inch-deep treads are close enough to 1 foot to slope each ¼ inch. You have one other adjustment to make. It's a good idea to slant the risers in about 1 inch to prevent stubbed toes. To make the slant adjustments, measure in 1 inch from the tread and riser intersections, as shown in the illustration. Then measure up ¼ inch for the slope adjustment.

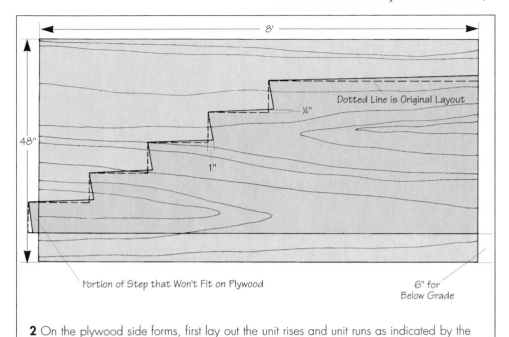

8'

48"

¼"

1"

Dotted Line is Original Layout

Portion of Step that Won't Fit on Plywood

6" for Below Grade

2 On the plywood side forms, first lay out the unit rises and unit runs as indicated by the dotted lines. Then adjust for drainage slope and slanted risers.

3 **Cut out the side forms.** Use a circular saw to cut out the first side form; then use the first form as a template to lay out the second form. Cut out the second form. For this example, you would then cut two 2x12 strips of ⅜-inch plywood to extend the bottom step where the 8-foot plywood sheet doesn't reach.

4 **Erect the side forms.** Position the side forms at each side of the entry, using a carpenter's square to make sure they are perpendicular to the walls of the house. Use a level to check that the back of the forms are plumb and the bottoms are level. Check across the forms to make sure they are at the same level. Drive 2x2 stakes into the ground about 1 foot apart. Except for the ones nearest the wall, make sure the stakes at the sides of the forms are shorter than the plywood so they won't interfere with screeding the concrete after it is poured. Leave the stakes nearest the wall about 4 inches taller than the tops of the forms; they will support a cross-tie that will be added later. In the example, 2x4 stakes are used at the bottom step to support the strips of plywood that extend the plywood sheet.

3 Use a circular saw to cut the first side form, then use the first form as a template to lay out the second side form.

To attach the stakes to the forms, drill ³⁄₁₆-inch-diameter pilot holes through the stakes to insert screws. You can use a piece of tape on the drill bit to make sure you don't drill through the plywood too. Insert 2-inch drywall screws into the pilot holes and drive them into the plywood.

5 Cut riser forms. Rip 2x8 lumber to the height of the risers (6⅜ inches in our example). When you make the cuts, bevel them at about 45 degrees. Use the bevel side as the bottom edge so that you will be able to reach and finish the entire

surface of the tread with your float and trowel. Cut the 2x8 riser forms equal to the width of your steps plus 1½ inches for the thickness of the forms. Predrill and screw the riser form boards as you did the side forms; this time use 2½-inch-long drywall screws to attach these boards.

6 Shore the forms against bulging. Shore the side forms using 2x2 or 2x4 stakes driven into the ground with 1x4 braces connecting them to the stakes on the side form.

For steps wider than 48 inches, reinforce the riser forms to prevent them

from bulging. First attach a 2x4 stake near the center of the bottom riser. Nail a length of 2x6 to this stake and angle-screw small cleats to the risers to hold the 2x6. Angle the ends of the cleats, as shown, so you can get your trowel in when finishing the concrete. Finally, nail a 2x4 cross-tie between the two side-form stakes nearest the foundation wall.

7 Paint on the mastic. To prevent the concrete from sticking to the foundation wall, paint or trowel a coat of mastic onto it. This will form an isolation joint and keep the concrete

4 Install the side forms in the excavation, supporting the forms with stakes. Screw the stakes to the forms.

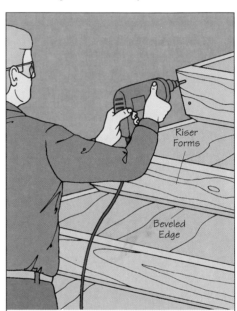

5 Make the riser forms from 2x8 lumber; rip them the riser height and create a beveled bottom edge. Screw the riser forms to the side forms.

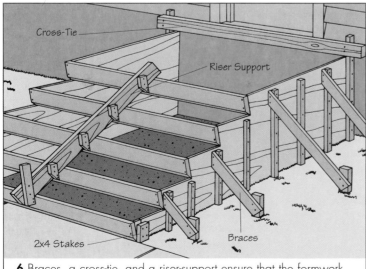

6 Braces, a cross-tie, and a riser-support ensure that the formwork will not bulge when the concrete is poured.

7 Apply mastic to the foundation wall to act as an isolation joint.

8 Fill the center of the step form with rubble to reduce the amount of concrete you'll need for the pour.

from cracking along this intersection when it shrinks during curing.

8 Fill the form with rubble. To reduce the volume of concrete that will be needed, fill the center portion of the step form with gravel, brick, stone, or broken concrete. Be sure to keep the fill at least 4 inches away from the side forms, the riser forms, and the top of the concrete. This will ensure that you get a minimum 4-inch thickness of concrete over and around the fill material.

Calculating Garden Steps

1 Determine the total run. Since garden steps don't abut a building, you usually have flexibility about where the top and bottom of the steps will be located. As a result, your design leeway is in the total run—the total horizontal distance the stairway will travel. On the other hand, the vertical distance the stairway must travel, called the total rise, is more fixed as it is determined by the change in grade you want to traverse.

With this in mind, start by driving a stake in the ground at the top of the grade, about where you want the top of the steps to be. Hook your tape measure over the stake and pull the tape

straight out until you reach the bottom of the grade. Stop at a nice even number if you can—say, 8 feet. This is your total run. Drive a longer stake into the

ground at this point. Use a level to check that the stake is plumb.

2 Determine the total rise. The vertical distance the stairs will traverse is called the total rise. To determine the total rise, tie string to the uphill stake. Mason's twine is best because it sags less than other string. Make sure the string is attached to the uphill stake at ground level. Stretch the string tautly to the downhill stake and put a line level on it. Adjust the string at the downhill side until it is level. When it is, mark where the string crosses the downhill stake. Now measure from the ground to the mark to get the total rise. Let's say you find the total rise to be 30 inches.

3 Determine the unit rise and run. As mentioned earlier, the ideal riser height (unit rise) for outdoor stairs is 6 inches. In the example, the total rise is 30 inches, which would give you five steps. Dividing the total run of 96 inches by five steps gives you a tread depth (unit run) of 19.2 inches. That's too deep for a comfortable stride.

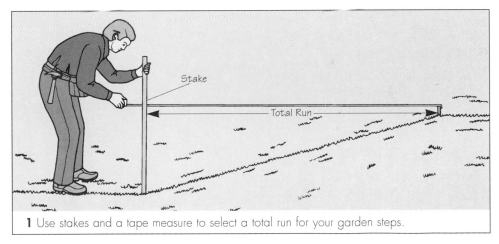

1 Use stakes and a tape measure to select a total run for your garden steps.

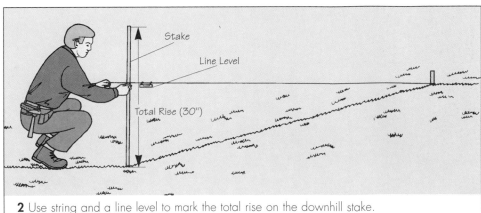

2 Use string and a line level to mark the total rise on the downhill stake.

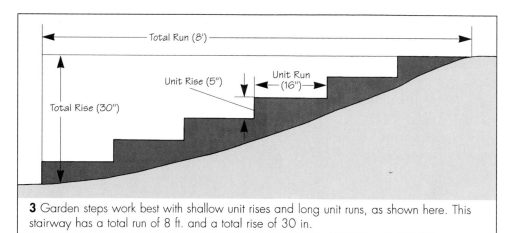

3 Garden steps work best with shallow unit rises and long unit runs, as shown here. This stairway has a total run of 8 ft. and a total rise of 30 in.

See what happens if you try six steps: 96 inches divided by six steps equals 16 inches for the unit run. With a total rise of 30 inches, six steps would give you 5-inch risers. The tread is a bit longer than ideal (which is 12 inches), but the rise is a bit shorter. The first stair-building rule of thumb says that twice the unit rise plus the unit run should equal between 25 and 27 inches to create a comfortable step. For our six-step design, the result is 26 (10+16), which means that the 5-inch unit rise and 16-inch unit run will be fine.

Excavating and Building the Garden Step Forms

All garden steps require a footing at the bottom. If there are more than three steps, tie the steps together by including a footing under the top step

Garden Steps to Span Long Distances

In outdoor construction, you may want to intersperse the steps with sections of sidewalk if there are a number of grade changes in the landscape. If you do this, try to make the sidewalk sections an uneven number of paces long. Of course, pace length varies according to each person's height and walking style, but 17 inches is a good average. So make the sidewalks 17 inches, 51 inches, or 85 inches long, if you can. This way walkers will alternate between left and right feet when stepping up, making the walk feel more natural and comfortable.

as well. The footing should be at least 2 feet deep or, in areas where freezing occurs, 6 inches below the frost line. Pour the footings before the steps and leave reinforcing bars sticking up to tie the steps to the footing. See "Concrete Footings," page 63.

1 Calculate the side form lengths. Make your side forms from 2x12s. Here's a quick and easy way to use your framing square and tape mea-

sure to determine how long the boards need to be.

Using a scale of 1 inch equals 1 foot, measure from the framing square's blade to its tongue to find the length of the form board. The example stairway has a total run of 8 feet, so start measuring from the 8-inch mark on the tongue. The example stairway's total rise is 30 inches (2½ feet), so measure up to the 2½-inch mark on the square's tongue. The measurement on the tape measure is about 8½ inches. Since lumber is sold in 2-foot increments, you know you need to purchase two, 10-foot 2x12s for your side forms.

2 Lay out and cut the side forms. Place one of the 2x12s on a pair of sawhorses and lay out the treads, risers, and top step full-scale. In the illustration, this layout is shown with dotted lines. Lay out these lines lightly; they won't be your final cutting lines.

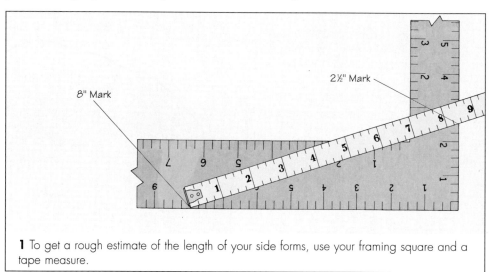

1 To get a rough estimate of the length of your side forms, use your framing square and a tape measure.

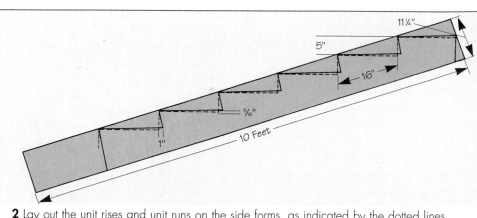

2 Lay out the unit rises and unit runs on the side forms, as indicated by the dotted lines. Then adjust the layout for tread slope and riser slant.

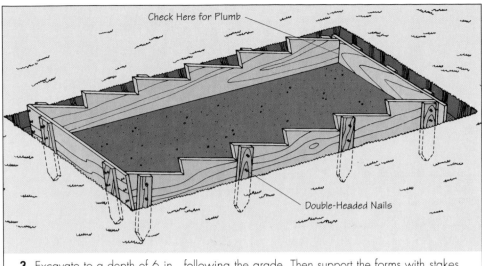

3 Excavate to a depth of 6 in., following the grade. Then support the forms with stakes fastened with double-headed nails.

Check Here for Plumb

Double-Headed Nails

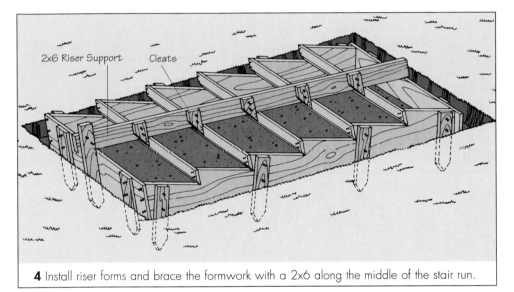

4 Install riser forms and brace the formwork with a 2x6 along the middle of the stair run.

2x6 Riser Support   Cleats

For drainage, the treads should slope downhill about ¼ inch per foot. The example steps have a run of 16 inches so slope each tread about ⁵⁄₁₆-inch. Also, it's a good idea to slant the risers in about 1 inch to prevent stubbed toes. To make the slant adjustment, measure in 1 inch from the tread and riser intersections, as shown in the illustration. Then measure up ⁵⁄₁₆-inch for the slope adjustment. Use a circular saw to cut out the first form; then use the first form as a template to lay out the second form. Cut out the second form.

3 Excavate the site and set the forms. The concrete will need to be poured to a depth of 6 inches below grade, so excavate the step site to that depth. The excavation need not be level at the bottom, it

should follow the slope of the natural landscape. Make the excavation about 12 inches wider and 12 inches longer than the steps to give you room to assemble the forms. You may need to excavate deep enough for a gravel base under the concrete if site drainage is poor.

Set the side forms into the excavation. Make sure the forms are plumb at the top of the steps, as indicated in the illustration. Cut enough 24-inch-long 2x4 stakes to space them every 2 or 3 feet. Pound the stakes into the ground and secure them to the form boards with 8d double-headed nails.

Cut two end form boards to 3 inches longer than the final step width. Nail one to each end of the side form boards with 10d double-headed nails.

4 Install the riser forms and bracing. Rip 2-by stock to equal the height the rise of the steps. For this example, rip 2x6s to 5 inches wide. When you made the rip cuts, set the blade of your saw to 45 degrees to create bevels. Placed to the outside at the bottom, this bevel will allow you access to the entire tread when you finish the concrete. Cut the riser forms to the width of the final steps plus 3 inches for the width of the side forms.

Nail the riser forms across the side forms. To brace the form, lay a 2x6 up the stairs, centered side to side, as shown. Attach the brace to a stake against the outside of the bottom end form with 8d double-headed nails. Cut cleats with ends angled at 45 degrees. Place a cleat against each riser form and nail it to the brace. Toenail the cleat to the risers.

Pouring and Finishing the Concrete

This section applies to both stoops and garden steps. Wear rubber boots, protective clothing, and gloves, because prolonged contact with concrete will burn your skin. See "Pouring and Placing Concrete," on page 27 for general information.

1 Place the reinforcing mesh. To provide added strength for your steps and to minimize cracking, place wire mesh reinforcement in the form. Reinforcing mesh must be completely

1 Place wire mesh reinforcement into the forms to minimize cracking.

embedded in the concrete. Use small stones, bricks or pieces of broken concrete or concrete block to support the mesh so that it will be in the middle of the pour. Allow 2 inches between the edges of the mesh and the edges of the form. Overlap the pieces of mesh by 6 inches and tie them together with wire.

Before you start mixing the concrete, check the formwork for correct size and depth. Once you're sure that everything is in its proper place, spray the inside surfaces of the forms, the rubble fill, if any, and the soil sub-grade with water from a garden hose. This will keep them from drawing moisture from the concrete, possibly resulting in a poor surface. Moistening the forms and soil is especially important on a warm, windy day.

2 **Place the concrete.** Mix your concrete as near the job site as you can or have the delivery truck park as close as possible. If you're lucky, the delivery truck's chute extensions will reach your form and you won't have to cart the concrete. Otherwise, move the concrete from the mixing area or from the truck to the project site with a wheelbarrow. Lay 2x12s across lawn areas to protect them from the weight of the wheelbarrow.

Start dumping the concrete in the bottom step, making sure to fill the form completely. Fill the next step, using a shovel if you are transporting with a wheelbarrow. Tamp the concrete with a shovel to fill in corners and remove air voids. Tap the outside of the form boards lightly with a hammer to settle the concrete around the perimeter of the forms.

As you place the concrete, lift up the wire reinforcing mesh with a hammer claw to make sure it is totally embedded. Continue transporting and dumping the concrete until the form is full.

3 **Screed the concrete.** Once you have filled the form with concrete, you can remove the middle brace. The danger of the forms bulging is greatest as the concrete is being placed into the form, and now that's finished. Begin to strike off, or

Wire Reinforcing Mesh

2 Place the concrete in the formwork beginning with the bottom step.

3 Use a 2x4 to screed the surface of the concrete level with the top of the form.

screed, the surface of the concrete level with the top of the form. To do this, drag a straight 2x4 that is slightly wider than the steps along the top of the form. Press both ends down on the form. Fill any hollow areas with a shovel, then level them.

4 **Smooth the surface.** Smooth the surface of the concrete for the first time with a darby or a float. Make large, sweeping arcs, being careful not to gouge the surface. Do not do anything else until the water sheen is gone from the surface. The waiting time depends on the tempera-

4 Smooth the surface of the concrete by making large, sweeping arcs with a darby.

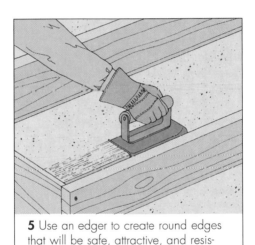

5 Use an edger to create round edges that will be safe, attractive, and resistant to damage.

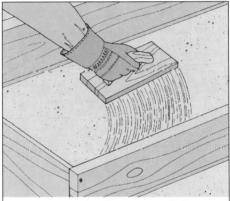

6 Use a wooden float to smooth the surface and bring a cement paste to the top.

ture, wind, and humidity as well as the type of cement used.

5 Separate and form the edges. Next, use the point of a small trowel to cut the top inch or so of concrete away from the face of the form, so concrete won't chip off when the form is removed. Then use an edger to round the edges so they will be attractive and resistant to damage. Run the edger back and forth to smooth the surface, being careful not to gouge the concrete.

6 Float, trowel, and broom the surface. The finishing operations are detailed in "Final Floating, Troweling, and Brooming," on page 29. The steps are summarized here.

Use a wooden float to smooth the surface and bring a cement paste to the top of the concrete of the treads and risers. Hold the float nearly flat and move it in wide, sweeping motions. Be sure to smooth over any marks or gouges. If water comes to the surface when you begin the floating, stop and wait a while before trying again. Go back over the edges with the edger to touch up after floating.

Floating can be the final stage in building a concrete step, as a floated finish yields a surface with good traction. There are, however, a few ways to make the steps even safer. One way is to pull a damp broom along the floated surface to texture the

concrete. Pull the broom across each step in one motion, parallel to the door. Another method is to sprinkle an abrasive material, such as silicon carbide or aluminum oxide, onto the treads after the floating and then float a second time. A third method is to install nonslip strips in the treads after the first floating.

Cure the concrete. After the concrete has cured for at least three days, carefully remove the forms. Do not pry or hammer against the concrete itself.

The concrete will continue to cure slowly for another month, until it reaches full strength but the steps can be used after the first week. If there are any holes or defective areas in the sides of the steps that were covered by forms, patch them with a stiff mixture of cement sand and water. Smooth the patch with a wooden float, and keep it moist for several days to cure.

The concrete will continue to cure slowly for another month until it reaches full strength, but the steps can be used after the first week. If there are any holes or defective areas in the sides of the steps that were covered by forms, patch them with a stiff mix of cement, sand, and water. Smooth the patch with a wooden float, and keep it moist for several days to cure. Keep all the concrete moist for seven days to allow it to cure properly, using one of the methods described in "Curing Concrete," on page 32.

Concrete Footings

Concrete footings are used to support garden walls of brick, block, or stone. Footings are also used below stairs, usually located below the lowest step, to anchor the structure to the ground. Footings are set below the local frost line depth to avoid damage from frost heave. The depth to which the soil freezes depends not only on climate and geographic location but also on soil composition, altitude, and weather patterns. In North America, particularly in western and northern locales, patterns of freezing can vary widely

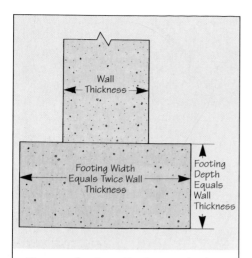

Concrete footings. The footing depth should be the same as the wall thickness, or a minimum of 8 in. The footing width should be twice the wall thickness, or a minimum of 16 in.

within a small area. It is imperative that you consult your local building department to determine frost line depth and how much farther a footing should reach below that line.

The following project is for building a footing under a masonry wall, but the technique is the same for a stairway or ramp footing. Simply make the footing as long as the stairway/ramp is wide and locate the footing at the bottom step or where the ramp ends.

Planning the Project

Building codes are very specific about footing requirements for various structures, so get information from your local building department before starting any work. In areas with extremely deep frost lines, it may not be practical to dig the wall footing below the frost line; you could end up with more wall beneath the ground than above it. In some cases, the code might allow the footing to sit on at least 8 inches of compacted, well-drained gravel that is laid above the frost line. If at all possible, however, it's always best to set footings below the frost line, where freezing and thawing soil won't push the wall up and down. In soil with poor drainage (regardless of frost line depth), place the footing on a tamped gravel base at least 6 inches thick. The gravel base prevents water

from accumulating beneath the footing, keeping soil movement to a minimum. If you are unsure of the soil type, ask your local building officials about the types of wall footings they recommend. Footings for walls must be sturdy and strong to support the weight they will carry.

The footing depth should be the same as the wall thickness, or a minimum of 8 inches. The footing width should be twice the wall thickness, or a minimum of 16 inches.

Wooden forms are used for shaping a footing. If you can dig a trench without the sidewalls crumbling, then the earth itself can be used as forms. In most cases, however, form boards are required to make accurate, level footings. Use wide boards (2x6s, 2x8s, 2x10s, etc.) that extend to the full depth of the footing, or, if the soil will hold a vertical edge, dig the rim of the trench wider to accommodate narrow boards, such as 2x4s, that will serve as guides for leveling the top of the concrete footing.

Poured concrete can exert considerable pressure on the forms, so they should be held in position with 1x4 stakes driven into the ground and nailed to the forms every few feet and 1x4 spreaders nailed every few feet along the top of the form boards. Use double-headed nails so that you

can dismantle the forms easily after the concrete has set.

Locating and Excavating

Once you've established where to build a wall, use stakes, string, and batter boards to mark the footing location and to guide you in excavating trenches and setting up any forms. You can use the following instructions for either a freestanding straight wall or for one with corners. If your wall will define property lines, be sure the footing is properly positioned according to easement regulations.

1 **Locate the wall ends and corners.** Drive stakes in the ground to represent both 90-degree corners of the wall or, for straight, freestanding walls, the outer corners of the wall at each end.

2 **Erect the batter boards.** Measure out 3 to 4 feet beyond each stake, and erect a set of batter boards, as shown. The batter board crosspieces (the horizontal members) should be at least 1 foot wider than the anticipated width of the footing trench, with the center roughly aligned to the center point of the proposed wall.

Using the stakes as guides, attach a string to the batter boards to represent the outside face of the wall. At

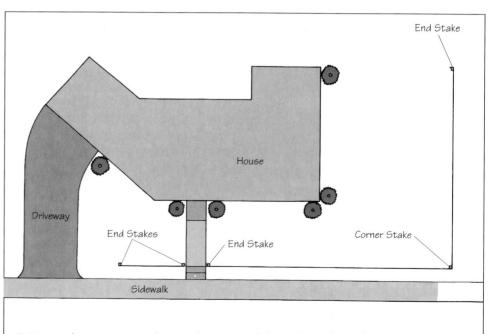

1 Drive stakes to represent the outside corners of the wall needing a footing.

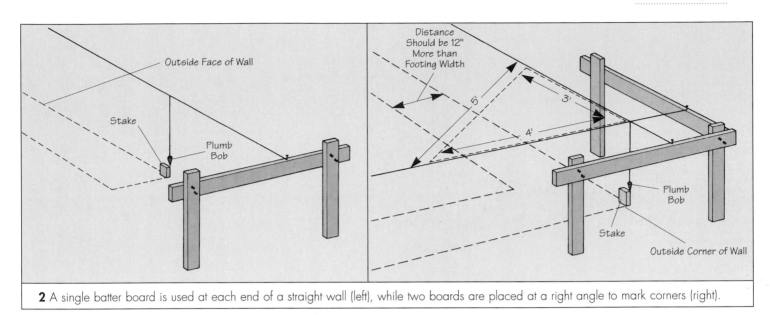

2 A single batter board is used at each end of a straight wall (left), while two boards are placed at a right angle to mark corners (right).

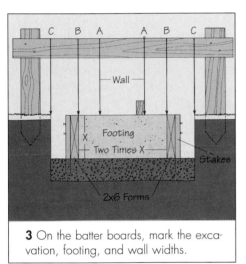

3 On the batter boards, mark the excavation, footing, and wall widths.

the corners, use the 3-4-5 triangulation method to make sure the strings meet at 90 degrees. See "Making Square Corners," page 24.

3 Set the strings and excavate.
On the batter board crosspieces, measure the wall width from the string and mark the other face of the wall (labeled A in the illustration); the inside and outside faces of the footing (B); and the outside edges of the footing trench (C). The footing width is twice the wall thickness. The trench should be 1 or 2 feet wider than the footing to provide room for installing the formwork. At each mark, drive a nail to tie the string to the board.

When the strings are set and squared, mark with sand below lines C to delineate the excavation for the trench. Then excavate to the depth of the footing and any required gravel base.

Footings without Forms

For footings in firm, dry soil, wooden forms can be eliminated and the concrete can be formed by the earth trench. Excavate a trench that is the exact width of the footing, using a spade to keep the edges straight. Make the trench deep enough so that the top of the footing will be about 2 to 3 inches below finished grade. Drive a row of wooden stakes down the middle to indicate the top of the concrete. Use a straight 2x4 and a level to make sure the tops of the guide stakes are level. When the concrete is poured, simply smooth the surface with a float so that it is even with the tops of the stakes.

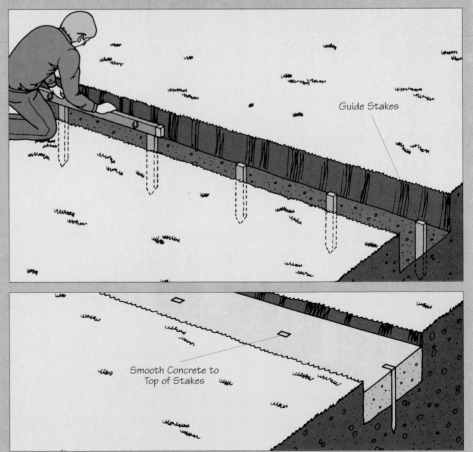

Building the Formwork

Before building the forms, add a gravel base, if needed. Add half the amount and tamp to level. Then add the rest of the gravel to provide adequate drainage.

1 Locate the footing corners. First, reattach the strings representing the edges of the footing (B strings) to the batter boards. At the ends of the footing, or where corner strings intersect, hang a plumb bob to the bottom of the trench. At these points, drive short lengths of rebar into the ground. Drive them deep below the proposed footing surface. These rebar stakes represent the ends of a straight footing or the inside and outside corners of an L-shaped footing.

2 Install the corner stakes. Hold a small piece of the form material against the rebar at the outside corners and drive two 1x4 stakes a few inches from the rebar. These stakes will support the corners of the outside form boards. The tops of the stakes should be level with each other and equal to the top of the form boards. If you're placing an L-shaped footing (a corner), you can, for now, ignore the rebar driven at inside corners.

3 Install the intermediate stakes. Stretch leveled strings between the corner stakes, and use the strings as guides to install intermediate stakes about every 4 feet to support the form boards. If the form boards are long enough to reach between the corner stakes, you may find it easier to attach and level the form boards first, then use them as a guide to install the intermediate stakes.

4 Install the form boards. Attach the form boards by driving double-headed nails or screws through the stakes into the boards. While nailing, place your foot against the inside of the board to keep from knocking the stake out of position. As long as the stakes are level, you can align the top edges of the boards with the tops of the stakes. Check the form boards

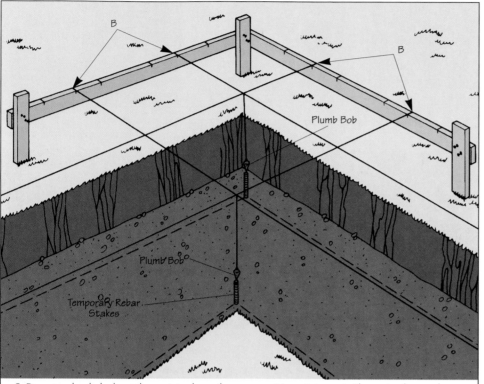

1 Drop a plumb bob at the point where the corner strings intersect. Place a rebar stake at this location.

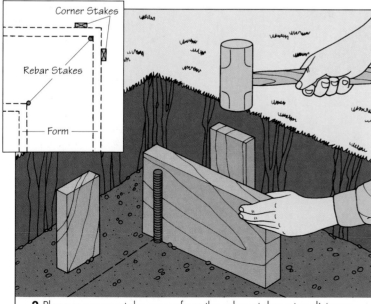

2 Place a corner stake away from the rebar stakes at a distance equal to the thickness of the form board.

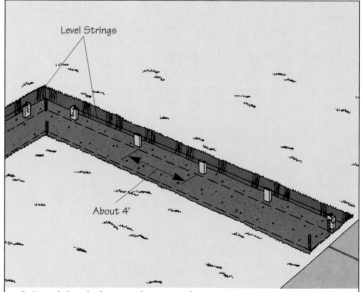

3 Stretch leveled strings between the corner or end stakes and use the strings as guides to install intermediate stakes every 4 ft. to support the form boards.

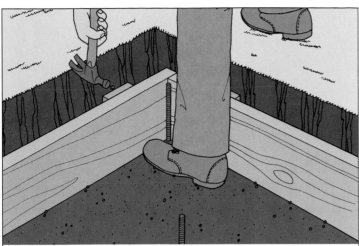

4 Attach the form boards to the stakes with double-headed nails. Check for level during the process.

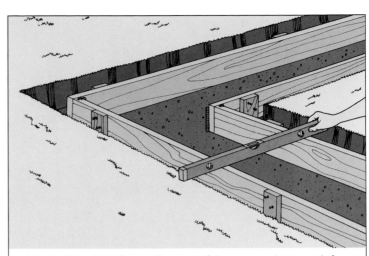

5 Set stakes along the inside edge of the corner; then attach form boards, keeping them level with the outside forms. The space between the inside and outside forms equals the footing width.

Stepped Footing Forms

Where the ground under a wall slopes slightly, you can build a level footing that is deeper in the ground at one end than the other. Where the ground slopes steeply, it is best to step the form down the slope so that the footing is in a series of level sections. For footings without forms, step the excavation down and form a dam with a board or piece of plywood and wooden stakes driven into the sides of the excavation. For footings with lumber forms, build two overlapping forms to create the change in height.

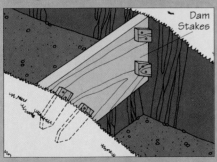

Dam Stakes

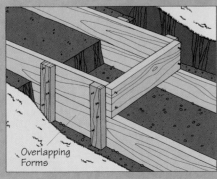

Overlapping Forms

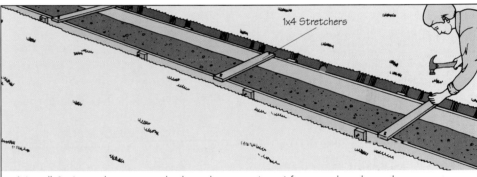

1x4 Stretchers

6 Install 1x4 stretchers across the board tops at 4- to 6-ft. intervals to keep the concrete from spreading the forms.

frequently with a 4-foot level to make sure they remain level.

5 Set up the inside forms. Use the outside form boards to locate the stakes for the inside forms. Beginning a few inches from the inside corner rebar, drive stakes every 4 feet or so. Locate the stakes so that when you attach the form boards, the space between the forms equals the footing width. Set the stakes along one edge of the footing first, making sure they are level. Then, at the inside corner, align a form board with the rebar and attach the board to the stakes. Every few feet, lay a level across the inside and outside form boards, as shown, to be sure they are level with each other.

Set the stakes for the adjacent inside form, then attach a form board. Butt the end of this board against the one that is already in place and toenail the top edge to keep the boards flush. Check for level and perfect square.

6 Brace the formwork. If the form boards are 2x6s or wider, install 1x4 stretchers across the board tops at 4- to 6-foot intervals to keep the concrete from spreading the forms. Deep forms that are built with multiple boards may require extra bracing.

Adding Reinforcement

Place horizontal rebar in the footing trench, according to local building codes. Footings require rebar; reinforcing mesh or ready-mix infused with fibers will not do. For shallow footings, use bricks to prop the rebar above the trench bottom; rebar should be about one-third the way up from the bottom of the footing. Keep the bars at least 3 inches away from the form boards or trench sides.

Where two pieces of reinforcing bar must be spliced together, lap them 30 times the diameter of the bar, or a minimum of 12 inches, and tie them securely together with twisted wire. For

Adding reinforcement. Rebar is laid in the footing form. Follow local building codes for proper reinforcement of footings.

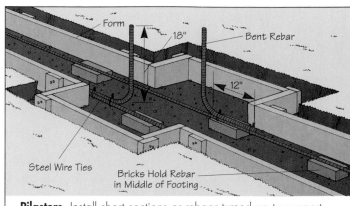

Form 18" Bent Rebar 12"

Steel Wire Ties Bricks Hold Rebar in Middle of Footing

Pilasters. Install short sections or rebaar turned up to support pilasters.

example, if the bar is ½ inch diameter, the overlap should be 15 inches (30x½). Intersecting reinforcing bars should also be tied to hold them together when the concrete is poured.

Pilasters. If your footing is for a masonry wall with pilasters, install short sections of rebar that will turn up into the masonry. The vertical leg should be at least 18 inches high, and the horizontal leg at least 12 inches long.

Handling and Pouring Concrete

Although instructions for making the pour are given here, please review "Pouring and Placing Concrete," on page 27, before pouring concrete in your footing.

First, check all formwork for proper grade and correct depth. Once you're sure that everything is in its proper place, spray the inside surfaces of the forms and the soil or gravel sub-grade with water from a garden hose. This will keep them from drawing too much water from the concrete, which can create a poor quality surface or weakened concrete.

Be sure to wear rubber boots, protective clothing, and gloves, because prolonged contact with fresh concrete will burn your skin.

Mix your concrete as near the job site as you can or have the concrete truck park as close as possible. Use a wheelbarrow to move the concrete from the mixing area or from the truck to the project site. Lay 2x12s across lawn areas to protect them from the weight of the wheelbarrow.

Start dumping the concrete at the farthest end of the forms, making piles that are slightly taller than the forms. Be sure to fill the forms completely. Fill low areas with a shovel; spade the concrete to fill in corners. Settle the concrete against the perimeter forms by tapping the outside of the form boards with a hammer.

As soon as the first section of the form is filled, begin leveling, or screeding, the concrete. Use a straight length of 2x4 that is slightly wider than the form. Drag it along the top of the forms, pressing down firmly. Fill any hollow areas with a shovel and strike them off level. Since the

concrete will not be exposed to view, no other finishing is required.

Cure the concrete. Keep the concrete moist for seven days to allow it to cure properly before starting to build the wall. Use one of the methods described in "Curing Concrete," on page 32.

After the concrete has cured for a day, carefully remove the forms. Do not pry or hammer against the concrete itself. The concrete will continue to cure slowly for another month until it reaches full strength, but it is safe to begin the wall construction after the first week.

Handling and pouring concrete. Start dumping the concrete at the farthest end of the forms. Fill the forms completely. Fill any low areas with a shovel; tamp the concrete to fill in corners.

Brick & Block

Brick walkways, arranged in zigzag or square patterns, contrast with the surrounding landscape to complement any setting. Brick steps, creating suspense as they make their way to a house, are inviting and serve to emphasize the front door's role as an architectural focal point.

Concrete pavers, commonly used for drive-ways, come in various shapes and colors that add texture and visual interest. Brick patios provide a cool surface on hot summer days and a secluded spot any time of year.

A substantial rounded coping atop a brick garden wall adds visual variety as well as preventing water from soaking into the wall. Interlocking blocks make it easy to create a cascade of rounded terraces. Concrete retaining walls lend a formal air to the landscape. Screen walls can be created by alternating bricks with spaces or by using screen blocks.

Stucco is a versatile material that can take on almost any shape, texture and color to harmonize with its surroundings. It can be applied with metal mesh over plywood or directly over concrete block or other masonry material to create a durable, weather-resistant surface.

Brick and Block Techniques

Brick has been used as a building material for several thousand years. It is laid in place by hand, one unit at a time, and doesn't require as much physical effort as working with heavier concrete block or stone. Bricklaying is easy to learn, and even a first-timer can produce a pleasing finished product. The techniques are simple and methodical, and there's a sense of accomplishment that comes with the steady progress of a brick project. Since the work is done a little at a time, even a big job is not such a daunting task.

Concrete block is a much newer material than brick, but it has become popular for its durability, versatility, and economy. This chapter covers the techniques of constructing garden walls, retaining walls, sidewalks, steps, and patios from brick, brick pavers, concrete block, and interlocking concrete pavers.

Both brick and concrete block are usually bonded together with mortar. Like concrete, masonry mortar contains cement, sand, and water. The difference is that concrete also contains gravel to increase its durability and compressive strength while mortar usually contains hydrated lime to improve its working characteristics. With mortar, bond strength and workability are more important than compressive strength. Some types of concrete block retaining walls are "dry-stacked" without mortar. These units are interlocked mechanically with pins or simply by shape.

Most masonry projects will also require accessories such as anchors, ties, or joint reinforcement. These materials anchor masonry to existing construction, tie intersecting masonry sections together, and control expansion and contraction. In addition, many projects call for flashing to prevent water penetration.

Types of Brick

Brick is made from clay that is molded to shape and fired at very high temperatures in a large kiln, or oven. The color of the natural clay determines the color of the brick, although some manufacturers combine more than one clay to produce a variety of colored brick from off-white to almost black. Brick textures vary, depending on the molding process. Since brick distributors handle the products of several manufacturers, there should be a wide selection of materials available to you.

Brick made in the United States and Canada today is extremely dense, hard, and durable. If the units are shaped by extruding the clay through a die, they usually have holes through the middle. These holes make the bricks lighter in weight and more economical, and they increase the bricks' bond to the mortar. This type of brick is used for wall construction where the holes are not visible.

The best way to choose brick for your project is to visit a local brick distributor where you can look at sample panels or project photographs—these will give you a good idea of what the finished masonry will look like. Colors and textures will vary from one manufacturer to another. A color that has a wide range of light and dark shades as well as "blends," which combine more than one color, will be more difficult to work with than a single color with relatively few shades. Light and dark units must be carefully mixed together as a project is built so that you don't accidentally create zigzag patterns or blotches of color.

Face brick. Face brick is used when consistency in appearance is required. A batch of face brick will be quite uniform in color, size, texture, and face surface. Face brick comes in three types, differentiated by appearance. Type FBA (architectural) brick has no limits on size variations or on the amount of chips and cracks that are permitted. This type includes hand-molded brick as well as extruded brick that is tumbled or rolled before firing to soften the edges or dent the surfaces. This is a popular type of brick for residential construction because the units resemble old brick. Type FBS (standard) brick is used in commercial applications more than on residences. The dimensions don't vary as much from one unit to the next, the edges are sharper, and there are fewer chips and cracks permitted. Type FBX (extra) brick has the tightest limits on size variation, chips, and cracks. The edges are very sharp, and the crisp outline gives these units a very contemporary look.

This type is not as popular, even for commercial projects.

Bricks similar to those used in historic buildings are produced by some manufacturers. The units are formed and shaped by pressing the clay into a mold by hand or by machine, giving the brick a weathered and rustic look. These molded bricks are relatively porous and will absorb more water than extruded bricks. Many suppliers also stock actual used brick. Molded bricks do not have "cored" holes in the center but may have an indentation called a "frog". Used brick has a charming irregular quality and is structurally sound, but unpredictable durability makes it risky for exterior use.

Building brick. Building bricks, or common bricks as they are sometimes called, are rough in appearance but structurally sound. The chips, cracks, and slight deformations in building brick create a rustic look and these units are less expensive than face brick.

Paving brick. Paving brick is always solid, because in paving, the widest faces are visible. The clay is machine pressed densely into molds and baked longer than either extruded or molded face brick units. This process reduces the amount of water that will be absorbed by the brick. With pavers, low absorption is critical, because the materials must be able to withstand repeated cycles of winter freezing and thawing as well as heavy traffic. Paving brick is classified by its appearance in the same way as face brick: PA (architectural), PS (standard), and PX (extra).

Firebrick. Firebrick is made of a special clay and is baked at an extremely high temperature to make the units resistant to high heat. Firebrick is used to line fireplaces, ovens, and furnaces. It is off-white and is installed with a special fireclay mortar. You won't need firebrick for projects in this book.

Sizes and Shapes of Brick

Building and face brick come in many different sizes, but the easiest size to work with is called modular brick. The basic unit is $3\frac{5}{8}$ inches wide, $2\frac{1}{4}$ inches thick, and $7\frac{5}{8}$ inches long. The measured dimensions of the units themselves are called the actual dimensions; the dimensions of a unit plus one mortar joint are called the nominal dimensions. When laid with standard $\frac{3}{8}$-inch mortar joints, the nominal length is rounded up to 8 inches. Three bricks laid with the large bed surface one on top of the other and with $\frac{3}{8}$-inch mortar joints between measure 8 inches high. By rounding up to include

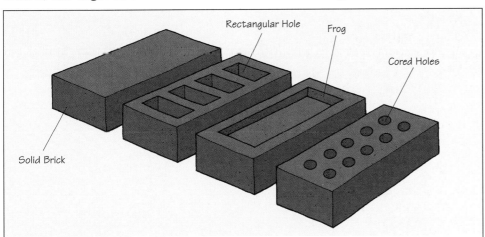

Building brick. Bricks (including building bricks) come solid or with rectangular holes or indentations called frogs. Some have a series of round "cored" holes.

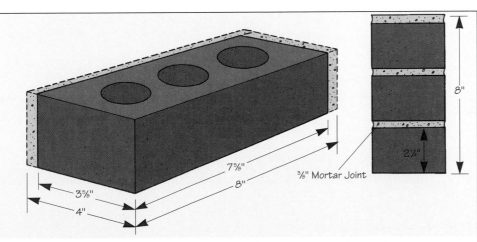

Sizes and shapes of brick. Modular bricks are sized to give you a 4x8-in. building module, which allows for $\frac{3}{8}$-in. mortar joints.

Brick Grading

There are two grades of face brick and three grades of building brick. Grading is based on how well a brick resists damage from freezing and thawing when it is wet. Grade MW (moderate weathering) can be used when the bricks will be exposed to moisture but not saturated when freezing occurs. Grade SW (severe weathering) should be used when the bricks are likely to be frozen when saturated with water. Grade NW (no weathering), available only in building brick, is for indoor use only. In all areas of the United States except southern Florida, southern Texas, southern Arizona, and southern California, Grade SW is recommended for outdoor use; and even in those areas, Grade SW is recommended for horizontal applications where the brick is in contact with the soil. Paving brick is divided into similar grades, designated as SX (for highest freeze-thaw resistance), MX (for use where freezing conditions are not a factor), and NX (for interior applications).

mortar joints, you can easily plan wall lengths and opening locations and minimize brick cutting. Rounding up also makes it easy to combine brick with other types of modular masonry units, such as concrete block.

Solid paving bricks that are designed to be laid with mortar have the same 3⅝ by 7⅝-inch face dimensions as ordinary bricks. Paving bricks that are designed to be laid butted together without mortar have a full 4 by 8-inch face size so that patterns will still lay out to a 4-inch module. Paving brick comes in several thicknesses. The most common are 1½ inches for light traffic areas such as patios and sidewalks and 2¼ inches for heavy traffic areas such as driveways and streets. Paving bricks never have holes through them.

Special shapes. Some brick manufacturers make special shapes such as wall copings, angled corner brick, and radial units for curved walls. Specially shaped units cost more, but they can add a distinctive touch to your designs.

Calculating Modular Masonry Units

Laying out brick units is simple when you set the length and width of walls, patios, or walks to a multiple of 4 inches. With nominal 8-inch brick, use a 4-inch module because that is the length of half a brick. The importance of brick halves is that they create a staggered layout in the bond pattern. For example, make a brick wall 80 inches long (a multiple of 4 inches) rather than 78 inches long. Likewise, make a brick sidewalk 36 inches wide rather than 30 inches because 36 is a multiple of 4. Any openings that are planned should also be located and sized on the 4-inch module. This will mean that only whole and half-size units will be needed, and a minimum number of units will have to be cut.

For estimating purposes, figure about seven bricks (nominally 4 by 8 inches) for every square foot of area in a wall. Area is determined by the length times the height of a wall. Remember to double the estimate for a wall that

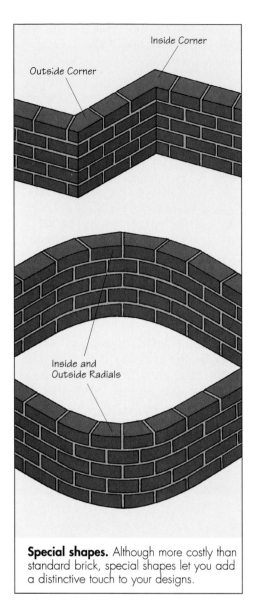

Special shapes. Although more costly than standard brick, special shapes let you add a distinctive touch to your designs.

is two brick widths (called wythes) thick. A wythe is a vertical section of a wall that is equal to the width of the masonry unit. Typical garden walls are two wythes wide. Estimate about 4½ bricks for every square foot when paving bricks are laid broad face, horizontally on the ground.

Water absorption. Some brick is very dry and will absorb a lot of water from the mortar. This causes a poor bond between the brick and mortar. To test a brick for excessive absorption, draw a circle the size of a quarter on the

Water absorption. If it takes less than one minute for the brick to absorb 12 drops of water, the brick is too dry.

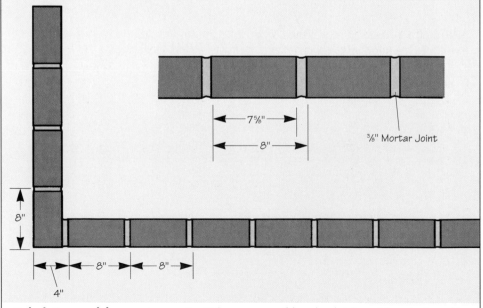

Calculating modular masonry units. Whenever possible, plan brick wall lengths in multiples of 4 in. to allow you to use only full and half bricks.

bed surface of the brick using a crayon or wax pencil. With a medicine dropper, place 12 drops of water inside the circle; time how long it takes for the water to be absorbed. If the water is absorbed in less than one minute, the brick is too dry. Thoroughly wet the bricks with a garden hose the day before you lay them. Let them dry for an entire 24-hour period.

Concrete Block

One of the most economical masonry materials is concrete block. These masonry units consist of an outside shell with a hollow center that is divided by two or three vertical webs. The ends of a unit may have flanges that accept mortar and join with the adjacent block, or they may have smooth ends for corners and the end of walls. Concrete block is manufactured throughout the United States and the exact design, texture, and color may differ slightly from area to area.

Although they are called concrete, these blocks are not the same as the concrete used for the walks, footings, and the other poured concrete projects found in this book. The blocks are composed of different materials including cement, sand, and a variety of very small aggregates such as gravel and cinders. There are various types of blocks, such as solid, load-bearing, and non-load-bearing. The heavy blocks made with sand and gravel or crushed stone can weigh more than 40 pounds each; working with them can be back breaking if you're not

accustomed to heavy lifting. Lighter units made with coal cinders, slag, and other aggregates may weigh as little as 22 pounds, but they are less resistant to moisture absorption. Be sure to ask your supplier about what type of block to use for your project.

Concrete block construction is as prone to shrinkage cracking as are concrete slabs and sidewalks. The shrinkage cracking in concrete masonry construction is controlled in the same way as they are in concrete slabs—with steel reinforcement and control joints. Approximately every 20 feet along a wall's length, a control joint takes the place of a vertical mortar joint to regulate cracking.

Concrete Block Characteristics

Standard concrete blocks have an actual face size of 7⅝ inches by 15⅝ inches. When you add the thickness of a standard ⅜-inch mortar joint, the block measures 8 by 16 inches—its nominal size. The most commonly used block thickness is also nominally 8 inches (7⅝ inches actual dimension), but you can get nominal 4-, 6-, 10-, and 12-inch thicknesses, too. Three modular bricks including their mortar joints are the same height as one nominal 8-inch concrete block; two nominal brick lengths equal one nominal block length.

Stretcher core styles. A basic concrete block unit is called a stretcher. Stretchers are cored with two or three holes per unit to reduce the weight as much as possible. The core holes

Stretcher core styles. The number and shapes of the holes vary, but all standard stretcher blocks are hollowed to save materials, to make them lighter and easier to handle, and to make room for steel reinforcing bars.

are tapered slightly to make it easier to remove them from the manufacturing molds and to provide a better grip for handling.

If your design will incorporate vertical reinforcing steel in the cores, the wall will be easier to build using special two-core units with open ends. These units are called A-blocks because they are shaped like the letter A. If A-blocks are not available from your supplier, you can make your own by sawing or knocking out the ends of regular units. This will let you place the blocks around the rebar rather than lifting and threading them over the top of the steel.

Screen blocks. Screen blocks are used to create walls with open patterns. Walls can be made entirely of screen blocks, or a few courses of screen blocks can top a solid wall or be worked into the wall in several places. Screen blocks come in a variety of shapes and patterns.

Consider your many options when

Images of concrete block cross-sections: Two-Core Block with Smooth Ends, Two-Core Block with Flanged Ends, Three-Core Block with Notched Ends

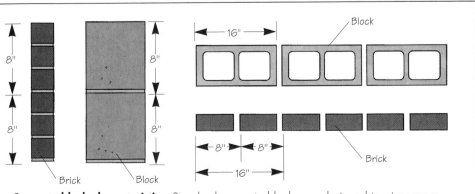

Concrete block characteristics. Standard concrete blocks are designed to give you a 8x16-in. building module, which allows for ⅜-in. mortar joints and works well with modular brick coursing.

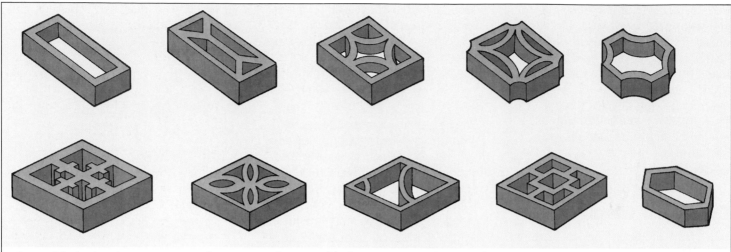

Screen blocks. Used to create open, decorative walls, screen blocks come in a wide array of patterns.

designing a concrete block wall. Some concrete blocks are gray and have flat faces with a texture that may range from coarse to relatively fine, depending on the aggregate used. Other blocks are more decorative and come in a variety of colors and textures. Most manufacturers now produce blocks that look more like natural stone and blocks with ribs, raised geometric patterns, or smooth-ground faces. Decorative colors range from creams, buffs, and browns to reds, pinks, and even greens. Some colors are produced by using colored stone aggregates, while others are made by adding pigments. Units made with colored aggregates are often brighter, and the color will not fade in the sun. Those made with pigments come in a greater variety of colors, but some may fade over time.

The interlocking retaining wall block is a fairly new type of concrete block material. There are several different types of systems marketed under a variety of trade names. They differ from traditional concrete block in that they are laid without mortar. Some systems interlock because of the shapes in which they are cast, others interlock with metal or plastic pins. The interlocking mechanisms also align the units correctly as they are stacked—it's like putting the pieces of a puzzle together. Building a retaining wall or a raised planter has never been easier. Some types of interlocking block can be used to build retaining walls as high as 12 feet. The

Tools for Brick and Concrete Block

Brick and block work doesn't require many specialized tools. For excavation you'll need a strong shovel and a spade. A wheelbarrow or mortar box, a sturdy plastic bucket, and a mason's hoe are needed for mixing mortar. For measuring and ensuring accurate building you need a framing square, a 4-foot level, a line level, a folding rule, and a chalk line. Line blocks and mason's string are used to keep the courses straight. A brick hammer and brickset, a circular saw with a masonry blade, a hawk or mortar board, a trowel, jointing tools, and brushes are needed for brick and block projects. You may also want a story pole to measure the correct height of the courses. Make a story pole from a piece of scrap 1x2 and mark the pole in increments equaling the courses of the brick or block—usually 8-inch increments. For more about these tools, see "Masonry Tools," beginning on page 7.

manufacturers furnish step-by-step instructions tailored to the specific requirements of their units. A project using this material is presented later.

Types of concrete pavers. Concrete masonry pavers, commonly used for driveways, patios, and sidewalks, come in a number of shapes and colors. These pavers are designed to be laid in a sand base without mortar; some interlock to form repeating patterns. Concrete pavers are much stronger and denser than ordinary concrete blocks, so moisture absorption and damage from repeated freeze/thaw cycles aren't a problem.

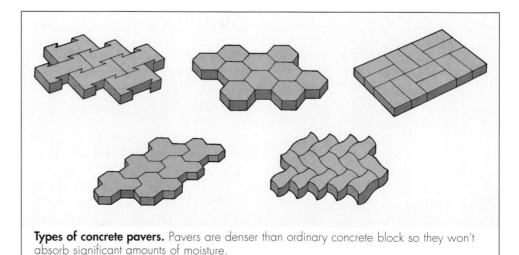

Types of concrete pavers. Pavers are denser than ordinary concrete block so they won't absorb significant amounts of moisture.

Portland Cement & Lime Mortars			
Mortar Type	Proportions By Volume		
	Portland Cement	Hydrated Mason's Lime	Mason's Sand
N	1	1	6
S	1	½	4½

Factory-Blended Masonry Cement Mortars		
Mortar Type	Proportions By Volume	
	Portland Cement	Hydrated Mason's Lime
N	1	3
S	1	3

Mortar

The mortar in a masonry structure constitutes only a small percentage of the materials, but its importance cannot be overlooked. A good bond between the mortar and bricks or blocks provides stability, provides resistance to wind pressure and other lateral loads, and helps prevent moisture penetration. While mortar is similar to concrete, the kinds of mixtures that produce a good bond do not necessarily produce the high compressive strengths that are common with concrete mixes. As mentioned before, it is more important that mortar be workable and produce a good bond than have a high compressive strength.

Mortar and concrete typically use the same types of portland cement. The most common is a Type I general-purpose cement. Lime is added to mortar mixes to make them retain water longer, to improve workability or handling, and to make the hardened mortar less brittle and less prone to shrinkage. The mortar used in historic buildings was made with lime and sand only, no portland cement. These lime mortars cured very slowly. The invention of portland cement in the late 1800s changed the way masonry mortar was made and speeded up construction. The trade-off is that the higher the portland cement content, the stiffer the mixture is when it is wet and the more rigid the mortar when it is cured. This makes the mortar a little harder to work with and a little more likely to crack if the masonry is not properly constructed.

There are two typical mortar mixes. For interior work, and outdoor work that is above grade, use a Type N mix. This mix is composed of 1 part portland cement, 1 part lime, and 6 parts sand. The lime should be a hydrated mason's lime, and the sand should be a well-graded masonry sand that has a range of grain sizes from fine to coarse. For below-grade construction and for paving projects, use a Type S mix. For flatwork, including patios, sidewalks, and driveways, an air-entrained portland cement will improve freeze-thaw resistance.

Mortar is usually mixed by volume proportions using a container of convenient size for consistent proportioning. Always use the same container for measuring ingredients so that the proportional volume of material is the same each time.

Ready-Mix Masonry Cements

Some manufacturers produce factory-blended masonry cements that are a combination either of portland cement and lime or of portland cement and natural or chemical agents. Masonry cements are available in Types N and S—these will produce a Type N or S mortar when mixed with sand in a one to three proportion (one part masonry cement to three parts sand). For small projects, masonry cements are more convenient than portland cement and lime mixes because all you have to do is add sand and water.

Masonry cements are also available with preblended pigments to produce a variety of mortar colors that range

from white, cream, buff, tan, and pink to chocolate brown. This is the easiest way to get colored mortars, and it is easier to produce consistently colored batches than by mixing pigments separately. When buying masonry cements, read the label to make sure it meets the requirements of ASTM C91 Standard Specification for Masonry Cement.

For very small projects, you may find it most convenient to buy a mortar mix that includes both the masonry cement and the sand. These mixes are a bit more expensive than mixing your own, but they require only the addition of water at the project site. A packaged mortar mix is a practical option only for small projects, repairs, and repointing jobs.

See the tables above, "Portland Cement and Lime Mortars" and "Factory-Blended Masonry Cement Mortars" for proper mixing proportions.

Mixing Mortar

One of the most important things in mixing mortar is consistency from batch to batch. Always use a container for measuring ingredients so that the proportional volume of materials is the same each time. A 1- or 2-gallon plastic bucket is a good size, and not too heavy when it's filled.

If you're using a portland cement and lime mortar in a Type N 1:1:6 mixture, measure out one bucket of cement, one bucket of lime, and six buckets of sand; one bag of portland cement plus one bag of lime mortar mix will lay about 300 bricks or 75 blocks. If you're using a bagged masonry cement, measure out one bucket of cement and three buckets of sand. A single-bag masonry cement mix lays about 125 bricks or 30 blocks. For smaller batches, simply use a smaller bucket for measuring. Don't pack the materials in the bucket, and don't mix more mortar than you can use in a couple of hours. You'll quickly get an idea of how much mortar you can lay before it sets up.

If you can't store materials close to where you'll be working, mix them in a wheelbarrow so you can move the

Mixing mortar. Use a mason's hoe to thoroughly mix the dry mortar ingredients before adding water.

Add water. To test if your mortar has the right amount of water, make a series of sharp ridges. The ridges should stay sharp without crumbling.

mortar easily. When using a mortar box, make sure it is placed level so water won't collect in one end or in a corner.

First measure all of the dry ingredients and mix them thoroughly with a mason's hoe. If you put half the sand in first, then the cement and lime, and then add the rest of the sand, blending will be a little quicker and easier. Alternately pull and push the materials back and forth until the color is even. Then push the mix to one end of the mortar box or wheelbarrow, or make a hole in the middle.

Add water. Pour 2 gallons of water in the empty end of the mixing box or the hole in the middle of the mortar mix; 2 gallons of water is about the right amount for one bag of portland cement and one bag of lime plus sand. (Start with approximately 2 gallons when mixing masonry cement with sand.) Measure the water. Don't use a garden hose—it's too easy to put in too much water. Mix the dry ingredients with the water, pushing and pulling the mix back and forth with a chopping motion until the consistency is uniform.

The amount of moisture in the sand will influence how much water you'll need to achieve the right mortar con-

sistency. If you buy bags of sand for small projects, it will be dry. If you buy sand in bulk by the ton for larger projects, it will probably be damp or wet. (Keep your sand pile covered so that the moisture content will not change drastically with changes in the weather.) You're aiming for mortar that is the consistency of soft mud and will hold a ball shape. If the mix is too dry after the initial 2 gallons of water, add more water in small quantities until the consistency is right. To check for proper consistency, make a series of sharp ridges in the mortar with the hoe or trowel. If the ridges appear dry and crumbly, more water is needed. If the ridges stay sharp without slumping, the mortar is the right consistency. It is very easy to add too much water. If you put in too much, add proportional amounts of the dry ingredients to bring the mortar back to the proper consistency.

Within the first two hours after mixing, mortar can be retempered with water to replace evaporated moisture and restore proper consistency. In hot, dry weather, the time limits on retempering may be shorter. About 2½ hours after initial mixing, mortar begins to harden and must be discarded because it will never develop good bond with the bricks or blocks. Don't

retemper colored mortar because it will dilute the pigments and result in uneven colors in the wall. Mix smaller batches of colored mortar so you can use up batches more quickly.

How to Work with Mortar

If you have never worked with mortar before, you may want to practice a little before beginning your project. Slicing off a chunk of mortar and spreading it is a skill that is learned with practice. The key is holding the trowel correctly.

1 Set up a practice surface. Lay a 2x4 flat across the top of two concrete blocks, buckets, or sawhorses. This is about the same width as a wythe of brick.

2 Use the proper grip. Grasp the trowel handle with your thumb extended on top of the handle, not over the end of it. Grip the handle firmly, but do not squeeze it.

3 Load the trowel. You can grab mortar directly from the mortar box or wheelbarrow by slicing a narrow V-shaped wedge of mortar with the trowel and lifting it out in a single scooping stroke away from your body. However, it is easier to place a small amount of mortar onto a hawk to

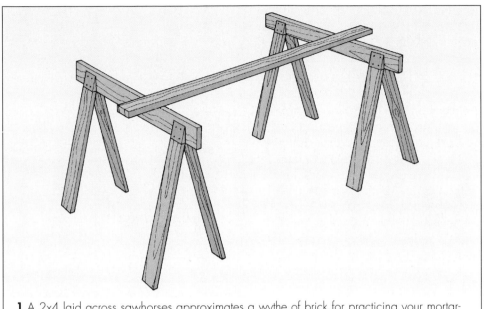

1 A 2x4 laid across sawhorses approximates a wythe of brick for practicing your mortaring technique.

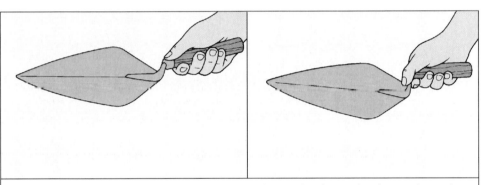

2 Shown at left is the proper way to hold a trowel. Don't hook your thumb over the end of the handle as shown at right.

then load the trowel. From the hawk, slice a piece off with the edge of the trowel and pull it away from the pile toward you. Scoop under to pick it up.

To keep the mortar from falling off the trowel before you're ready, "stick" it to the surface with a quick, slight snap of the wrist upward. Mortar of the correct consistency will not slide off.

4 Lay the mortar. Hold the loaded trowel over the 2x4, and with a sweeping motion, turn it and snap the mortar out along the board. A full trowel load of mortar is usually enough to lay three or four bricks or a couple of blocks. When you first begin, though, you may want to pick up smaller amounts. It will take some practice before this becomes a smooth motion and you are able to spread the mortar without throwing it off the sides of the board.

5 Shape the mortar. Use the edge of the trowel to cut off excess mortar at the sides of the 2x4. Then make a shallow furrow in the middle of the mortar bed. Don't make the furrow too deep. In practice, you won't furrow the mortar below the first course, only the second and subsequent courses.

Scrape the mortar off the 2x4 and return it to the batch, then repeat

3 Put some mortar on your hawk, then slice and scoop a trowel-load.

4 Snap the mortar onto the practice 2x4. Start with small amounts of mortar until you get the hang of it.

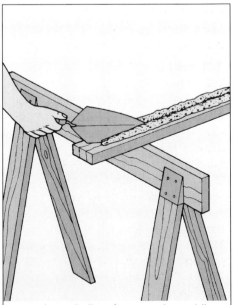

5 Make a shallow furrow in the middle of the mortar bed.

the steps until the feel of the trowel and the spreading motions become more comfortable.

Ties, Flashing, and Reinforcement

Masonry construction usually requires accessory items such as ties to bond multiple wythes of masonry, flashing to limit water penetration, and reinforcement for lateral strength.

Ties. Multiple wythes of masonry in a wall must be tied together either with header bricks or metal ties. Header bricks are laid perpendicular to the wall length, overlapping both wythes and creating a pattern bond in the wall surface. Metal ties can be used in walls of parallel, unconnected wythes. The ties are embedded in the mortar to join wythes. A Z-shaped wire tie is used for solid masonry units such as brick; a rectangular wire tie is used for hollow masonry units such as concrete block or to tie concrete block and brick wythes together. Rectangular ties and Z-ties are ³⁄₁₆ inch in diameter. For extra protection against corrosion, use ties that are hot-dip galvanized.

Veneer walls. Brick can be used as a non-load-bearing wall veneer. The wall is built 1 inch away from the house sheathing. If the framing is wooden, the brick can be attached to the structure with corrugated veneer anchors. Anchors are connected to wood framing, metal studs, or concrete at every 16 inches vertically and every 32 inches horizontally.

Reinforcement. There are two types of masonry reinforcement. The first is a prefabricated wire joint reinforcement that is used primarily in the mortar beds of concrete block walls to help control shrinkage cracking. For residential projects, the side wires should have a 9-gauge thickness. The width of the joint reinforcement should always be about 1 inch less than the width of the blocks, so that it is covered on each side of the wall with ½ to ⅝ inch of mortar.

The second type of masonry reinforcement are heavy steel reinforcing bars like those used in concrete construction. Called rebar, these bars are used in masonry to strengthen supporting members such as piers, lintels, and bond beams.

Masonry ties, anchors, and joint reinforcement should always be placed in the mortar bed rather than lain on the unit. This will provide better embedment of the metal and better performance of the masonry.

Flashing. Masonry flashing can be made of metal, rubberized asphalt sheet membranes, or other materials.

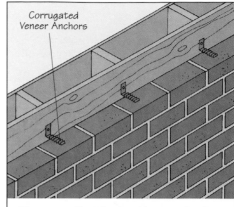

Veneer walls. Non-load-bearing brick veneer walls are connected to wood framing with corrugated veneer anchors.

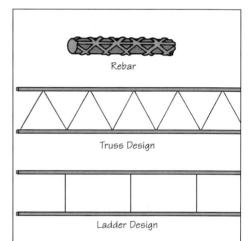

Reinforcement. Prefabricated wire reinforcement is laid in mortar beds. In masonry unit construction, a steel reinforcing bar is usually required to strengthen supporting members such as pilasters, lintels, and band beams.

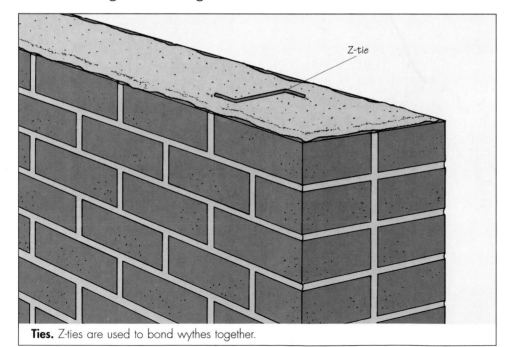

Ties. Z-ties are used to bond wythes together.

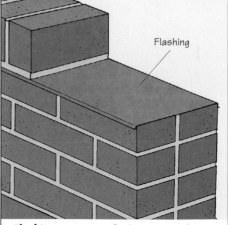

Flashing. Masonry flashing is used to keep water out of walls or to direct it to weep holes.

It is used to control moisture in masonry walls either by keeping the top of a wall dry or by collecting water inside a wall so that it can be drained out through weep holes.

Brick Terminology

To understand the procedures in this book, you must first learn some terminology used by masons. Like any trade, there are a few terms that are specific to the craft.

As mentioned before, a wythe is a vertical section of a wall that is one masonry unit thick. Typical brick garden walls are two wythes thick. Another basic term is course. A course is simply a horizontal row of masonry units. A garden wall 4 feet tall has 18 courses of 2¼-inch-thick bricks plus mortar joints.

Brick positions. A brick that is laid lengthwise in the course is called a stretcher. When standing upright with the edge facing out, the brick is called a soldier, when the face is positioned out, a sailor. A stretcher unit that is rotated 90 degrees in a wall so that the end is facing out is called a header. If the unit is then stood on its edge, it's called a rowlock. With modular brick, no matter which way you turn the units, they will work to a 4-inch module. A header unit is exactly the same width as a wall built of two wythes of brick with a ⅜-inch mortar joint in between. Concrete blocks are normally laid only in the stretcher position. As you will see, using alternating stretcher and header units, you can easily create patterns and designs in a wall—called the wall's bond pattern.

Joint positions. Horizontal joints are called bed joints, vertical joints between individual bricks or blocks are called head joints, and the vertical joint between wythes is called a collar joint.

Partial bricks. A brick cut in half lengthwise is called a bat. One that is halved in width is called a soap, and one that is halved in height is called a split.

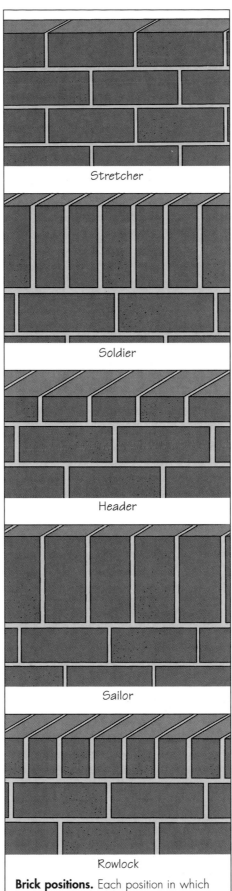

Brick positions. Each position in which bricks may be laid has its own name. You'll need to know these names to understand descriptions of brick patterns.

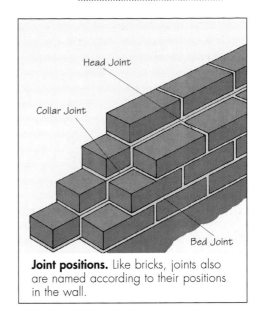

Joint positions. Like bricks, joints also are named according to their positions in the wall.

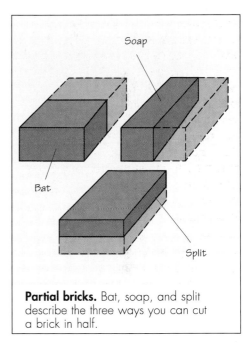

Partial bricks. Bat, soap, and split describe the three ways you can cut a brick in half.

Expansion Joints

Allowances must be made in masonry construction for expansion and contraction. All construction materials, including brick and block masonry, expand and contract with changes in temperature. Clay brick also expands with the absorption of moisture; concrete masonry shrinks with loss of residual moisture from the manufacturing and construction process.

To prevent cracking from expansion and contraction, masonry walls are built with vertical expansion joints (for brick walls) and control joints (for block walls). A masonry expansion joint is a soft, mortarless joint that is designed to accommodate the natural expansion of brick. The exact locations are dictated by design features such as openings, offsets, and intersections. In brick walls, expansion joints are located near corners because the opposing push of intersecting walls can cause cracking. For both brick and concrete masonry walls, joints should be located at points of weakness or high stress concentration such as abrupt changes in wall height or thickness, at columns and pilasters, and at one or both sides of windows and doors. Short freestanding walls that are not connected to other structures may not require control or expansion joints as they can expand and contract independently.

Locate expansion and control joints. If you are working with a wall that is more than 30 feet long, you will need

to install at least one expansion joint. If either end of the wall is built against an existing structure such as a house, garage, or other wall, install an expansion joint between the two elements. If the wall is long and straight, place expansion joints no more than 30 feet apart. For L- and U-shaped walls, locate expansion joints near the corners.

There are several ways to build control joints in concrete block walls. The most common methods are illustrated in the concrete block garden wall project on page 111.

Install expansion and control joints. Make an expansion joint ⅜ to ½ inch wide. To keep mortar from accidentally blocking the joint during construction, fill the joint with a soft foam pad or piece of ⅜- or ½-inch plywood. The foam pad will stay in place; the plywood will be removed. If you use

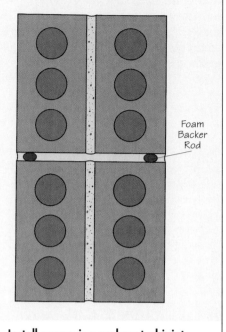

Install expansion and control joints. These flexible joints are made with foam backer rod and sealed with silicone sealant.

a foam pad, be sure its edges are recessed from the wall face about ¾ inch so that you can caulk the joint with silicone sealant (matched to your mortar color) after the wall is finished. Continue the expansion joint up through the wall cap or coping. Remember to install a foam backer rod to form the back side of the caulked joint. Buy closed-cell backer rods and silicone sealant from a building supply company. Smooth the surface of the sealant to compress it firmly into the joint.

Steel joint reinforcement can also be used to restrain movement and reduce the number of control or expansion joints needed. This reinforcement is routinely used in concrete block walls to reduce shrinkage and is also sometimes used in brick walls to control expansion. For concrete block walls, prefabricated wire reinforcement is usually placed in every second or third bed joint.

Bond Patterns for Walls

The pattern in which the bricks are laid is called the bond pattern. The most common bond pattern is one where bricks are laid flat on their

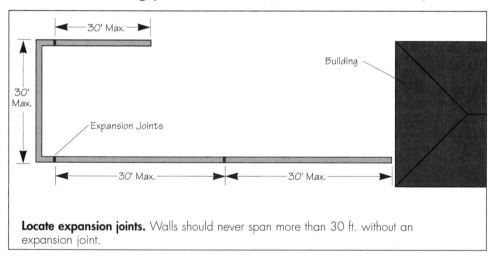

Locate expansion joints. Walls should never span more than 30 ft. without an expansion joint.

Bond patterns for walls. The most common pattern for walls of brick or stretcher blocks is the running bond, which staggers vertical joints every other course.

widest surface and turned lengthwise in the wall in the stretcher position. Each brick in a course of stretchers (a horizontal row) is offset one-half brick from the bricks in the courses above and below. The pattern formed by overlapping the brick in this way is called a running bond. If the bricks are offset one-third or one-quarter brick in each course, the pattern is called a one-third or one-quarter running bond, and the appearance differs slightly. The running bond pattern goes well in any landscape and is easy to keep consistent.

Using headers. As mentioned before, bricks turned perpendicular to the stretcher courses are called headers. By alternating header and stretcher bricks in different ways, you can create a variety of patterns, and since header units help hold the two wythes of a wall together, they are functional as well as decorative. There are a number of decorative bond patterns that mimic the look of historic masonry buildings, so the style goes well with older homes and newer homes of traditional design.

Popular bond patterns. The common, or American, bond is similar to the running bond, except it has courses of headers spaced every sixth course. The English bond consists of alternating courses of stretchers and headers; the headers are centered over the stretchers, and the vertical joints of all the stretcher courses align. A stack bond lays all the bricks as either headers or stretchers with all joints aligning vertically. The stack bond requires great precision to lay correctly and is used for veneer surfaces only—it is not permitted for load-bearing or structural walls. The Flemish bond is a complex pattern in which every course has alternating stretchers and headers. The pattern is offset by courses, so that the headers center over stretchers and vice versa.

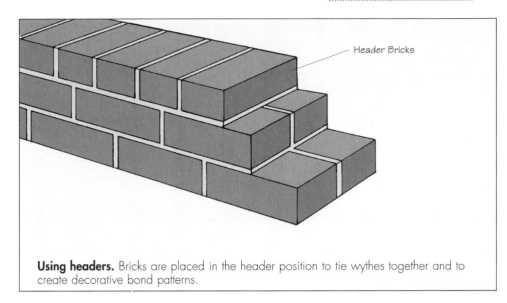

Header Bricks

Using headers. Bricks are placed in the header position to tie wythes together and to create decorative bond patterns.

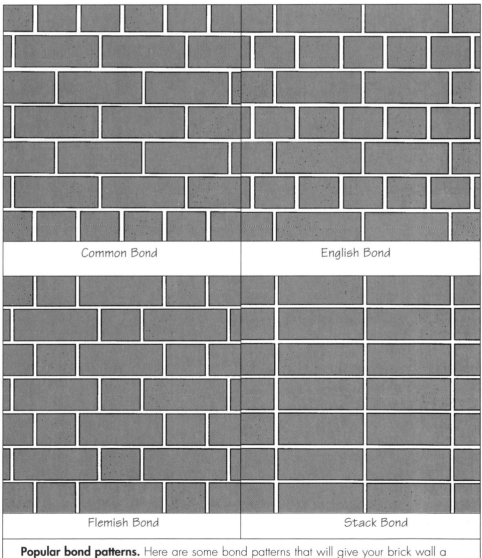

Common Bond

English Bond

Flemish Bond

Stack Bond

Popular bond patterns. Here are some bond patterns that will give your brick wall a distinctive look.

Brick & Block Projects

Included in this section are examples of double-wythe brick garden walls, a gently curving brick wall, a block screen wall, mortar-bed and dry-laid paving, and brick steps. These projects illustrate the basic design and construction methods for brick and block, which you can then adapt to your own needs and embellish with a creative touch using the ideas contained here. You will also need to build a reinforced concrete footing to support some structures—read about forming and pouring concrete footings in "Concrete Footings" on page 63.

Brick Garden Wall

You don't need to be an experienced mason to build an attractive brick garden wall. You'll quickly learn the necessary skills as you go, and as you become more proficient with a trowel and mortar, your work will get faster and more efficient.

A brick garden wall can provide privacy for a patio, define the perimeters of a lawn or garden area, or screen out street noise. Brick walls can be built in a vast array of styles to suit any landscape. The most common type of garden wall is two wythes thick and

Drainage. You may have to reshape the ground around your wall so you don't dam natural runoff paths.

laid with the brick in straight, parallel rows in a running bond pattern. A double-wythe brick wall has a finished thickness of about 8 inches, which provides enough stiffness for a wall height of at least 6 feet. This is the maximum that most building codes allow without reinforcing steel. Remember to include expansion joints every 30 feet, near corners, and where the wall abuts existing construction.

Drainage. Study the slopes and drainage patterns in your yard to make sure the wall will not dam natural storm water runoff paths. If necessary, reshape the ground to drain water away from the wall.

Lay out the wall. Planning the wall layout will be easiest if you use a modular-size brick: 7⅝ inches long, 3⅝ inches wide, and 2¼ inches thick when laid flat as a stretcher. When laid in the wall with standard ⅜-inch mortar joints, the nominal length is 8 inches, and the nominal width is 4 inches. Since three courses of bricks with mortar joints measure 8 inches high, all your dimensions can be planned as multiples of 4 inches (the nominal length of half a brick). Using a piece of graph paper, draw a plan of the wall to scale, making each brick twice as long as it is wide. Draw the plan of the wall using only whole and half bricks.

Also draw a side view, or elevation, of the wall. Figure three courses of modular brick with horizontal mortar joints for every 8 inches of height. This would mean that a 4-foot-high wall has 18 courses of brick, and a 6-foot-high wall has 27 courses.

Add pilasters for strength. Masonry walls must have supporting pilasters to keep them from falling over. Pilasters are thicker wall sections added at regular intervals to add stiffness to the wall. Factors such as the wall's height and the wind pressure exerted on the wall dictate the placement of pilasters. The usual spacing of pilasters is at a distance 18 times the thickness of the wall. Follow this guideline if you are building a wall less than 6 feet high with a continuous concrete reinforced footing. This means that a 4-inch-thick unreinforced masonry wall must have pilasters every 72 inches (18 times 4 inches = 72 inches). An 8-inch-thick wall would require pilasters every 12 feet, and a 12-inch-thick wall every 18 feet. Check with your local building department to find out what the rules are in your area. If you live in an area that is subject to earthquake activity, you should use a special seismic design and will need the services of a structural engineer.

In a short wall, pilasters can be used as decorative features even when they're not needed for extra strength, because they break up the line of a brick wall. Small pilasters can be built to project on only one side of the wall; larger pilasters can project on both sides. The small pilasters are adequate for walls up to 4 feet high, and the large ones for walls up to 6 feet high. Alternating courses of brick in the wall must overlap the brick in the pilaster to form a strong interlocking structure.

Design the footing. Brick walls need a concrete footing for stability and support. The thickness of the footing is the same as the thickness of the wall. The concrete footing must be twice as wide as the wall's thickness. For an 8-inch-wide double-wythe wall, the footing is 16 inches wide. Remember that the footing must expand in width around any pilasters. If you are building along a property line, the full footing width must be inside your property line. If you are building adjacent to an existing patio or sidewalk, plan ahead so the full width of the footing can be poured next to the existing slab with a small space in between to separate the two.

Consider frost depth. The footing must be built below the frost depth

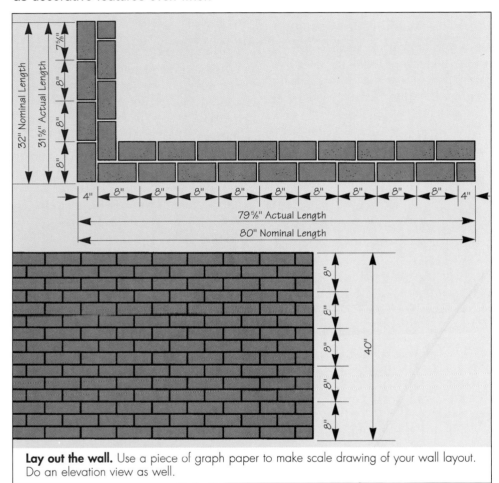

Lay out the wall. Use a piece of graph paper to make scale drawing of your wall layout. Do an elevation view as well.

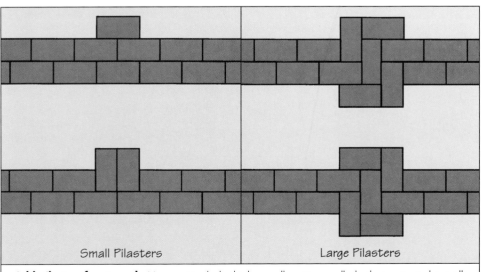

Small Pilasters — Large Pilasters

Add pilasters for strength. You must include thicker wall sections called pilasters to make walls strong enough to withstand strong winds without toppling.

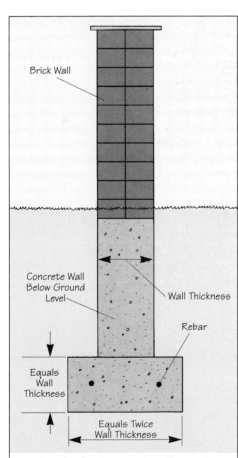

Design the footing. Brick walls need concrete footings that are twice as wide as the wall and as thick as the wall is wide. The footing must go below the frost line in your area.

so that it will not heave or tilt when the soil freezes and thaws each year. For footings that must be set very deep, it is much more economical to first build a concrete wall on the footing up to ground level rather than building many courses of brick below the ground surface. See "Concrete Footings," on page 63.

Step down slopes. If the ground slopes substantially along the length of the wall, both the concrete footing

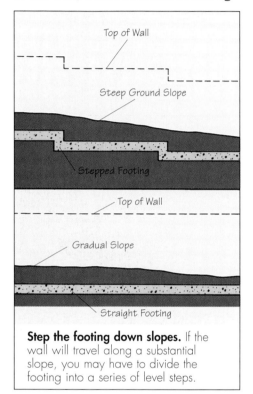

Step the footing down slopes. If the wall will travel along a substantial slope, you may have to divide the footing into a series of level steps.

Estimating Materials Needed

Estimate the number of bricks you will need by multiplying the number of units in the wall length times the number of courses in the wall height. For decorative bond patterns, draw an elevation of the wall to scale on graph paper, and then count the number of stretcher and header units. Remember that for double-wythe walls, you must double the number of stretcher units to account for the two wythes. Estimate 28 cubic feet of mortar for every 100 square feet of wall surface. Refer to "Mortar," on page 79, to estimate individual mortar ingredients.

and the brick wall may have to be stepped to follow the slope. Stepped footings are also described under "Concrete Footings" on page 63. For flatter slopes, build a footing that is deep enough so that its bottom is below the frost line and its top is level for the full length of the wall.

Mark the Wall on the Footing

The following project is an example of how to build a two-wythe brick wall with a corner. The wall uses a running bond pattern, the easiest-to-build and most common style. The sample wall section starts near a garage and runs 35 feet, turns 90 degrees, and runs another 20 feet. The wall is 4 feet high, so it has 18 courses of bricks. The wall is built with brick measuring a nominal 4 by 8 inches, so in the outside wythe, the 35-foot-courses contain 52 and a half bricks, and the

20-foot-courses contain 30 bricks. The inside wythe measures one half brick less for each course. As for placing the pilasters, 18 times the thickness of the wall (8 inches) equals 12 feet. This wall needs pilasters at a spacing of no greater than every 12 feet. Aesthetically, the wall will look best if the pilasters are evenly spaced at shorter distances. It's fine to use spacings shorter than required. In this sample project, there is no pilaster at the corner so that you can learn how to interlock a running bond corner. However, you might like the way the wall looks if you include a pilaster at the corner. As a plus, the wall will be a bit stronger, too.

This project begins after you've plotted the site and built the concrete footing for the wall. See "Concrete Footings," on page 63, for how to do this.

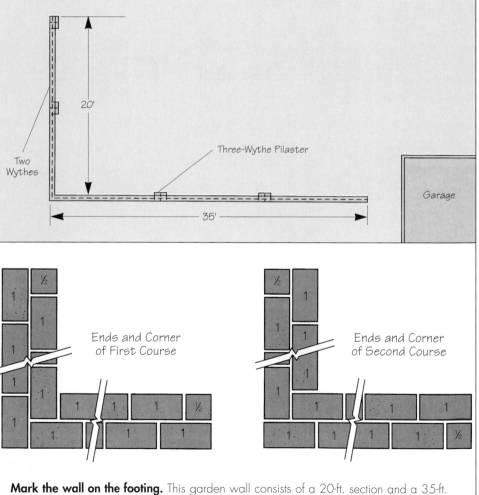

Mark the wall on the footing. This garden wall consists of a 20-ft. section and a 35-ft. section that meet at a corner as shown at top. The drawing at bottom shows how to lay out the first and second courses at the corner.

1 Snap a chalk line. After your concrete footing has cured for at least seven days, brush all debris from the surface. Measure and mark the location of the outside face of the wall, being careful to center the masonry across the width of the footing. For an 8-inch-wide wall on a 16-inch-wide footing, simply measure 4 inches in from the footing edge at both ends of the wall and snap a line between these measurements to mark the outside face of the wall.

Square the corners and snap a chalk line along the length of the footing. To ensure that the corners are square, use the 3-4-5 triangle method. From the outside corner point, measure up 4 feet along one leg of the footing, and 3 feet along the other leg. The two lines are square when the diagonal between the two points measures 5 feet. To square the line of a wall against an existing wall, again use the 3-4-5 triangle method.

2 Lay the outside wythe in a dry run. Check the wall length and design by laying out a dry course of brick. Lay the outside wythe of bricks as stretchers along the chalk line. Start at one end, dry lay a few bricks, then move to the other end. Use whole bricks and fill in toward the middle. Use a small scrap of ⅜-inch plywood to space the units. Adjust the size of the joints between the ends of the bricks (called head joints) to make up for slight variations in the size of the bricks. Every brick and head joint combination should be 8 inches long. If you are using rough or antiqued brick, which varies more in size, you will have to take up the slack at the joints to achieve the correct overall length. Use the edge of a level to periodically check for proper alignment along the chalk line. When you get to the middle of the wall, go back to the other end and complete the dry run of the outside wythe.

3 Lay the inside wythe in a dry run. Now lay out the stretchers of the inside wythe parallel to the outside wythe. Begin at the ends, using half-bricks, and allow about ⅜ inch between the two wythes for a collar joint. Notice that the head joints are

1 Snap a chalk line to indicate the front of the wall.

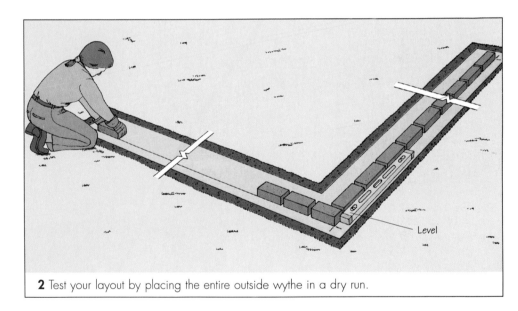

Level

2 Test your layout by placing the entire outside wythe in a dry run.

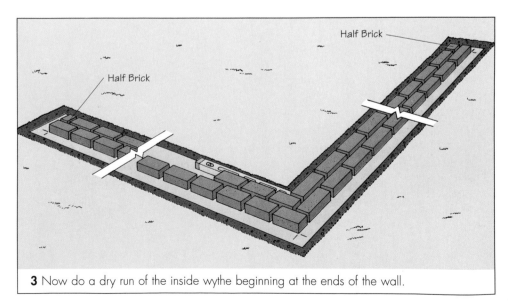

Half Brick

Half Brick

3 Now do a dry run of the inside wythe beginning at the ends of the wall.

offset by a half brick length in the two wythes. This makes the wall stronger than if the joints were aligned. If your wall is straight and does not have a corner, lay out the inside wythe beginning and ending with a half brick to create this same offset. Remember to lay the pilasters where indicated on your layout.

4 **Mark the joint locations.** Adjust the head joints if necessary for even spacing, and mark the joint locations on the footing when all the bricks

are dry laid. Using a marker, pencil, or chalk, make long slash marks at all the joints so that you will be able to confirm the spacing of the first course as you work. Make some type of distinctive mark to locate expansion joints. Check the wall width periodically by laying a header brick perpendicular to the stretchers. The width of the wall should be exactly the same as the length of the header brick.

Creating the Brick Leads

After marking the joints and moving the dry run bricks out of the way, you'll begin wall construction by building leading sections, or leads, at the ends and corner. Masonry walls are always laid from the ends first and filled in toward the middle; the leads help establish the correct spacing and coursing heights for the rest of the wall. The first course of a corner

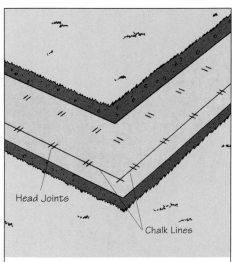

4 Adjust the head joints if necessary for even spacing. Mark the joint locations on the footing.

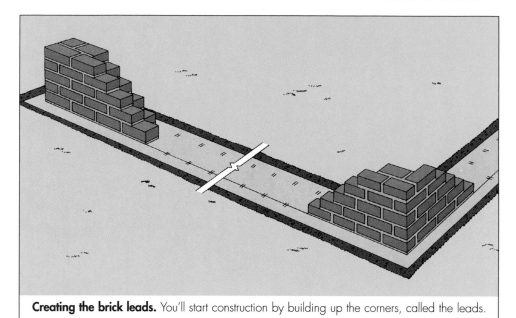

Creating the brick leads. You'll start construction by building up the corners, called the leads.

Cutting Bricks in Advance

The wall shown here will use only whole and half bricks. Cut a number of half bricks now, so you won't have to stop and start during wall construction. Soft brick can usually be cut with a quick downward blow from a brick hammer. Experienced masons can split bricks exactly using this technique. However, this method may be difficult for a novice. A better technique is to place the brick on firm ground, score it on all four sides with a brickset, then sever the brick with a final sharp blow.

Hard brick such as pavers, can be cut with a circular saw equipped with a masonry blade. Be sure to clamp the paver to a work bench and wear eye protection when cutting. For even quicker cutting, you can rent a mechanical cutter, called a guillotine, at a tool-rental shop.

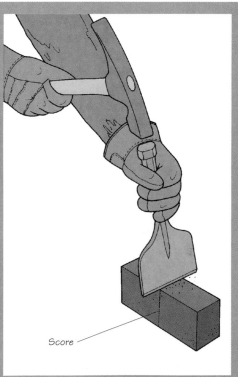

Tool head joints first. The joints will look best if you tool all the head joints before tooling the bed joints with one smooth stroke for each course.

Preparing Line Blocks

To fill in the masonry between leads, you need to stretch a string line to mark each course as you build up the wall. Use line blocks and mason's twine to do this. (Mason's twine is better than cotton string because it will stretch tight without sagging.) Secure the twine by first pulling it through the slot in the middle of the block and wrapping it around the right side of the block. Pull the line through the center slot again and wrap the line around the left block. Hook the block around a corner brick and stretch the twine to the opposite corner. Pull the twine tight in the slot of the other block, hook around the block edges, and secure it around a corner brick of the same course. The line must not sag in the middle.

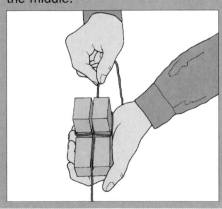

the bed joints—this will leave a smooth, unbroken line on the bed joints. Don't wait until you have finished a large section of wall before you tool the joints. Check the mortar frequently, and tool the joints a few at a time when the surface is just the right consistency. As the joints are tooled, small pieces of mortar called "tailings" will be squeezed out at the edges of the joints. Remove these with the edge of the trowel.

Filling between Leads

1 **Set the string line.** Hook one line block on the corner of the lead so that the string is level with the top of the brick in the course you're working on. Stretch the string to the opposite corner lead and hook the other line block at the same height. Check the line with a line level. The line blocks hold the string about 1/16 inch away from the face of the wall. The masonry in between the leads can now be "laid to the line" to keep the wall straight and the brick course level.

2 **Fill in first course.** Fill in the first course between leads, checking the face of the bricks to make sure they are correctly laid along the chalk line and with the proper head joint thickness. Work on the outside wythe

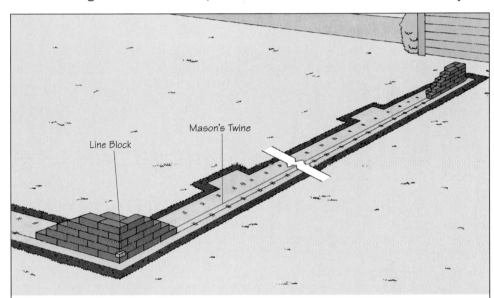

1 The line block will keep the string taut and about 1/16 inch away from the way so you can lay brick accurately to the line.

2 Fill in the wall, working on the outside wythe first. Be especially careful to get the first course straight and level.

first. It is critical that the first course of brick be level and plumb, because it is the base for the entire wall. You can correct slight irregularities in the concrete footing by varying the thickness of the first mortar bed, up to a maximum of about ¾ inch. You can allow for slight variations in brick length by adjusting the thickness of the head joints between the ends of the units, but try to keep the head joints fairly uniform in size. Remember to account for any expansion joints in a wall over 30 feet long. See "Expansion Joints," on page 83.

3 Lay the closure unit. The last brick to be put into place in a course is called a closure brick. You should have just enough space left for this brick plus a head joint on each end. To make sure you get full head joints, butter the ends of the adjacent units and butter both ends of the closure brick. Lower the brick into place from above, being careful not to dislodge the adjacent bricks. Now complete the inside wythe of the wall. Completely fill between the wythes with mortar.

Note: Remember that ties will begin here, on top of the first course.

4 Completely fill between leads. As you work on successive courses, continually check the tops of the brick with a 4-foot level to make sure that each course is level. Tap down any bricks that are set too high. Remove bricks that are set too low, cut away the mortar, and lay the unit with fresh mortar. Any brick that is dislodged after it is initially set must be removed, the mortar cut away, and the unit relaid with fresh mortar. Also check that the bricks are plumb. Use the side of the level as a straightedge to align the face of the units in each course.

5 Build up new leads. When you have filled in the courses between your leads, build up the ends or corners of the walls again to form new leads. Continue to place the ties and fill the collar joint just as you did in the first section of wall. Repeat the process of filling in courses and building up leads until you reach the final wall height.

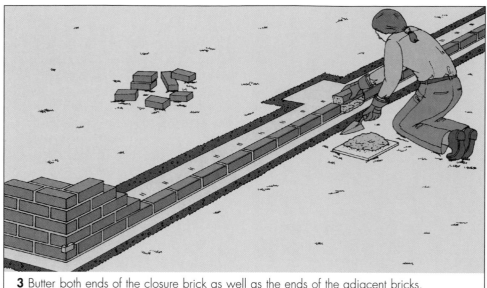

3 Butter both ends of the closure brick as well as the ends of the adjacent bricks.

4 Fill in the rest of the bricks between the leads, tapping bricks into place with your trowel handle where necessary to level them.

5 If your wall will continue higher, begin again with new leads, filling them in just as you did between the first leads.

Install a Wall Coping

When the wall is at the final height, the top is finished with a final course called the coping. Coping on a brick wall ties the masonry units together and helps retard water penetration. When water penetrates the joints, it can freeze and do severe damage to a masonry structure. The coping can be a course of rowlock header bricks, stone slabs, or specially molded brick or concrete units. For this project, a rowlock coping is used. For the course immediately below the coping, use solid brick without cores, or fill the cores with mortar. It is also important that the collar joint between the wythes be entirely filled to eliminate voids in which water could collect and freeze.

1 **Install flashing.** For maximum weather protection, install flashing immediately below the wall coping. Stainless steel flashing is the most resistant to corrosion. Copper flashing also resists ordinary corrosion, provides an excellent moisture barrier and is easy to shape. To save money, you can also use self-adhesive rubberized asphalt flashing, or a plastic flashing that is rated as resistant to degradation from ultraviolet light, or a laminated combination flashing.

Except for self-adhesive flashing, place a thin bed of mortar on top of the wall, center the flashing over the two wythes, and press it down into the mortar. Work with relatively short sections of flashing (about 4 feet), so your mortar doesn't dry out, and overlap the flashing sections about 4 to 6 inches. Seal lap joints with non-hardening mastic or caulk. If you are using metal flashing, extend it ½ inch or so beyond the faces of the wall and turn it down to form a drip edge. Flexible flashings won't hold a bend, so extend them past the wall and later trim them flush with the joint. Self-adhesive flashing can be installed directly on the brick, and laps are self-sealing.

2 **Lay the coping.** Lay a bed of mortar on top of the flashing, then butter one side of your coping

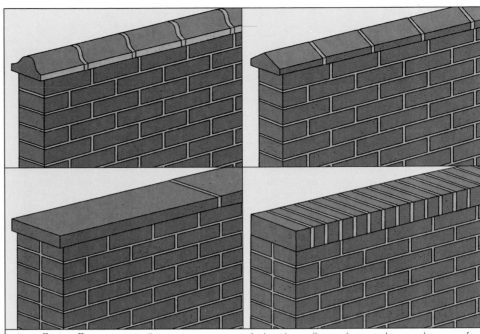

Install a wall coping. Wall copings vary in style but they all are designed to tie the top of the wall together while preventing water from penetrating the wall.

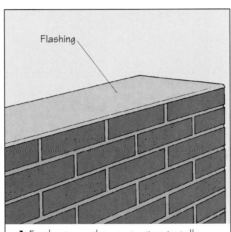

1 For best weather protection install flashing in the mortar bed just below the coping.

2 Put mortar on top of the flashing and lay the coping in the mortar.

units and lay them as the top course of the wall. If you are using brick, lay the bricks on edge in the rowlock position to form a brick coping. Use solid bricks without cores at the ends where the side of the brick is exposed. Make sure the joints are completely filled and then tooled to compress the surface of the mortar. Check for level and alignment by holding a 4-foot level to the rowlocks. Be sure to install expansion joints in the coping to prevent the wall from bowing and cracking.

Clean the wall. After the wall has set for about a week, brush the surface with a stiff natural- or synthetic-bristle brush to remove mortar drips and dust. Use a plastic or wooden scraper and then a brush to remove large mortar splatters. If necessary, clean completed red brick walls with a diluted solution of muriatic acid (mixed 1:10 with water). Don't use muriatic acid on white, cream, buff, gray, or brown brick, because it can leave ugly green or brown stains—check with the brick manufacturer or distributor. Before applying an acid cleaning solution, thoroughly wet the wall with a garden hose. Wearing rubber gloves, apply

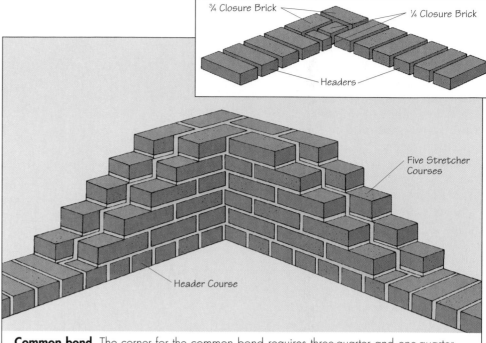

Before filling in the excavated area around the base of the wall, the bricks below ground must be treated against moisture penetration. There are two methods for doing this.

The first and easiest method involves brushing on a heavy bituminous coating that is composed of asphaltic materials. The coating is applied as if it were thick paint. Use an old throw-away brush or roller. Do not go above ground as the black tar-like coating is unattractive.

The second method is to parge (coat) the bricks below ground with a ¼-inch layer of cement plaster to form a protective shield against moisture. Trowel on the cement as you would apply plaster to a wall.

Either method is effective. Once completed and dried according to the manufacturer, fill in the excavation and tamp the soil solidly.

Common bond. The corner for the common bond requires three-quarter and one-quarter closure bricks. Headers are used every six courses.

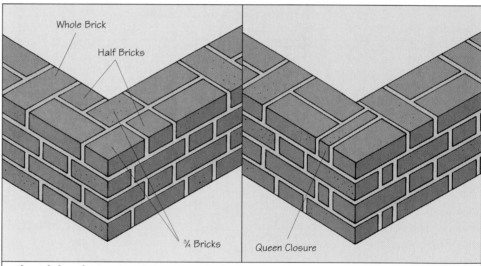

Flemish bond. The Flemish bond can be built with a Dutch corner, as shown at the left, or with an English corner, as shown at the right.

the acid solution carefully with a special acid brush available from masonry suppliers. Scrub lightly, then thoroughly rinse the wall with the garden hose. Be extremely careful when working with acid to avoid burns and other injuries. Don't use metal tools or buckets, because the acid will corrode them. Always pour the water in the bucket first, then add the acid.

Making Corners for Decorative Bonds

The project just described was built with a running bond pattern. However, you may prefer a decorative bond pattern that requires some extra planning. In a double-wythe wall with a decorative bond pattern, brick headers will connect the wythes instead of metal ties. Refer to "Bond Patterns for Walls," on page 84, for details.

Common bond. The common bond pattern uses header units in every sixth course. With common bond, it is customary to begin with a header

course at the base of the wall; one-quarter and three-quarter closure units are required to make the corner pattern. It is important to build the inside and outside wythes at the same time so that the header units can be set in place properly. The long joints between header units should be buttered with mortar as you would normally butter a head joint between stretchers. Hold the brick in one hand and scrape mortar onto the side with the trowel from all four directions, making sure you get enough mortar to completely fill the joint. Be sure

also to completely fill the collar joint between stretcher wythes as each course is laid so that the wall is the same thickness as the length of the header units.

Flemish bond. The Flemish bond pattern uses alternating stretcher and header units in every course. There are two ways of forming the corner pattern for a Flemish bond wall. One is called a Dutch corner and uses cut half-length and three-quarter-length units. The other option is called an English corner, which uses a field-cut closure brick called a queen closure.

Serpentine Brick Wall

A serpentine, or S-shaped, brick wall is both unusual and attractive. It is a style made famous by Thomas Jefferson in the gardens that he designed at the University of Virginia in Charlottesville.

While most brick walls require a double thickness of brick for strength and stability, serpentine walls can be built with a single wythe of units because of the curved shape. If you try to stand a piece of cardboard on its edge, it will fall over, but if you fold or bend the cardboard into an S or a zigzag, it will stand up by itself. This same principle permits the use of single-wythe brick for building serpentine walls.

The brick-laying technique for a serpentine wall is the same as the previous brick garden wall project. A line is drawn on the center of the footing to mark the middle of the brick wall; the bricks are dry-laid, and then the first course is set in mortar. Courses are filled between leads, joints are tooled, and the wall is capped off. The only difference is in the layout of the wall on the footing and the use of a single wythe. The design specifics of a serpentine wall are explained here.

Design specifics. Since serpentine walls depend on their shape for stability against overturning, it is important that the radius and depth of the curve be just right. A design rule of thumb based on proportional relation-

ships can be used: The radius of the curve cannot be more than two times the wall height, and the depth from front to back must be at least one-half the wall height. The maximum height for a serpentine wall is no greater than 15 times the wall thickness.

You can build curved walls using ordinary rectangular bricks laid lengthwise in the stretcher position. If the radius of the curve is too small, though, the corners of each brick will stick out slightly and create a basket weave effect. The minimum radius required to produce a smooth curve with brick stretchers is about 8 feet.

Serpentine walls should be built on flat ground, as they do not lend themselves well to sloping terrain. Don't plan to build a wall that must be altered to curve around obstructions. It is complicated to build and requires an architect. The graceful curves and shallow recesses of a serpentine wall lend themselves to distinctive landscaping.

Leave at least 1 inch between the ends of the wall and any adjacent construction to allow for expansion of the brick.

Planning a Serpentine Wall

Let's say you want to build a 4-foot-high serpentine wall that uses an 8-foot-radius curve and has a depth from front to back of 4 feet. (The radius is equal to twice the height,

and the depth is equal to the height, so the design meets our rule-of-thumb criteria.) You can make the length whatever you want, starting and stopping at any place along the curve, but it is easiest to work from the centerline of one curve to the centerline of another. Use modular brick measuring nominally 4 by 8 inches. With an 8-foot radius and 4-foot depth, the distance from the center of one curve to the center of the next is 10 feet 9 inches. The wall is built in a running bond and is 18 courses tall.

Curved footings. As with other types of brick walls, the serpentine single-wythe wall needs a concrete footing to support it. The footing must be wide enough to prevent overturning and deep enough to resist frost heave in the soil. A footing for this type of wall should be 6 inches thick, 12 inches wide, and follow the same curved shape as the wall. For footings that must be set very deep, it will be much more economical to build a concrete wall up to within a few inches of grade rather than building several courses of brick below ground level. Follow the instructions in "Concrete Footings," on page 63, for how to build concrete footings. You'll need to use 1x6 lumber for the forms as they will bend to the gentle, long curves.

Mark the footing. When the footing has cured for a week, draw a line down the exact center of the footing. Since the footing is 12 inches wide,

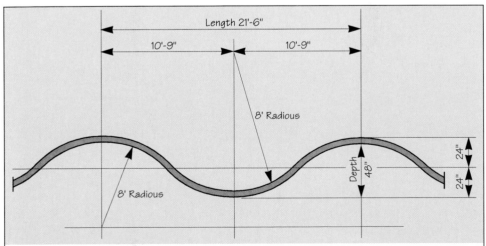

Planning a serpentine wall. In designing the wall, make sure that the radius of the curve is no more than two times the wall height and the depth from front to back is at least half the wall height.

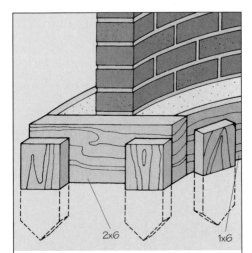

Curved footings. Bend 1x6 lumber in the gentle curves you will need for the footing under the serpentine wall.

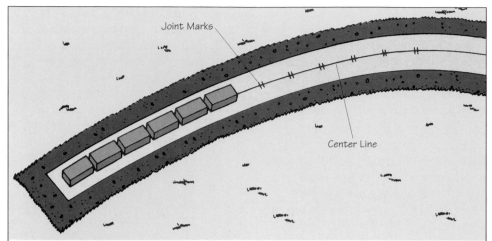

Mark the footing. Draw a line along the center of the footing to indicate the center of the wall's single wythe. Place the first course of bricks in a dry run; then mark the joint locations.

measure and mark 6 inches from either side at about every 3 feet, then make a line to connect the marks. This line will be used to center the wythe of bricks. As with the garden wall project, begin to lay the first course in a dry run and mark the joint locations on the footing.

Estimate the number of bricks you will need by multiplying the number of units in the wall length times the number of courses in the wall height. Estimate 14 cubic feet of mortar for every 100 square feet of wall surface. Refer to "Mortar," on page 79, to estimate individual ingredients. Now that the footing has been marked with the location of the first course, the wall is built just like any other brick wall. Simply begin from "Creating the Brick Leads," on page 90, and continue through the steps to the end of the garden wall project to build a serpentine wall. Since you can't stretch a string line along the curve, check level and plumb frequently with a 4-foot level and keep the coursing accurate with a story pole.

Brick Screen Wall

By omitting bricks to form a pattern of openings, solid brick can be used to build what are called screen walls. A screen wall provides privacy while still allowing light and air through the wall. This type of wall works well to hide a large air-conditioning unit

or to shield a trash can area while still allowing ventilation. You can alternate pierced sections of wall with solid brick sections to make the wall stronger; if necessary, you can add supporting pilasters.

There are several different styles of brick screen wall. One of the simplest to build and most attractive consists of two rows or wythes of brick laid in the English bond pattern, shown on page 85. In this pattern, the courses of brick alternate between stretcher and header courses. When modified to create a pierced screen wall, every other header brick is omitted to form the opening pattern. The remaining headers tie the two wythes together

and provide support for the stretchers. The first five courses in the illustration are laid as a solid wall to form a good base. The middle courses are then laid in the screen pattern with solid areas between for visual interest. The upper portion of the wall is finished with three more solid courses then a rowlock coping.

Use a modular size brick—one that is 7⅝ inches long, 3⅝ inches wide, and 2¼ inches tall. When laid in the wall with standard ⅜-inch mortar joints, the nominal size of this brick is 8 inches long and 4 inches wide. When laid as a header, the length of the brick is the same as two stretchers with a joint between, so the header fits exactly across the width of the two-wythe wall. Three courses of bricks with mortar joints are also 8 inches high, so all of your dimensions can be planned as multiples of 4 inches, which is the nominal length of half a brick. Before doing any construction, draw a plan of the wall to scale, making each brick twice as long as it is wide. If you make the wall 7 feet 4 inches or 8 feet long rather than 7 feet 6 inches, you will need only whole and half bricks.

Build a two-wythe screen wall. A brick screen wall with two wythes is built with supporting pilasters every 12 feet to make the wall stronger. Small pilasters can be built for walls

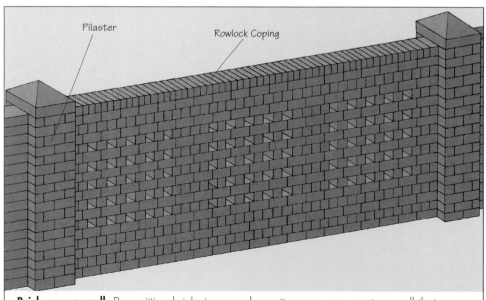

Brick screen wall. By omitting bricks in a regular pattern you can create a wall that blocks the view while still permitting ventilation.

Build a two-wythe screen wall. For the screened section omit every other brick in the header courses, leaving the ones that will support the ends of the stretcher units for the next course.

no higher than 4 feet; larger pilasters are used for taller walls. Alternating courses of brick in the wall must overlap the brick in the pilaster to form a strong interlocking structure. See "Add pilasters for strength," on page 86, for more information. Plan to adjust the footing for the additional width of the pilasters.

To build a screen wall, follow the instructions for a brick garden wall starting on page 86 and continue to the end. When you've reached the header courses of the screened section, simply omit every other brick, leaving only the ones that will support the ends of the stretcher units in the next course. Center the headers over the joints between the stretcher units below so that they will provide about 2 inches of bed surface for each stretcher they will support in the next course. In this way, you'll create the screen pattern. Tool the mortar joints in the "voids" of the screen pattern as you would all the other bed and head joints of the wall.

Masonry-Unit Paving

Brick paving is both attractive and durable—some types are strong enough to support even heavy truck traffic. The paving system includes the base, the setting bed, and the paving material. The type of paving system that will work best for you depends on the desired appearance and what kind of traffic the surface must bear.

Note: The projects illustrated in this section are walks, both dry-laid in sand and mortared on a concrete slab. However, the technique for masonry-unit paving is the same for making a patio or a driveway.

For driveways made of dry-laid brick paving, choose a pattern that does not have continuous joints in the same direction as the path of travel. The herringbone pattern is a good choice. Otherwise, the pavers will eventually slide forward or backward because of the repeated braking and acceleration of cars. If you do use a pattern such as the running bond, be sure that the continuous joints are laid perpendicular to the path of vehicles.

Bond Patterns

There are many bond patterns for paving, including some that are not seen in vertical brick structures. Some are more difficult to lay than others, but all require careful planning and layout to avoid misaligned joints or partial bricks along the edges. Before

you lay the bricks, do a dry run to spot any potential layout problems.

Stack bond. Also called jack-on-jack, this pattern is symmetrical and easy to create. Starting at one end of the walk, place a single brick in a corner, then place remaining bricks in stair-step fashion, in the sequence shown. If possible, plan the walk width to avoid cut bricks. If you can't do this, cut partial bricks all at once to the same size. Place cut bricks along the least conspicuous edge of the walk.

Running bond. This is the most popular brick pattern and is easy to lay out. Also, the pattern visually minimizes any minor variations in brick sizes. Place the first course of bricks as stretchers across the walk. Start the second course with a half brick, set whole bricks end to end, and place a final half brick. Repeat this alternate pattern for successive courses so that end joints fall midway between bricks in the previous course.

Herringbone. This pattern looks best with patios and driveways. On narrow walks (3 feet or less), the pattern may appear confusing. As with the running-bond design, a herringbone pattern requires partial bricks along the walk edges and ends, which are best cut in advance. Starting at one corner, place full bricks in a step pattern, using half bricks as needed to fill in along the edges. Use a framing square to align the bricks where they meet at 90-degree angles.

Basket weave. Basket-weave designs look best when you use modular bricks with a width that equals exactly half their length (with allowance for mortar joints, if used). To make a simple two-brick basket weave, lay two bricks side by side to form a square in one corner of the walk. Working across the walk, lay a second square of two bricks at right angles to the first. Alternate the direction of each square until you reach the other side of the walk. Install the second course by laying two bricks at right angles to the square above it. Continue in this manner to create the pattern shown. Variations include a half basket weave and double basket weave.

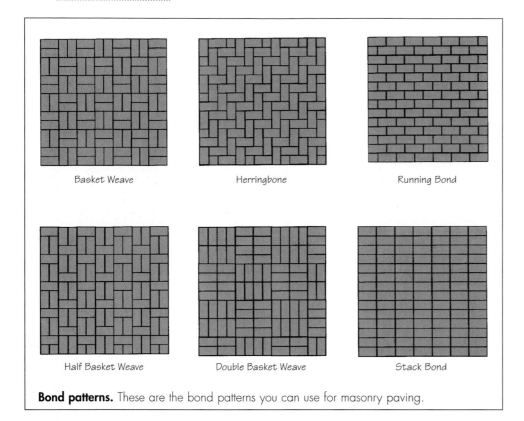

Basket Weave   Herringbone   Running Bond

Half Basket Weave   Double Basket Weave   Stack Bond

Bond patterns. These are the bond patterns you can use for masonry paving.

Paving Materials

Paving materials include brick, concrete paver units, and interlocking concrete pavers. Among these choices, some materials are cut to more precise sizes and shapes than others; some materials are better suited to particular climates. However, construction techniques and required substrates are similar for most pavers.

Paving brick. Bricks provide a beautiful walk surface that will last for many years, provided that you choose the right kind of brick. Some are designed for interior applications, and won't hold up under wet or freezing conditions; some have smooth or glazed surfaces that can make for a dangerously slippery walk when wet. The ideal brick is hard, is dense, and has a slightly rough surface to provide good traction in wet weather. Paving brick meets these criteria; it is designed especially for walks and patios. The next best choice is solid face brick.

Paving bricks designed to be laid with mortar joints are 3⅝ inches wide by 7⅝ inches long, so that with a standard ⅜-inch mortar joint, they make a nominal 4 by 8-inch module. Paving bricks designed to be laid butted together without mortar joints are 4 by 8 inches, forming the same module.

Designed especially for ground contact use, paving brick has a high resistance to abrasion and moisture penetration. Some paving bricks, called repress pavers, have chamfered or rounded edges on one or both faces. Repress pavers are better for cold climates because the chamfered edges facilitate water runoff, and are less likely to get chipped. Bricks are also rated for their intended uses. Type II is suitable for residential driveways and entry walks. Choose a brick suited to your particular climate; Class SX for severe weathering, or Class MX for moderate weathering.

Concrete pavers and interlocking pavers. Interlocking pavers are modular concrete units manufactured to lock in a tight pattern that won't shift with heavy traffic. Available in a wide variety of sizes and shapes, most pavers are 2⅜ to 2½ inches thick, about the same as a standard brick. Some driveway concrete pavers are 3⅛ inches thick. One type, called a grass paver, has an open-grid shape for planting grass or other ground cover. Grass pavers provide a durable, natural-looking walk surface, and the turf helps hold the pavers in place.

Concrete masonry pavers are always laid on sand. The sand acts as a cushion and as a leveling bed. If the soil is naturally well drained and stable, the sand bed can be placed directly on the excavated subgrade, if the natural drainage is poor or the soil is soft, you will need a 4-inch gravel drainage base below the sand bed. If you like, you can place a layer of landscaping fabric, black plastic or 15-pound roofing felt below the sand to prevent weeds from growing between the bricks and to keep the sand from settling down into the gravel layer.

Interlocking pavers are butted together with swept-sand joints over a sand bed. Some pavers have small tabs on one side and one end to ensure consistent joint spacing. Where soil conditions and climate permit, the sand bed may be laid directly on well-tamped and leveled soil without the gravel drainage base. Depending on the shape of the paver, you may end up with voids or chinks along the edges of the walk. Some manufacturers make special edging pieces to fill the voids and create a straight edge. Otherwise, you'll have to cut the pavers or fill the voids with mortar to make straight edges.

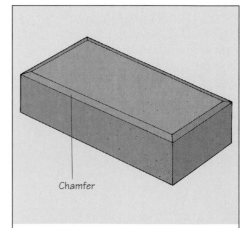

Paving brick. Paving brick is dense to resist moisture penetration and abrasion. Some pavers have chamfered top edges to prevent chipping and facilitate water run-off.

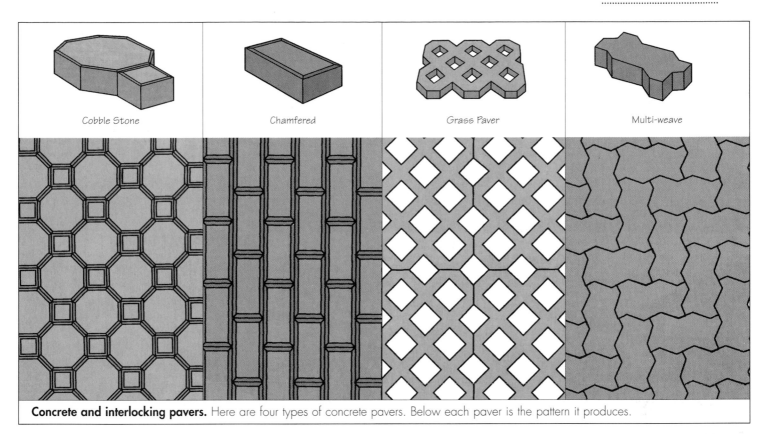

Cobble Stone   Chamfered   Grass Paver   Multi-weave

Concrete and interlocking pavers. Here are four types of concrete pavers. Below each paver is the pattern it produces.

Dry-Laid Walks

In dry-laid walks, the unit paving materials are laid on a bed of tamped sand, usually over gravel. No concrete or mortar is required. This type of construction is called flexible paving and is applicable for brick pavers, concrete pavers, and interlocking pavers. The pavers fit together tightly and fine mason's sand is swept into the thin joints. This creates a stable and durable walk, even in climates subject to some frost heave. With this system, it's easy to replace damaged paving materials, fill sunken portions of the walk, or remove sections of the walk to access buried utility lines or pipes. However, the sand must be replenished as it gradually washes away.

A flexible base usually consists of compacted gravel with a sand setting bed. The sand acts as a cushion and a leveling bed to compensate for minor irregularities in the base surface. If the soil is naturally well drained and stable, the sand bed can be placed directly on the excavated subgrade. If the natural drainage is poor, you will need a gravel drainage base below the sand bed.

The required thickness of the gravel base depends on the strength of the underlying soil or your area. For residential walks, patios, and driveways with light traffic, a 4-inch-thick gravel or crushed stone base plus a 2-inch sand setting bed are required. Mortarless paving systems can also be laid on existing asphalt or concrete if a 2-inch sand setting bed is added on top.

Edging Options

Mortarless brick paving requires some method of containment at the edges to keep the units from sliding. A course of bricks set on end (either straight or at an angle), treated wood held by stakes, concrete curbs, or a preformed edging system will provide the required stability. Metal or plastic edging systems are simple and easy to install; since the preformed edging

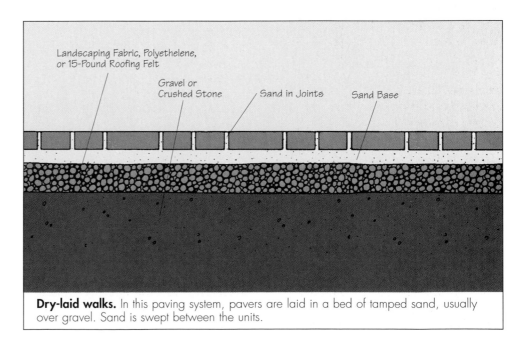

Landscaping Fabric, Polyethelene, or 15-Pound Roofing Felt

Gravel or Crushed Stone

Sand in Joints

Sand Base

Dry-laid walks. In this paving system, pavers are laid in a bed of tamped sand, usually over gravel. Sand is swept between the units.

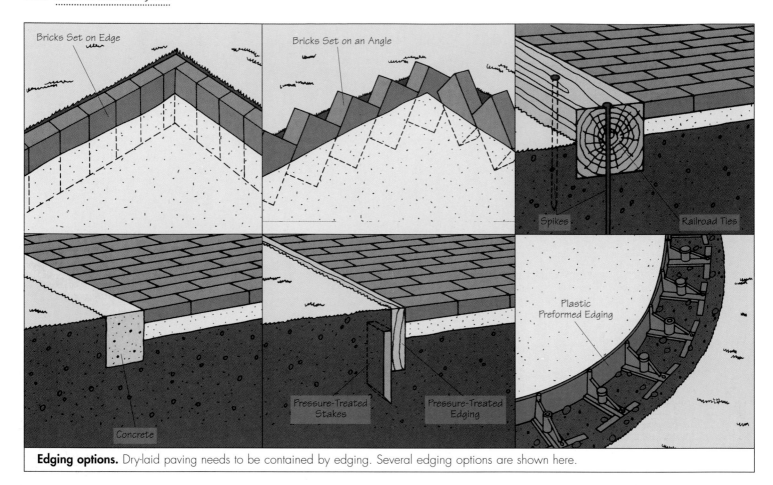

Edging options. Dry-laid paving needs to be contained by edging. Several edging options are shown here.

is concealed below the ground, it does not change the appearance of the bond pattern in the masonry paving. Interlocking pavers may not need an edging material—check the manufacturer's literature.

To construct a dry-laid walk you need compactable gravel, sand for the bed, mason's sand for the joints, and the paving material. You'll begin with the excavation of the site. Next, you'll install the edging, add compactable gravel (if needed), lay landscaping fabric, provide a sand bed, and finally install the pavers.

1 Mark the area with string.
Measure and lay out the size and shape of the brick paver walk using wooden stakes and string. Set stakes adjacent to any existing construction to mark where the edge of the paving will be and set stakes for the outside corners a little beyond the proposed paving edge. Remember to account for the thickness of any edging material. Check for square by using the 3-4-5 method as explained in "Making Square Corners," on page 24.

2 Excavate the soil. Sprinkle sand under the string lines to mark the shape of the required excavation, then untie the strings.

The finished paving surface should be about 1 inch above the adjacent ground and 1 inch below the sill of any adjacent doors. You must also provide drainage by sloping the walk away from the house at a rate of 1 inch for every 4 feet of length. Plan your excavation depth to these parameters, accounting for the gravel (if needed), the sand bed, and the paver thickness below ground. Usually brick pavers will sit about 1 inch above ground. Excavate along the sand marking lines, removing all grass, sod, roots, and large rocks to the depth necessary to accommodate the thickness of the base, sand bed, and pavers.

Although you might get away with setting your paving materials directly on the ground, the walk will last longer, and fare the elements better, when built on a subbase consisting of 2 inches of sand over 4 inches of

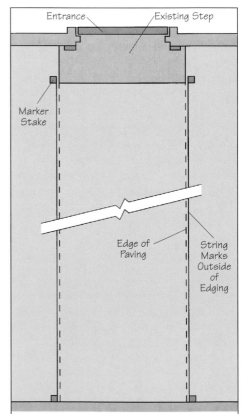

1 Lay out the area to be paved with stakes and string. Use the 3-4-5 method to ensure square corners.

gravel. Site drainage may in fact make the use of gravel mandatory. The type of gravel you should use is called compactable because you can tamp it to form a well-drained firm subbase. Crushed limestone, with stones sized ¾ inch or less, is ideal for this application; avoid smooth river run or pea gravel. When you buy the gravel, figure on using 1 cubic yard for every 50 square feet of walk area. Lay half the gravel, tamp with a hand tamper, then add the rest and tamp again.

3 Install brick edging. Retie the string line between the wooden stakes to act as a guide for the height and alignment of the edging. For this project, the edging is a row of bricks set as sailors. You must dig a deeper, narrower trench around the perimeter of the excavation to account for the gravel, sand, and 8-inch height of the brick sailors (not the same depth as the pavers). Place the bricks on end with the flat side against the string line. Tamp the pavers down with a trowel handle to get the right height. Fill in around the edging with sand. The units should stick up above the excavation high enough to cover the depth of the 2-inch sand bed plus the thickness of the pavers when they are laid flat (2¼ or 1½ inches). Butt the edge units snugly against one another.

At this point, before the sand bed is laid, do a dry run of your bond pattern inside the edging bricks. It is time well spent to check how the bricks will fit. Complete a pattern of a few square feet, then remove the bricks.

4 Install a weed barrier. To keep weeds from growing up between the unmortared paving joints, install a layer of landscaping fabric roofing felt, or polyethylene between the soil or gravel base and the sand bed. Roll out sections of fabric and lap adjoining pieces by at least 4 inches. You can lay a few bricks behind you to keep the fabric in place. If your project includes a gravel base, the weed barrier between the gravel and the sand will keep the sand from settling.

5 Spread and screed the sand bed. Fill the excavated area inside the

2 Sprinkle sand under the string to delineate the excavation, then remove the string before excavating.

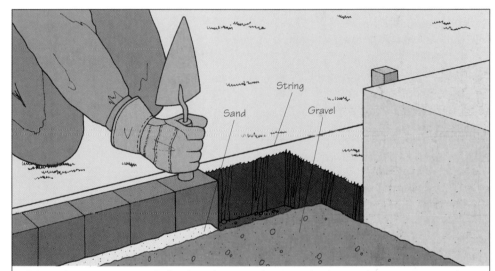
3 Retie the string as a guide for the edging. In the example shown, the excavation is deepened at the perimeter to make room for edging bricks set as sailors.

4 Place landscaping fabric, roofing felt, or polyethylene plastic on the soil or gravel base.

edging with construction sand. When ordering sand, figure on using 1 cubic yard for every 150 square feet of walk area. Tamp the sand to a level that allows for the thickness of the pavers so that the paving surface will be 1 inch above final grade. Use a straight length of 2x4 longer than the edging is wide and attach to it a length of 1x4 to screed the sand. The 1x4 is screwed to the 2x4 with drywall screws.

If your project is a patio or other wide project that a 2x4 screed cannot easily stretch across, simply drive stakes in the sand bed to hold a temporary 2x4 form board 12 feet from the edging. Pull the screed between the form board and the edging. When you remove the stakes, fill the holes with sand and tamp level. Work in one direction so you never walk on the screeded sand.

6 **Install pavers.** Begin placing the pavers on the tamped sand, butting them tightly together and tamping them into place with a rubber mallet or a trowel handle. Use a string line to maintain the coursing in straight lines. (Interlocking pavers fit together like a jigsaw puzzle, but a string line still helps.) If you have to kneel on the sand bed at first to lay the brick, put down a piece of ½-inch plywood to keep from making holes in the sand. After you have laid a few courses, you should be able to move around and kneel on the pavers instead.

7 **Check for level and bed the pavers.** After setting several square feet of pavement, lay a 32-inch length of 1x6 on the walk, and tap the wood over the entire surface with a hammer or mallet to uniformly bed the pavers into the sand. If individual units are slightly tilted or too high, tap them gently into place with a rubber mallet. If a unit sits too low, lift it up, place sand underneath, and reseat the brick. Periodically check the surface of the paving with a 4-foot level to ensure that the pavers are level or are sloping uniformly in the correct direction.

If you're doing a large driveway or patio, rent a vibrating tamper. At the

5 Place sand in the excavation and screed it to a level that will bring the pavers level with the edging.

6 Lay the pavers in the sand and use a rubber mallet or a trowel handle to tap them tightly together. Use a string line to keep courses straight.

7 After every several square feet, check the paving for level and tamp the pavers to set them in the sand. Rent a vibrating tamper for large jobs.

end of each workday, tamp the units to compact the sand bed and settle the pavers into place.

8 Fill the joints with sand. When all the paver units are in place, spread a thin layer of dry mason's sand evenly over a 5 or 6-foot section of walk. With a stiff broom, sweep the sand into the cracks between the pavers. Sweep in all directions to fill all of the joints completely. Sweep excess sand into a pile, and scoop it into a bucket for future use. Then lightly spray the walk with water to pack down the sand, and wash it off the surface. Do not use a heavy spray, or you will dislodge sand from the joints. Allow the surface to dry, then repeat the process until all of the joints are completely filled and compacted.

8 Use a stiff push broom to sweep sand into the joints between pavers.

Brick Walk in Mortar

A brick walk laid in mortar provides a more formal look than the dry-laid walk with sand joints. Mortar is used as a bed for the bricks and fills the ⅜-inch joints. The mortar bed for the pavers must be placed on a concrete slab, which can be newly poured or already in place.

Concrete slabs for rigid brick paving should be 4 inches thick and reinforced with wire mesh. A 4-inch layer of gravel under the slab may be required for drainage. If not, use 2 inches of sand as a leveling bed. Be sure to excavate deeply enough to allow for the thickness of the concrete slab and base plus the thickness of the mortar setting bed and the pavers. Paving brick comes in several thicknesses, the most common of which are 1½ inches for areas such as patios and sidewalks, and 2¼ inches for driveways. The mortar setting bed is ½ inch thick. (Concrete construction techniques are fully described in "Concrete Techniques," on page 17.) Finish a new concrete surface with a slightly rough texture so that it will form a good bond with the mortar setting bed. Always allow a new slab to cure properly before laying the mortar bed.

Existing concrete slabs can also be used to support rigid brick paving as long as there are no major structural cracks. Minor cracks will not be harmful, but you must patch them.

Estimating mortar amounts. The quantity of mortar you will need for the mortar bed depends on the size of the walk and the size of the paving material. The amount of mortar you will need to fill the joints depends on the size and number of joints and the size of the paving material. Also, consider the depth of the joints. With 2¼-inch-thick bricks, one 80-pound bag of mortar will fill joints for about 160 modular bricks with ⅜-inch joints, or about 110 standard bricks with ½-inch joints. Order one 80-pound bag of mortar mix for every 15 square feet of mortar bed.

Drainage for mortared brick paving. Patios, sidewalks and driveways should all be sloped ¼ inch per foot to drain water off the surface. Depending on the size and shape of your project and the contour of the ground around it, the surface can slope to one side or be crowned in the middle to shed water off both sides. Relocate any downspouts that would drain onto the paving or use flexible drain pipe to route the water runoff around the paving. The finished paving should be about 1 inch above the surrounding grade (slightly higher in poorly drained areas). If necessary, shape the surrounding grade to make sure that runoff drains around rather than over the paving.

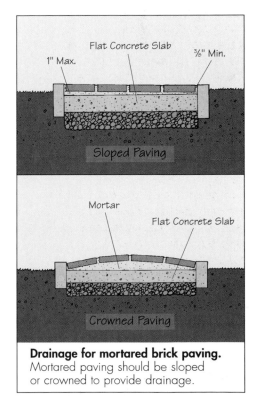

Drainage for mortared brick paving. Mortared paving should be sloped or crowned to provide drainage.

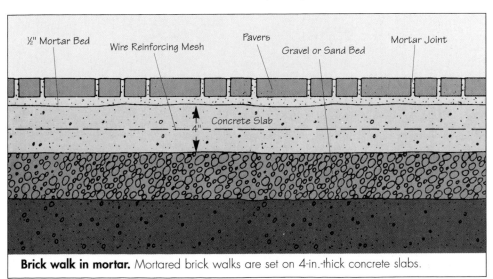

Brick walk in mortar. Mortared brick walks are set on 4-in.-thick concrete slabs.

Here's how to lay a mortared walk:

1 Install brick border. As with the dry-laid walk, the options for edging are explained in "Edging Options," on page 101. Don't use a plastic or metal edging system with mortared paving; it's unnecessary and adds nothing to the look. If you choose a concrete edge, place an expansion joint between the edge and existing slab.

For this project, the edging material is a row of sailors—bricks on end in a row. Dig a narrow trench around the outside edge of the slab. Make the trench ½ inch wider than the brick thickness. Dig the trench so that the units stick up above the slab high enough to cover the ½-inch mortar bed plus the thickness of the pavers when they are laid flat (2¼ or 1½ inches).

Spread mortar on the edge of the slab and on the lower half of the brick sailor. Also mortar the edge of the brick where it butts the next sailor. Place the brick pavers on end with the flat side against the edge of the concrete and press them into place. Tamp dirt against the outside faces to hold them in place. Use a ⅜-inch scrap of plywood to space out the mortar joints between units. Keep the tops level and at the right height by checking frequently with a 4-foot level and a ruler. The joints are ready for tooling when the mortar is "thumbprint" hard, meaning that you can press your thumb against the mortar and leave a print impression without any mortar sticking to your thumb.

2 Lay out the paving bricks. Lay out the paving bricks without mortar to check the spacing and the bond pattern. Use a piece of ⅜-inch plywood to gauge the thickness of the mortar joints. Cut some half bricks now if needed. When you're satisfied with the bond, remove the bricks. Be sure you don't knock the edging out of place if the mortar hasn't cured fully.

3 Lay mortar setting bed. Clean the top of an existing concrete slab with a commercial cleaner or a solution of one part trisodium phosphate (TSP) to five parts water. Scrub

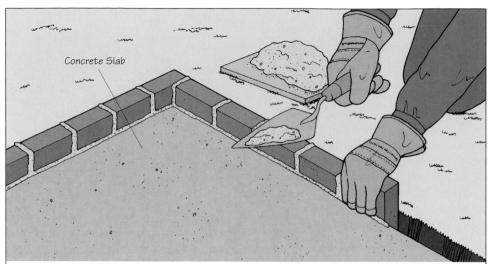

1 Border bricks for mortared paving are installed in a manner similar to dry-laid paving. In the example shown, the only difference is that mortar is placed between the sailor bricks.

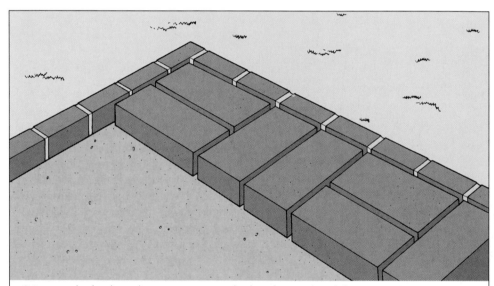

2 Lay out the bricks without mortar to test the bond pattern and the joint spacing.

3 After screeding the mortar bed, make grooves with a notched trowel.

briskly with a push broom or heavy bristle brush, rinse, then allow to dry.

Apply a mortar setting bed using a Type S or mortar. This setting bed will hold the pavers in place and also help to compensate for minor irregularities in the slab surface. If you are working on an existing slab and it is not properly sloped to drain water, use the mortar bed to get a ¼ inch per foot drainage. Maintain a minimum thickness of ⅜ inch and a maximum thickness of 1 inch for the bed. Place the mortar in an area small enough so that you can lay the bricks before the mortar begins to dry out. Screed the surface of the mortar bed as you would the sand in a dry-laid walk. Then score the surface with the notched edge of a rectangular metal trowel.

4 **Use twine to maintain coursing.** Wrap mason's twine around a brick, stretch it across the outside edge of the first course, and wrap the other end around a brick on the opposite side. This line will help guide the coursing for straight rows. On small projects, such as a narrow sidewalk, lay the pavers in complete courses, working across the slab. On larger projects, such as patios, lay the pavers in smaller, rectangular sections for convenience.

5 **Install the pavers.** If the pavers have high absorption (see "Water Absorption," page 76), soak them with a garden hose before you begin, then allow them to dry for 24 hours. Place the pavers and fill the joints in one of three ways:

■ Using a conventional mason's trowel, butter one end and one side of each paver and set it firmly into the mortar setting bed. If necessary, tap the pavers down with the trowel handle. Remove excess surface mortar with the edge of the trowel.

■ Place the bricks on the mortar setting bed leaving the joints open. After the pavers have been installed and have set for a day or two, wet them with a garden hose, let them dry a little, and fill the joints with a thin mortar mix about the consistency of sour cream. Use a coffee can or other small contain-

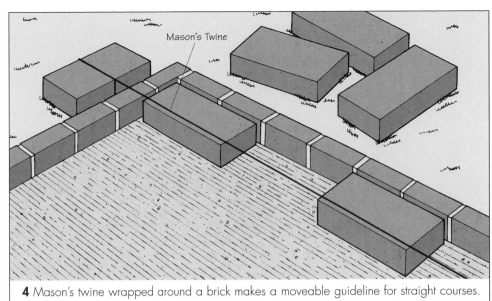

4 Mason's twine wrapped around a brick makes a moveable guideline for straight courses.

5 There are three ways to lay brick in mortar: (A) Butter the bottom and one side of each brick as you place it. (B) Lay the bricks in mortar and fill the joints in place with a thin mortar mix. (C and D) Sweep a sand and portland cement mixture into the joints; then spray with a fine mist from a garden hose.

er that can be squeezed to form a spout, and work the mortar into the joints with the point of a trowel. Use a wet sponge or cloth to clean excess mortar off the brick surfaces before it dries.

■ Instead of the usual mortar setting bed, lay the bricks on a cushion of 1 part dry portland cement and 3 to 6 parts damp, loose sand. Leave the joints open, spacing the units with your finger or a scrap of ⅜-inch plywood. After all the pavers are in place, sweep the open joints full of the same dry portland cement and sand mixture. Be careful, especially at first, not to dislodge the pavers as you sweep. Sweep excess material from the surface, then spray the paving with a fine water mist until the joints are completely saturated. Keep the paving moist for at least three days to ensure proper curing of the cement-sand mix.

6 Tool the mortar joints. Regardless of which mortar method you use to set the pavers, you will need to tool the joint surfaces when they are thumbprint hard. Using a rounded jointer, tool the short joints first and then the long joints. Keep the joints approximately flush with the brick surface. Deep joints are hard to clean. Scrape excess mortar off the pavers with the edge of the trowel.

Clean the walk. After the walk has set for about a week, brush the surface with a stiff natural- or synthetic-bristle brush to remove mortar drips and dust. Use a plastic or wooden scraper and then a brush to remove large mortar splatters. If necessary, clean the completed project with a diluted solution of muriatic acid (mixed 1:10 with water). Don't use muriatic acid on white, cream, buff, gray, or brown brick, because it can leave ugly green or brown stains—check with the brick manufacturer or distributor. Never clean concrete masonry pavers with muriatic acid because it will etch the surface of the units and make them more susceptible to water absorption and freeze/thaw damage. Before applying an acid cleaning solution, thoroughly wet the pavers with a garden hose. Wearing rubber gloves, apply the acid solution carefully with a special acid brush (made with polystyrene or polmyra bristles, available from masonry suppliers). Scrub lightly, then thoroughly rinse with the garden hose. Be extremely careful when working with acid to avoid burns. Don't use metal tools or buckets, because the acid will corrode them. Always pour the water in the bucket first, then add the acid.

Brick Steps

If a brick walk traverses a sharp change in grade, you might need to build a set of brick steps. For maximum stability and economy, the steps are installed in a mortar bed over a concrete base, even if the walk is dry-laid paving on a sand bed. Brick steps can also be built to access a porch or stoop.

To build brick steps, you need to figure out the total height the steps must climb, called the rise, and the total length the steps traverse, called the run. The rise and run of the steps must then be broken into the number and height of the vertical risers as well as the depth of the horizontal treads. Certain rules of thumb dictate the relationship between riser height and tread depth based on what is safe and comfortable for walking. Generally, twice the height of the riser plus the depth of the tread should equal between 25 and 27 inches. Another universal rule for steps is that all the risers must be identical in height and all the treads must be identical in depth—otherwise people may trip.

One more design criterion: For flights of stairs less than 30 inches high, make each riser 7½ inches or less and each tread at least 11 inches. For flights of stairs higher than 30 inches, risers should be 6 inches or less and treads at least 12 inches. Stair width is equal to that of the walk, but never less than 36 inches wide. This project leaves the sides of the steps as exposed concrete. If you want to brick the sides, simply make the concrete base thinner by the width of two bricks plus two mortar joints (one brick width on each

6 Use a rounded jointer to tool the short joints first and then the long joints.

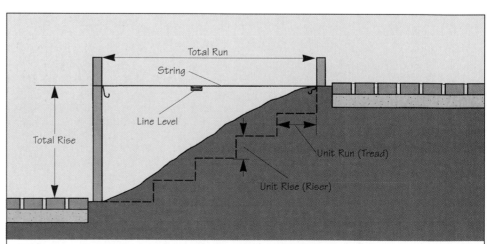

Brick steps. The total run is the total horizontal distance the steps will travel. To find the total rise, place a plumb stake at the bottom of the total run. Run a string from a stake at the top of the run to the stake at the bottom. Use a line level to level the string.

side). These criteria are guidelines to shoot for. With a garden step you generally have some leeway in the step design as there are often no hard boundaries defining the top and bottom of the steps.

Brick step design. The illustration shows four different ways of creating brick risers and treads by using different paver thicknesses (1½ or 2¼ inches), laying the bricks flat, setting them on edge, and varying the mortar joint thickness (⅜ to ½ inch). These options give you some flexibility in achieving the exact riser height you need so that the risers add up to the correct overall height. The exposed length of the pavers shown produces a tread of 12 inches.

Tread design. Steps should be at least as wide as the sidewalk leading up to them. A width that is a multiple of 8 inches will accommodate the use of whole bricks. Two 3⅝-inch-wide pavers laid flat plus two ⅜-inch mortar joints equals 8 inches. Three 2¼-inch-thick pavers laid on edge plus three ⅜-inch mortar joints is also nominally 8 inches (rounded up from 7⅞ inches). If you draw a plan of the treads, you will be able to figure the number of paving bricks you'll need.

Build the Concrete Base

There are two ways to build a concrete base for brick steps. A 4-inch-thick slab reinforced with wire mesh can be

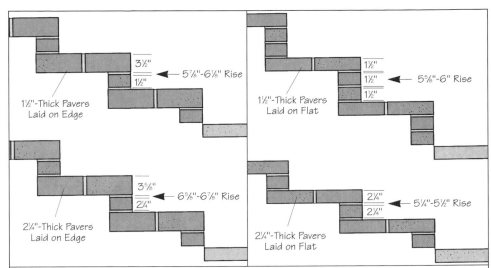

Brick step design. Here are four designs that use standard bricks to achieve proper rise-to-run ratios. Mortar joints can be ⅜ in. or ½ in.

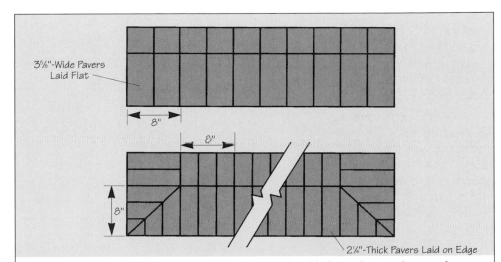

Tread design. Here are two tread designs that are divisible by eight to make use of whole bricks. Of course, the mitered corners of the design at the bottom still require quite a bit of brick cutting.

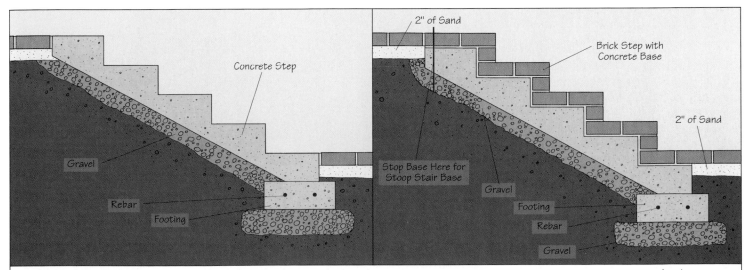

Build the concrete base. A concrete base for a brick step is built in the same way as a concrete step except you must account for the dimension of the bricks when forming the base.

used to support tiers of brick stacked and mortared to form the steps. If you need only two or three steps, use a flat slab, but this method takes a lot of brick. For a more economical installation, a 4-inch-thick stepped base reinforced with wire mesh is used to support a single layer of brick pavers. This method is used in the garden step project shown here.

You'll learn all about step design, determining unit rise and run, and making the concrete base in "Concrete Steps," on page 54. For brick steps, follow those instructions exactly but add to your excavation depth the height of the pavers and their mortar joints. For example, if your treads will be made from 2¼-inch-thick pavers laid flat on a ½-inch mortar bed with ⅜-inch mortar joints, drop the entire concrete structure (gravel base, footing, and form) 3⅛ inches. If you are building a stoop instead of a garden step, shorten the top tread as shown in the illustration at the bottom of page 109.

Finish the concrete surface with a slightly rough texture so that it will form a good bond with the mortar setting bed. Always allow new concrete to cure for about a week before laying the mortar bed for pavers.

Setting the Bricks on the Steps

Now that you've built the concrete base for the brick steps, the project is simply a matter of laying the bricks in the correct pattern and keeping the joints a consistent size.

1 **Dry-lay the units.** To check the size of the base and the spacing of the pavers, lay out the units without mortar on at least two steps. Adjust the width of the mortar joints as necessary to get the best fit.

2 **Install the mortar setting bed.** Clean off the concrete surface and apply a mortar bed using a Type S mortar. This setting bed will hold the pavers in place and also help to compensate for minor irregularities in the concrete surface. Make the mortar bed about ½ inch thick. Place the mortar and then smooth the surface with the flat side of a rectan-

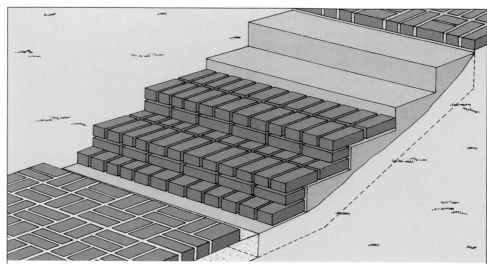

1 Do a test run, laying out the bricks on the steps to check the size of the base and the spacing of the pavers.

2 Clean the concrete surface and lay a ½-inch thick mortar bed working on one tread at a time.

3 Spread mortar on the sides of the bricks and set them in the bed.

gular metal trowel; score the surface with the notched edge. Start with the bottom step and mortar one tread at a time.

3 **Set the brick.** Spread mortar on the sides of the pavers with a trowel, and place them on the mortar setting bed, forming joints that are about ⅜ inch wide. Cut off excess mortar with the edge of the trowel. Check the surface with a level and tap the units gently with the trowel handle, if necessary, to bed them in the mortar.

4 **Tool the joints.** The joints are ready for tooling when the mortar is "thumbprint" hard, meaning that you can press your thumb against the mortar and leave a print impression without the mortar sticking to your thumb. Using a rounded jointer, tool the short joints first and then the long joints to produce a concave-shaped joint. Then finish the remaining steps. Mortar the next tread and lay the brick as previously discussed, until you finish the top step.

Clean the steps. After the steps have set for about a week, brush the surface with a stiff natural- or synthetic-bristle brush to remove mortar drips and dust. Use a plastic or wooden scraper and then a brush to remove large mortar splatters. If necessary, clean the completed project with a diluted solution of muriatic acid (mixed 1:10 with water). Don't use muriatic acid on white, cream, buff, gray, or brown brick, because it can leave ugly green or brown stains—check with the brick manufacturer or distributor. Before applying an acid cleaning solution, thoroughly wet the pavers with a garden hose. Wearing rubber gloves, apply the acid solution carefully with a special acid brush (made with polystyrene or polmyra bristles, available from masonry suppliers). Scrub lightly, then thoroughly rinse with a garden hose. Be extremely careful when working with acid to avoid burns. Don't use metal tools or buckets, because the acid will corrode them—use plastic. Always pour the water in the bucket first, then add the acid.

4 When the mortar is thumbprint hard, use a rounded jointer to tool the mortar joints.

Concrete Block Garden Wall

Concrete block styles have changed so much recently that block has become almost as popular as brick for home masonry projects. Attractive colors and textures as well as new products such as interlocking retaining-wall blocks offer new opportunities to use this material. The appearance of ordinary grey concrete block can be enhanced by applying a stucco coating or the block can be veneered

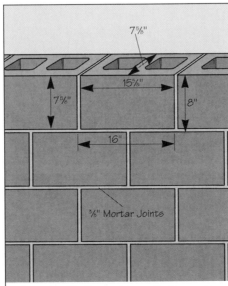

Concrete block garden wall. Concrete block is designed to be used in modules of 8x16 in., including mortar joints.

with a course of brick or stone attached with metal ties. Block projects are simple to build, easy to start and stop at your leisure, and extremely durable. The techniques for laying block are similar to those used to lay brick, but block is hollow and is usually laid in a single wythe, so there are some specific points to remember.

The most common size of concrete block has actual unit dimensions of 7⅝ inches high by 7⅝ inches wide by 15⅝ inches long. When laid with standard ⅜-inch mortar joints, the nominal face dimensions for each module are 8 by 16 inches. Plan the length of the wall as a multiple of 8 inches, which is the nominal length of half a block plus a mortar joint.

Decorative block. Decorative block (such as those with rugged stone faces, ribs, or geometric patterns) have only one decorative face, so if you want a wall with a decorative finish on both sides, you must use two wythes of thinner blocks. These units have the same face dimensions as an 8 by 16-inch block, but they are only 3⅝ inches thick. Two wythes with a ⅜-inch mortar joint in the middle measure 7⅝ inches, which is the same as the actual thickness of the

Decorative block. Decorative block is sized so that two wythes will give you a wall thickness equal to a single wythe of standard block.

nominal 8-inch block. This makes it easy to finish the top of the wall with a nominal 8-inch cap block.

Footings. You need to build a reinforced concrete footing to support a block wall. Once you have designed the wall, you can design a concrete footing to support it. The footing must be wide enough to prevent overturning and deep enough to resist frost heave in the soil. The thickness of the footing is the same as the thickness of the wall. The width of the footing should be should be twice the wall thickness. A typical block wall is 8 inches wide, so a footing for it should be 8 inches thick and 16 inches wide. Consult with your local building department about the correct depth for a footing in your area, then read "Concrete Footings," on page 63 for information about forming and pouring concrete footings.

Control Joints for Concrete Block

Concrete masonry will crack when it loses residual manufacturing and construction moisture and shrinks. This is unavoidable. Control joints are continuous vertical joints purposely made weaker than the rest of the joints so that the cracking will occur in straight lines rather than randomly. Because of the way they are formed, these joints maintain a wall's lateral strength. To make the control joints continuous,

you'll need to interrupt the running bond with half blocks, as shown.

Cracking is likely to occur at changes of height in the wall (such as with a stepped footing) or the thickness of the wall (such as at a pilaster). Usually, you'll place control joints where the wall abuts other structures and at a spacing of two and a half times the wall height for joint reinforcement located in every third bed joint or three times the wall height for joint reinforcement located in every

second bed joint. Control joints are created by using tongue-and-groove blocks, placing a Michigan joint, or using a premolded joint material.

Tongue-and-groove blocks. These blocks are specially shaped units that fit together without any mortar. Their matched design holds the wall laterally but allows for shrinkage. Plan for the use of these blocks when designing the wall and ordering materials.

Michigan joint. This is a control joint between two ordinary flanged con-

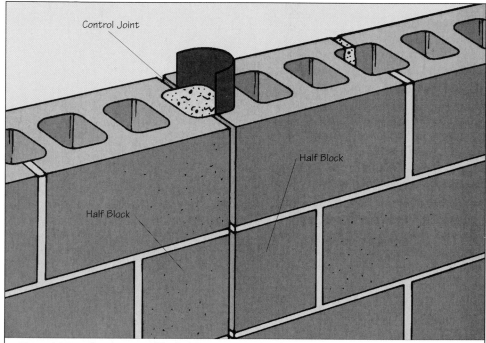

Control joints for concrete block. Like any concrete masonry, concrete blocks will crack and require continuous control joints to control where the crack will occur.

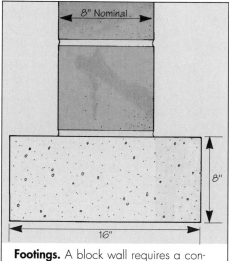

Footings. A block wall requires a concrete footing that is twice as wide as the wall is thick and deep enough to reach below the local frost line.

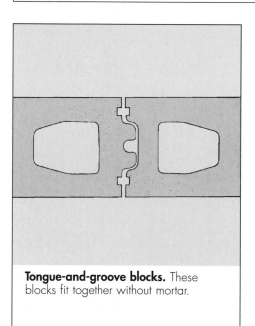

Tongue-and-groove blocks. These blocks fit together without mortar.

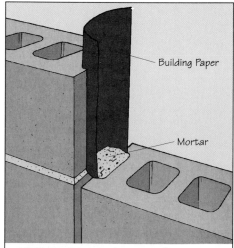

Michigan joint. In this type of joint, a piece of roofing felt is used to prevent a bond between blocks while allowing mortar to bond to one block.

crete blocks. A strip of roofing felt is folded on one side of the joint and the hollow core is filled with mortar. The building paper allows the mortar to bond to only one side. The mortar creates a plug that provides lateral strength. This type of joint may require cutting more blocks.

Premolded control joints. Use rubber inserts shaped like a plus sign (+). They fit into grooves formed in specially made blocks. Again, plan the use of these blocks when designing the wall and ordering materials.

Control joints in concrete block walls must be sealed against moisture. To do this, caulk the edges with a silicone sealant. Be sure to place closed-cell backer rod (available from masonry suppliers) behind the sealant to maintain the right depth for the sealant.

Joint reinforcement. Every block wall should have steel joint reinforce-

ment to minimize shrinkage cracking. Beginning with the second course, spread mortar only on the edges of the blocks. Place wire joint reinforcement between the first and second course and in every second or third bed joint after that.

Installing joint reinforcement can be awkward. When mortar is spread the length of two or three blocks, as is customary, only part of the length of the joint reinforcement can be embedded. The remainder rests on dry block and must be embedded as subsequent blocks are laid by laying mortar on top and jiggling the wire to get mortar to flow under it. Where joint reinforcement must be overlapped to splice two sections, nest the wires together in the joint, overlapping them about 16 inches.

The width of the joint reinforcement should be about 1 inch less than the width of the blocks so that it is protected by a good cover of mortar on both sides of the wall. Joint reinforcement must stop on either side of a control joint. It cannot continue through it.

Estimating materials needed. Estimate the number of blocks you will need by multiplying the number of units in the wall length times the number of courses in the wall height. You can use units with flanged ends for most of the work, but at wall ends and corners, you will need units with flat ends. Unlike brick, which is moistened before use, concrete blocks must remain dry. Store them on site in a dry location, under plastic. Remember to include joint reinforcement and control joint blocks or building paper to create control joints. Estimate 6 cubic feet of mortar for every 100 square feet of wall surface. Refer to "Mortar," on page 79, to estimate individual mortar ingredients.

Locating the Wall on the Footing

Design the wall on a piece of graph paper, making each block twice as long as it is wide. Take into account the use of control joints and reinforcement in your design. Begin to build the wall following these steps.

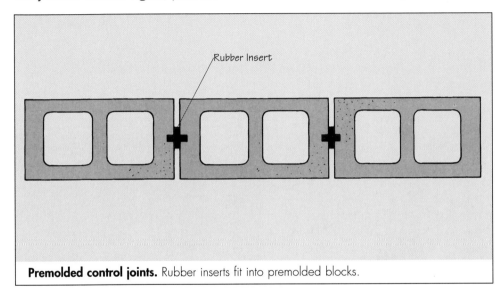

Premolded control joints. Rubber inserts fit into premolded blocks.

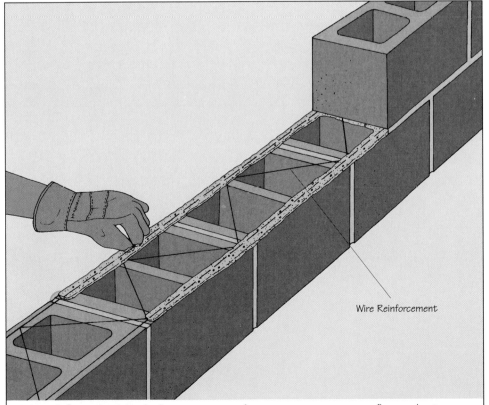

Joint reinforcement. Jiggle the wire joint reinforcement to get mortar to flow under it.

1 Marking the wall location.

After your concrete footing has cured for at least seven days, brush all debris from the top surface. Measure and mark the location of the outside face of the wall, being careful to center the masonry in the middle of the footing. As with the footing, batter boards and string are used to determine the corner locations. Square your corners and snap a chalk line along the length of the footing locating the wall. To ensure that the corners are square, use the 3-4-5 triangle method. From the outside corner point, measure up 4 feet along one leg of the footing and 3 feet along the other leg. The two lines are square when the diagonal between the two points measures 5 feet. Read "Making Square Corners" on page 24 for more details. To square the line of a wall against an existing wall, use a carpenter's square against the line and the wall.

2 Cut half blocks.

The wall construction is easiest using only whole and half blocks. You can purchase half block units, or cut half-size blocks now, as needed for the ends, with either a brickset or a circular saw with a masonry cutting blade. To use a brickset, place the block on sand or loose soil. With a hammer, strike the brickset to mark the cut on both faces of the block. Then work along the line again, striking harder until the block breaks. Always wear protective eyewear when cutting blocks.

3 Dry-lay the block.

Check the wall length by laying out a dry course of block. Start at the corners and work from both ends toward the middle. Use a piece of ⅜-inch plywood to space the units. Adjust the size of the joints between the ends of the units (called head joints) to take up slight variations in the size of the blocks. Using a marker, pencil, or chalk, make long slash marks on the footing at the head joints so that you will be able to confirm the spacing of the first course as you work.

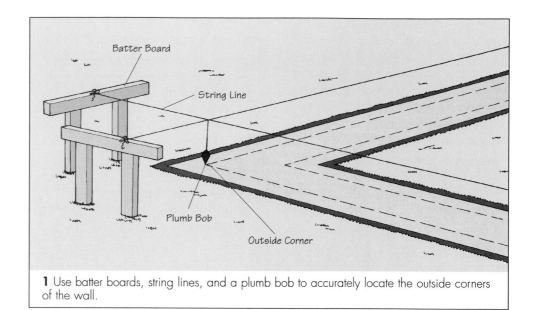

1 Use batter boards, string lines, and a plumb bob to accurately locate the outside corners of the wall.

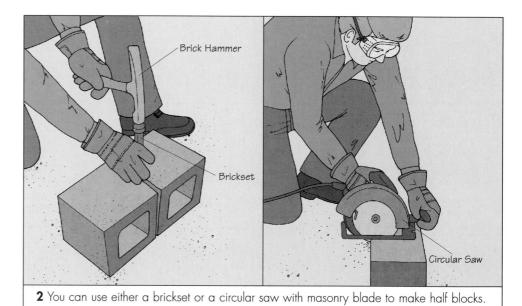

2 You can use either a brickset or a circular saw with masonry blade to make half blocks.

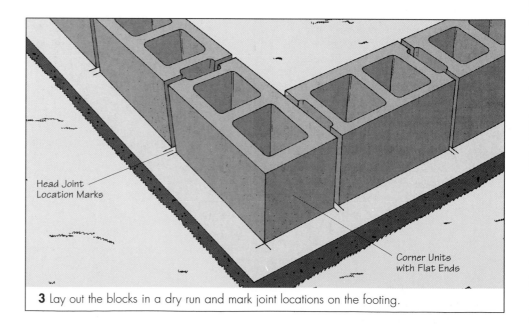

3 Lay out the blocks in a dry run and mark joint locations on the footing.

Building the Wall Leads

Begin wall construction by building leading sections, or leads, at the ends or corners. Masonry walls are always laid from the outside ends or corners toward the middle, which helps establish the correct spacing and coursing heights for the rest of the wall. The first course of a corner or end lead for a block wall should be three units long. The second and successive courses are set back one-half block in each course. This establishes a running bond pattern in which the units of one course are offset one-half block from the courses above and below.

1 **Lay the first block.** Mix a batch of mortar and begin the first course of the lead at one end of the wall. Pick up a trowel full of mortar, and spread it along the chalk line marking the wall's outer face. Use enough mortar to make a bed that is ½ to ¾ inch thick, slightly wider than a block, and about three blocks long. Don't skimp on the mortar or you'll wind up with voids under the blocks, which will substantially weaken the bond. Lay the corner or end unit first, pressing it firmly down into the mortar. Measure to make sure the resulting mortar bed is about ⅜ inch high; tap the unit lightly with the trowel handle if necessary. You can correct slight irregularities in the concrete footing by varying the thickness of the first mortar bed, up to a maximum of about ¾ inch, to keep the block course level. Use a 4-foot level to check that the block is both level and plumb. This is the most important block of the wall.

2 **Butter the block flanges.** Butter the head joints of concrete block by standing the units on end and swiping mortar onto the flanges with the edge of the trowel. When you set the block, place the wider ends of the flanges up to hold more mortar. Lift the block by the ends and place it gently on the mortar bed and firmly against the adjacent block. Mortar should squeeze from both the head and bed joints. Remove the excess mortar from the face of the blocks with the trowel blade. In this way, lay the three blocks for the first course of the lead section and check for level and plumb.

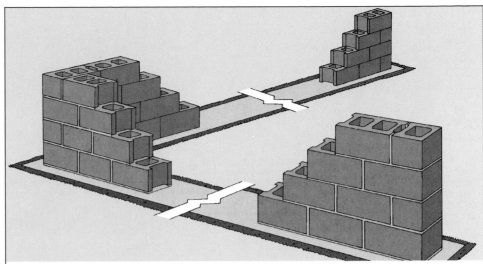

Building the wall leads. You will begin construction by building the corner leads, and then in toward the middle.

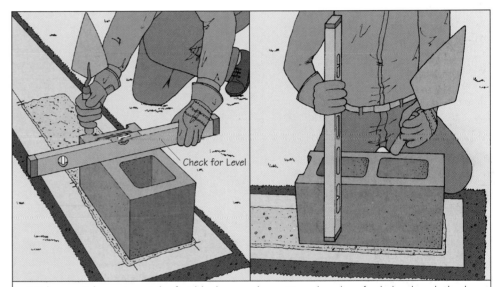

1 Take special care to get the first block properly positioned and perfectly level and plumb.

Check for Level

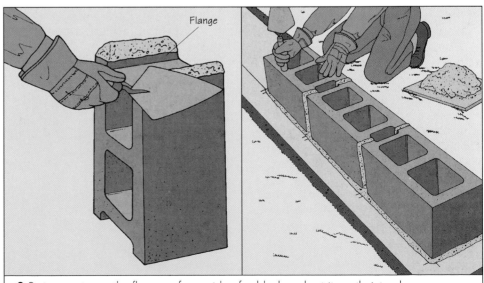

Flange

2 Swipe mortar on the flanges of one side of a block and set it gently into place.

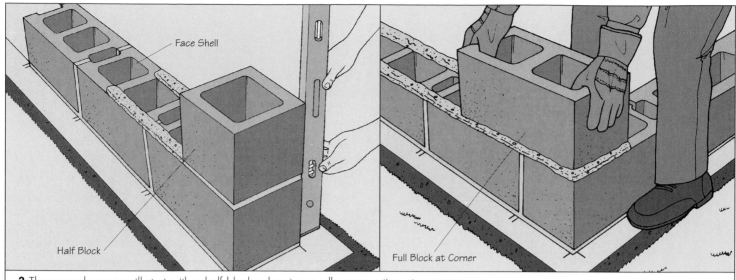

3 The second course will start with a half block unless two walls are meeting at a corner.

4 Check the "rack" of the leads with a level or straight 2x4.

3 Mortar the face shells. While the first course of a concrete block wall is laid in a full mortar bed, the rest of the wall is laid with what is called face-shell bedding. The 8x16-inch outside surfaces of a concrete block are called the face shells. Mortar is placed along the top of the face shells, which is about 1½ inches wide. Place the mortar with a downward swiping motion of the trowel. This is more difficult than laying mortar beds for brick, because the bed is narrower. Mortaring block will take some practice.

Spread mortar for the next bed joint on top of the face shells of the three blocks in the first course. If your wall has joint reinforcement between the

first and second courses, install it now. See "Joint Reinforcement" on page 113.

The second course will start with a half block to establish the running bond. The second course of a corner will start with a whole block. Butter the flanges of each block in the second course before it is laid. Set the blocks firmly into the mortar bed and against the adjacent units. Mortar should squeeze out of both the bed and head joints.

4 Finish the leads. Lay the rest of the leads, setting the blocks back one-half unit in each course of the end leads to establish the running bond pattern. Scrape excess mortar off the blocks with the trowel's edge. A 4-foot level or straight 2x4 laid carefully along

the "rack" of the lead should touch the corner of each block when placed on the flanges, and should be perfectly plumb when placed on the sides of the block. Use a story pole to set the vertical coursing as you build your leads. Build the leads four courses high.

Build Up the Block Wall

As with any masonry unit project, the wall is built by filling in between leads and then starting over with new leads built higher and higher. Here's how to complete the wall:

1 Prepare a string line. To fill in the masonry between leads, stretch a line to mark the top of each course as you build up the wall. Use line blocks and mason's twine to do this. (Mason's twine is better than

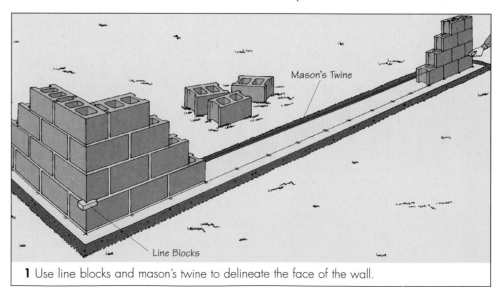

1 Use line blocks and mason's twine to delineate the face of the wall.

cotton string because it will stretch tightly without breaking.) Prepare the line blocks as explained in "Preparing Line Blocks," page 93. Hook one line block on the corner of the lead so that the line is level with the top of the block in the course you're working on. Stretch the line to the opposite corner lead and hook the other line block at the same height. Check the line with a line level. The line blocks hold the string about 1⁄16 inch away from the face of the wall. The masonry between the leads can now be "laid to the line" to keep the wall straight and the block course level.

2 Fill in first course. Fill in the first course between leads, buttering the flanges as you lay blocks in the mortar on the footing. Check the face of the units to make sure they are correctly laid along the chalk line and have the proper head joint thickness. As you work, continually check the tops of the blocks with a 4-foot level to make sure that each course is level. Tap down any units that are set too high. Remove units that are set too low, cut away the mortar, and lay the unit with fresh mortar. Check the blocks with a level to make sure they are plumb; use the side of the level as a straightedge to align the face of the units in each course. Any unit that is dislodged after it is initially set must be removed, the mortar cut away, and the unit laid with fresh mortar. It is crucial that the first course of block be level and plumb because it is the base for the entire wall. You can allow for slight variations in block length by adjusting the thickness of the head joints between the ends of the units, but try to keep the head joints uniform.

3 Lay the closure block. The last block to be put into place in a course is called the closure block. You should have just enough space left for this block plus a head joint on each end. To make sure you get full head joints, butter the ends of the adjacent blocks and both ends of the closure block. Lower the block into place from above, being careful not to dislodge the adjacent blocks.

4 Tool the mortar joints. As you lay the concrete blocks, remove excess mortar from the face of the joints with the edge of the trowel blade. After the mortar has begun to cure, however, the surfaces of the head and bed joints need to be tooled to compress the mortar and

2 Fill in the blocks between the leads. Check frequently that the blocks are plumb and level.

3 Put mortar on the flanges at both ends of the closure block as well as the ends of the blocks it will meet.

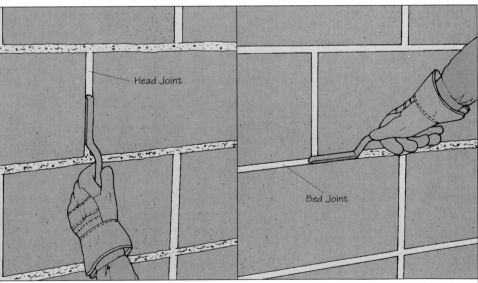

Head Joint

Bed Joint

4 Use a rounded tool to make concave joints doing the head joints first and then the bed joints.

decrease moisture absorption at the surface. It is important that joints be tooled at a consistent moisture content so that they do not appear light in some areas and dark in others. The joints are ready for tooling when the mortar is "thumbprint" hard, meaning that you can press your thumb against the mortar and leave a print impression without mortar sticking to your thumb.

Use a rounded jointing tool to make concave joints. Tool the head joints first and then the bed joints. Do not wait until you have finished a large section of wall before you tool the joints. Check the mortar frequently, and tool the joints a few at a time when the surface is just the right consistency. As the joints are tooled, small pieces of mortar, called tailings, will be squeezed out at the edges of the joints. Remove them with the edge of the trowel.

5 Fill between the leads. After laying the closure block and confirming the first course is level and plumb, the wall can be built up rapidly. Simply continue the process of buttering the flanges of each block as you lay it and placing it on the previous course on which a face-shell bed of mortar has been spread.

When you get comfortable with the block-laying process, you can set three or four blocks on end, mortar their flanges, mortar the bed joint, and lay a number the blocks in rapid succession. Just be sure to never disturb the line blocks and to check for level and plumb often. Scrape off any excess mortar.

When you have filled in the courses between your leads, build up the ends or corners of the walls again to form new leads. Repeat the process of filling in courses and building leads until you reach the next-to-last course of block below the coping.

Finish the Top of the Wall

The top of a concrete block wall requires a coping to protect the wall joints from water penetration. A coping is particularly important in cold climates with a lot of rain

5 Fill between the leads. If the wall will continue higher, build new corner leads.

or snow. When water trapped in a wall freezes, it expands and can cause serious damage to the block and mortar.

1 Place the wire netting. Before the coping is added, the cores of the top course of block are filled with mortar. To prevent this mortar from falling into the wall below, lay

strips of wire netting in the bed joint below the top course of block. Cut the wire netting about a ½ inch short of the edge of the face-shell. Nestle the wire netting in the middle of the mortar. Lay the top course of block as described above.

2 Fill the block cores with mortar. Fill the cores of the top course of

1 To prevent the mortar from falling farther into the wall, place wire netting on top of the course below the top course.

2 Mix a batch of soupy mortar and use a coffee can to fill the last course's cores.

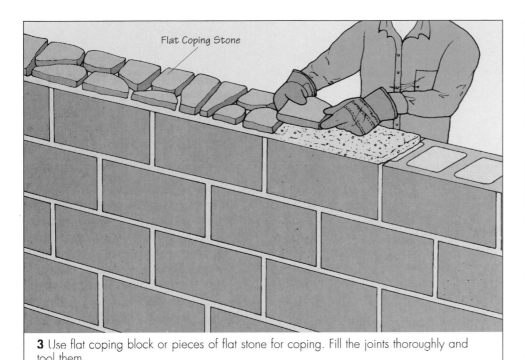

3 Use flat coping block or pieces of flat stone for coping. Fill the joints thoroughly and tool them.

4 Use a small chunk of concrete block to scrape residue off the wall.

block with mortar. Mix a batch of mortar with a little more water than usual so it will pour into the cores easily. Fill all of the hollow cores as well as any spaces between blocks. Stir the mortar in the cores a little to get rid of air bubbles. If the mortar settles, add more to bring it flush with the top surface of the block.

3 Lay the coping. Before installing the coping, install flashing as described in "Install Flashing" on page 95. Cap the wall with flat coping block or with pieces of flat stone. Make sure the joints between coping units are completely full, then tool them to compress the surface of the mortar as described previously. Be sure to continue control joints through the coping.

4 Clean the wall. Remove mortar splatters with the trowel when they are almost dry, then rub the wall with a small piece of concrete block to remove any residue. Caution: Do not use muriatic acid on concrete masonry because it will dissolve the cement in the block face, etching the surface.

Screen Block Wall

Decorative concrete block screen walls create a wall with a pattern of openings that provide both privacy and ventilation. There are more sizes and shapes of decorative screen blocks than can be mentioned here. However, the most common size of concrete block has actual face dimensions of 7⅝ by 15⅝ inches. When

laid with standard ⅜-inch mortar joints, the nominal face dimensions for each unit module are 8 by 16 inches. The face dimensions of some screen blocks are (nominally) 12 or 16 inches square. Screen blocks come in thicknesses of 4, 6, or 8 inches. Choose a style of block that you like and that is readily available in your area; then plan the length and height of a wall to be a multiple of the block length so that you will use only whole units.

Screen wall pilasters. Block screen walls are usually built with supporting pilasters for added strength. A pilaster is a column of masonry that is built as part of a wall. One of the simplest ways to build pilasters is to use special pilaster blocks. These

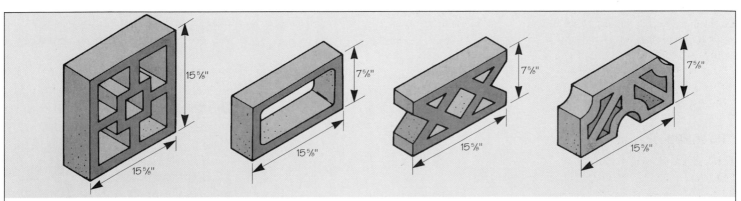

Screen block wall. Screen blocks come in a variety of sizes, although most are designed to work with an 8x16-in. building module, including joints.

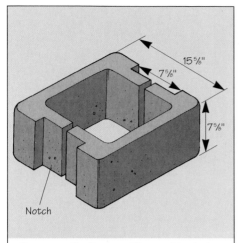

Screen wall pilasters. Pilasters blocks have two parts. When assembled, they form notches that fit around the screen blocks.

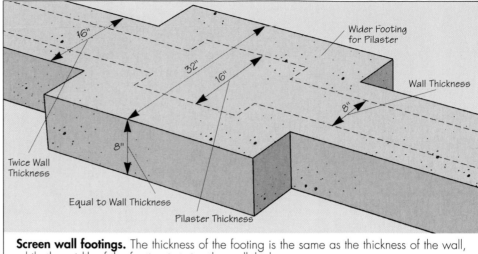

Screen wall footings. The thickness of the footing is the same as the thickness of the wall, while the width of the footing is twice the wall thickness.

units have notches, into which the screen block can be nestled, and a center core for reinforcing steel embedded in mortar.

The distance between pilasters is proportional to the nominal wall thickness. As a rule, a 4-inch-thick wall has pilasters every 6 feet, a 6-inch-thick wall has pilasters every 9 feet, and an 8-inch-thick wall has pilasters every 12 feet.

On a piece of graph paper, draw an elevation (side view) of your wall, and use it to calculate the number of screen block and pilaster units you will need. Since the pilaster block are

made in halves, remember to double the number of units shown in the elevation to account for both sides of the wall.

Screen wall footings. Once you have drawn your wall plan, you can design a concrete footing to support the wall. The footing must be wide enough to prevent overturning and deep enough to resist frost heave in the soil. The thickness of the footing is the same as the thickness of the wall. The width of the footing is twice the thickness of the wall. For example, if the screen block is 8 inches thick, the footing is 8 inches thick

and 16 inches wide. At the pilasters, the footing must be wider. For a nominal 16 by 16-inch pilaster, widen the footing to a 32-inch square.

Install rebar. Place two extra ⅜-inch steel reinforcing bars in the concrete footing and bend them upward to fit inside the pilaster block. Rebar can be ordered from the supplier bent to any angle. You may also be able to rent a tool that bends rebar. (The tool is similar to a hickey used to bend electrical conduit.) These rebar "dowels" must be long enough to stick out the top of the footing by at least 18 inches. Make the horizontal leg of the rebar dowels at least 12 inches long, and tie them with steel wire to the rebar in the footing. Rebar can be cut with a reciprocating saw.

Calculate and measure the spacing of the dowels carefully so that the rebar will align properly within the pilaster cavity. If necessary, lay out a dry course of block on the ground next to the footing forms before you pour concrete in them. Read "Concrete Footings," on page 63, and build a footing as directed.

Building the Screen Wall

The following project shows how to build a straight length of screen wall. The project has five courses of 16-inch-square screen block and four pilasters set at 12-foot intervals. Although not shown here, you can build a screen wall with corners.

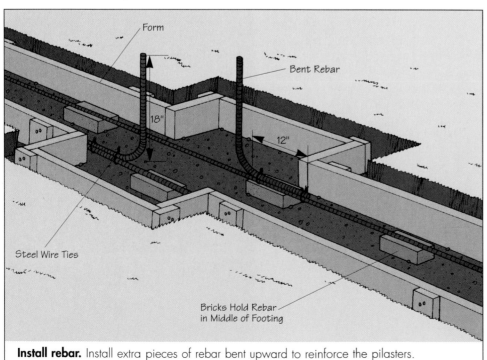

Install rebar. Install extra pieces of rebar bent upward to reinforce the pilasters.

Corners are made with pilaster units shaped to accept screen blocks at a 90-degree angle. Ask your building supply dealer about the availability of such blocks.

1 Snap a chalk line. After your concrete footing has cured properly, brush off the top surface. Measure and mark the location of the outside face of the wall, being careful to center the masonry in the middle of the footing. Snap a chalk line along the length of the footing. (If you have corners in the wall, follow the instructions in "Making Square Corners," on page 24 before snapping the lines.)

2 Dry-lay the screen blocks. Without any mortar, set a whole pilaster block on the footing with the rebar in the center, and check the wall length by laying out a dry course of screen block. The wall is built by starting at the pilasters and working the blocks from both ends toward the middle. Use a piece of ⅜-inch plywood to space the units. Adjust the size of the joints between the ends of the blocks to take up slight variations in the size of the block. Using a marker, pencil, or chalk, make long slash marks at the head joints to confirm the spacing of the first course as you work. Remove the pilaster and screen blocks.

3 Set rebar for the pilasters. After laying out the dry run and marking chalk lines on the footing, you are ready to begin building the pilasters. The reinforced pilasters are built as hollow shells around the reinforcing steel and then mortared solid. Mix a batch of mortar with a little more water than usual to pour in the pilasters. Before building the pilasters, attach a length of #3 rebar (⅜-inch in diameter) onto the dowels that were left protruding from the footing. Cut the rebar with a reciprocating saw or hacksaw so that it will extend 2 inches below the top of the last course of pilaster blocks. Overlap the rebar and dowel at least 12 inches and tie them together tightly with steel wire. The steel in the pilaster must be held upright until it is embedded in mortar.

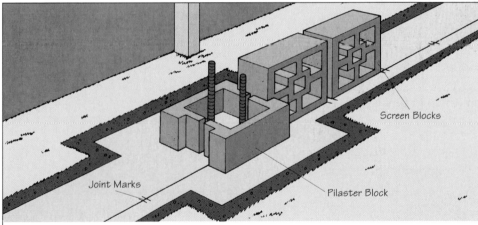

1 Snap a chalk line to delineate the outside face of the screen wall.

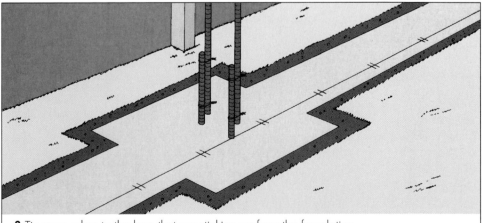

2 Lay out the first course of blocks, including the pilasters, to see how they fit on the foundation. You may have to adjust the mortar joint size slightly to make the blocks fit. When you are satisfied, mark the joint locations on the footing.

3 Tie more rebar to the bars that are sticking up from the foundation.

4 Build the pilasters to four courses before laying the screen block.

5 After every four courses, allow the piers to set overnight. Then fill them with mortar before continuing to build them up.

4 **Lay the pilaster blocks.** Build the pilasters before you begin laying the screen block. Place mortar on the horizontal surface of the footing to form bed joints and on the head joints between the front and back block; then set the blocks firmly into the mortar and against one another. Hold a 4-foot level on the side of the blocks to confirm plumb, and check the top for level. Build four courses of pilaster blocks (32 inches high), and stop.

Clean excess mortar off the blocks with the edge of the trowel. Tool the joints when they're "thumbprint" hard. See "Tooling Mortar Joints," page 92.

5 **Mortar the pilasters.** After building four courses, allow the mortar to cure overnight. Then fill the cavity solidly with a mortar mix to which extra water has been added. Stop each pour about 1 inch below the top of the fourth course. This will form a "key" with the next pour and make the pilaster stronger. Use a length of rebar to stir the mortar slightly to make sure that all the corners and recesses are filled and that there are no pockets of trapped air. Let it cure for a week before building the next four courses of the pilaster. While

Roofing Felt

6 Use roofing felt to create control joints between the pilasters and screen blocks.

you're waiting, fill in the screen blocks between the pilasters.

6 **Prepare control joints.** Control joints are continuous, weakened joints designed to accommodate the natural shrinkage of concrete masonry in such a way that cracking will occur at these joints rather than at

random locations. To make a control joint in this project, line one side of the pilaster block with roofing felt or building paper before mortaring in the screen block. Locate a control joint on one side of each pilaster.

7 **Lay the first course of screen block.** Mix a batch of mortar and

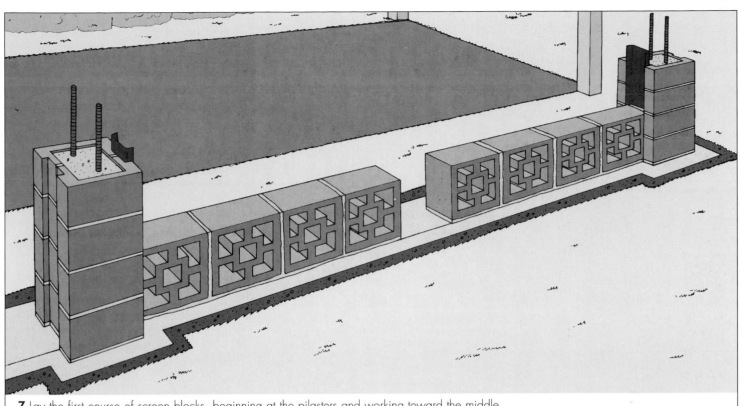

7 Lay the first course of screen blocks, beginning at the pilasters and working toward the middle.

begin to lay the first course of screen block. Spread mortar along the chalk line on the footing and on the side of the screen block that will be nestled in the pilaster. Begin at the pilasters and work toward the middle. It is important that this first block course be level—correct slight irregularities in the concrete footing by varying the thickness of the first mortar bed. Use a 4-foot level to check that the block is both level and plumb and that the faces are aligned to the mason's twine.

Mortar the entire side of the screen block for the head joints and maintain a ⅜-inch joint size. Remove excess mortar at the face of the units with the edge of a trowel.

8 Fill in the first course. The last unit to be put into place in a course is called the closure block. You should have just enough space left for this block plus a head joint on each side. To make sure you get full head joints, spread mortar on the ends of the adjacent block and on both ends of the closure block. Lower the block into place from above, being careful not to dislodge the adjacent blocks. See "Tooling Mortar Joints," page 92.

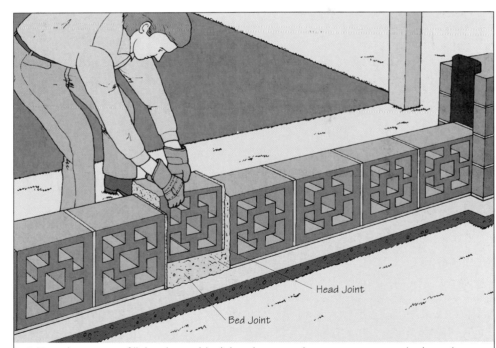

8 To make sure you fill the closure block head joints with mortar, put mortar both on the sides of the closure block and the sides of the adjoining blocks.

Head Joint

Bed Joint

9 Install joint reinforcement. Screen walls require reinforcement in every bed joint. Spread mortar on the top of the screen blocks, and place wire joint reinforcement in the first bed joint. This can be awkward: If mortar is spread the length of two or three blocks as is custom-ary, only part of the length of joint reinforcement can be embedded. The remainder rests on dry block and must be embedded by spreading mortar on top and jiggling the wire to get mortar to flow under it.

If joint reinforcement must be overlapped to splice two sections, nest the

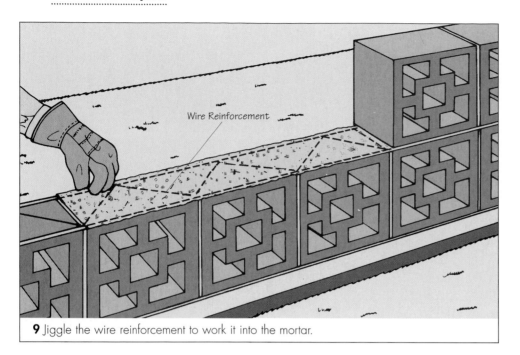

Wire Reinforcement

9 Jiggle the wire reinforcement to work it into the mortar.

wires together in the joint and overlap them about 16 inches. The width of the joint reinforcement should be about 1 inch less than the actual width of the units so that it will be protected by a good cover of mortar on both sides of the wall. Stop joint reinforcement on either side of control joints—do not continue it across the joint.

10 Continue to build pilasters and lay courses. As with all masonry-unit projects, the building process for the screen wall is simply an exercise in repetition. Continue to build the pilasters, fill them to an inch from the top and then fill in the screen block courses. Lay reinforcement in each bed joint, and tool the joints as you progress. Continue until you've reached final height as per your design.

10 When four courses are completed, build another four courses of pilasters, let them cure, fill the piers, and build up the screen just as you did for the first four courses.

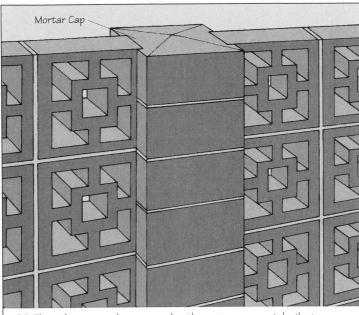

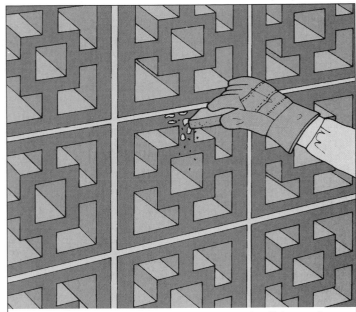

11 The pilaster can be capped with mortar, a special pilaster cap, or a flat piece of stone.

12 Remove splatters with a trowel and then rub off the residue with a scrap of concrete block.

11 Cap the pilaster. Cap the top of the pilaster with a bed of smoothly troweled mortar. Slope the mortar from a center point downward to shed rain and snow. You may choose to buy a piece of flat stone and mortar it to the top of the pilaster for a decorative look. A specially molded concrete pilaster top is another option to consider.

12 Clean the wall. Remove mortar splatters with the trowel when they are almost dry, then rub the area with a small piece of block to remove the residue. Do not use muriatic acid on concrete masonry because it will dissolve the cement in the block face, etching the surface.

Interlocking Concrete Block

Interlocking concrete blocks are a system of mortarless masonry units that have become popular in recent years. The construction process couldn't be simpler, and there are many uses for this type of concrete block. The units lock together to form retaining walls. These walls can stabilize an earth embankment and halt erosion, create terraces in a sloping yard, form a tree well, provide raised planting beds, and serve many other landscaping

applications. Sold under a number of different trade names, the systems are available through concrete block manufacturers, masonry distributors, and building materials distributors throughout the country.

While no mortar is required for interlocking systems, some include fiberglass rods or pins to hold the individual units together, while others have flanges that overlap. The units usually have a rough, stone-like texture and

are made in colors ranging from gray to buff or earth tones. Check in your area to see which system or systems are available.

Choose a system. When choosing a system, first determine the height and length of wall you want to build. Each brand of wall system will have a different size unit, so you should consult your supplier to determine the total number of units required. Some systems can be laid in curved

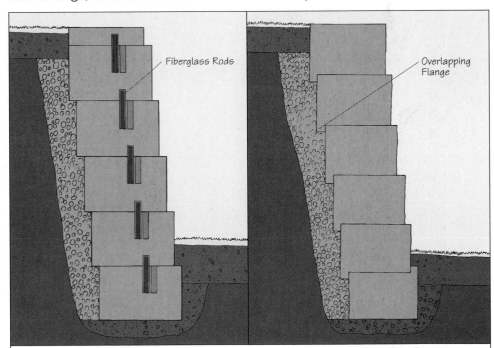

Fiberglass Rods

Overlapping Flange

Interlocking concrete blocks. Some interlocking systems use fiberglass rods, others use overlapping flanges.

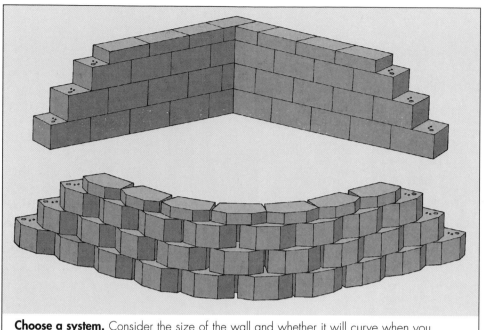

Choose a system. Consider the size of the wall and whether it will curve when you choose an interlocking block system.

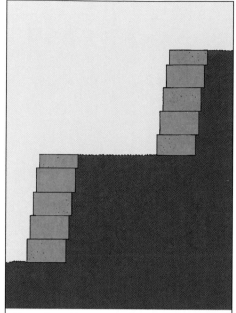

Terracing. Most interlocking systems can be built to about 36 in. high. To build higher build two walls with a terrace between.

lines, but others are limited to straight walls and 90-degree corners.

Terracing. With most systems, you can build a retaining wall up to 36 inches high without the need for reinforcing or special soil-retention accessories. For higher walls, systems may have special components to increase the strength of the wall and allow for drainage. As an alternative to a single high wall, consider two shorter walls stepped back against the slope.

Building a Tree Well

The following project has been designed using a kind of interlocking block that uses fiberglass pins for connectors. The step-by-step instructions illustrate the process of building a retaining wall to create a tree well, but because the design of interlocking concrete blocks differs among manufacturers, the block you buy may have different construction criteria. Every brand of interlocking block will come with manufacturer's specifications regarding height limitations, loading strength, and base requirements. Read these specifications carefully before building.

Protect the tree. When building a tree well, it is important to set the wall far enough away from the tree

Protect the tree. For most trees, the roots cover about the same diameter as the limbs. So avoid the roots by building the tree well outside the reach of the limbs.

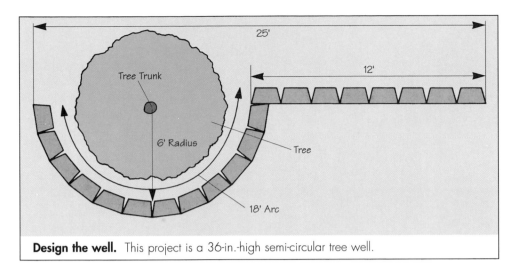

Design the well. This project is a 36-in.-high semi-circular tree well.

backward into the hill until you've reached a 36-inch vertical rise. Continue excavating until the vertical embankment falls away at an angle of 30 to 45 degrees from 90 degrees to allow for any soil that may fall forward. Make sure you cut the embankment to make a flat base on which the units can sit and to allow placement of the required gravel backfill.

2 **Excavate the trench.** Some interlocking block systems have the first course level to the grade; however, as mentioned before, this 36-inchhigh wall will have one course of

so that you won't damage the root system when you are digging the footing, and the roots won't undermine the footing once the wall is in place. For most trees, the diameter of the root system equals the spread of the limbs, so lay out a wall that is outside the reach of the limbs.

Designing the well. In this project, you'll build a 36-inch-high semi-circular tree well using interlocking concrete units that measure 4 inches high and 12 inches square. The total wall length is 30 feet, including a 12-foot straight section and a curve with an 18-foot arc length. The 18-foot arc length is half the circumference of the circle defined by the tree's limbs. Circumference of a circle is found by multiplying the diameter by pi (3.14). Divide this number by two to get half the circumference.

The 36-inch wall height requires nine courses of units (9x4 inches = 36 inches), and the 12-inch blocks make each course 30 units long. With this system, the top course consists of special solid capping blocks. You'll also need one course of blocks below grade. Figuring 11 courses times 30 units per course, the wall will require 330 units, 30 of which will be cap blocks. At about 30 pounds each, the units are fairly light in weight but still heavy enough to make a hard day's labor for those unaccustomed to lifting. Be sure to lift with your legs to avoid a painful back injury or unnecessary strains.

1 **Excavate the embankment.** As shown in the illustration, excavate

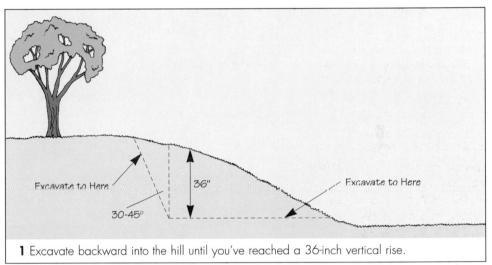

1 Excavate backward into the hill until you've reached a 36-inch vertical rise.

2 For well-drained soils, excavate a trench along the edge of the embankment to the depth of one course of blocks.

3 For soils that drain poorly, excavate deep enough to put 4 inches of gravel or stone under the wall. Cover the bottom of the trench with landscape fabric.

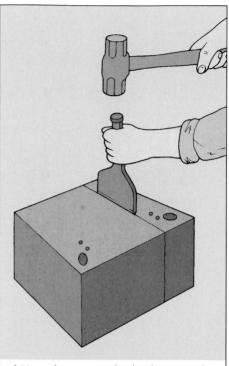

4 Use a hammer and a brickset to make half and three-quarter blocks.

block below grade. In well-drained areas, excavate a trench along the length of the embankment 6 inches deep (4-inch-thick block plus 2 inches of sand) and 24 inches wide (12-inch-wide block plus 12 inches of gravel backfill). Remove all grass, sod, roots, and large rocks, and tamp to make the bottom of the trench level and firmly packed. Place landscape fabric in the bottom of the trench. Overlap sections by at least 6 inches. Place a 2-inch bed of sand on the fabric. The sand aids in leveling the units. Smooth the top of the sand with a piece of 2x4, and use a level to make sure the surface is flat.

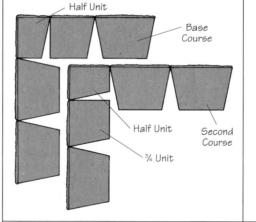

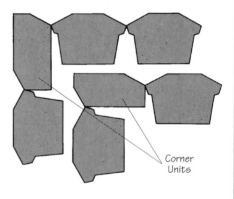

5 In systems such as the on the left, you alternate the positions of half and three-quarter blocks. In other systems you alternate the positions of corner units.

3 **Add a drainage bed if needed.** In dense soils, or soils with high clay content, or in areas with poor drainage, excavate the trench 10 inches to place 4 inches of ⅜- to ¾-inch gravel or crushed stone on the earth. This will create a drainage bed below the wall. Level the gravel drainage bed with a rake and tamp to compact it. Place a layer of landscape fabric over the gravel, then add 2 inches of sand as in Step 2 above. Use this gravel bed only if your soil has high moisture levels—it makes leveling the wall more difficult. Check

with your local building department as to the base needed.

4 **Split units for corner.** Some systems may come with specially shaped blocks, making cutting corner units unnecessary. If not, split half- and three-quarter units for the corners using a hammer and brickset. First score the unit all the way around, then break it with a few sharp blows. To avoid eye injury, be sure to wear safety glasses when splitting blocks.

5 **Set base course corner.** Starting at the 90-degree corner between

the straight and curved wall sections, lay the first course of units, butting each unit snugly against the next. To form the corner, you'll alternate the half- and three-quarter units in each course. Or follow the directions for using a manufacturer's prefabricated corner units. Set only the first course now. In some systems, subsequent corner courses are bonded to the course above and below with a masonry adhesive as recommended by the block manufacturer.

6 **Lay the first course.** For this sample project, the first course

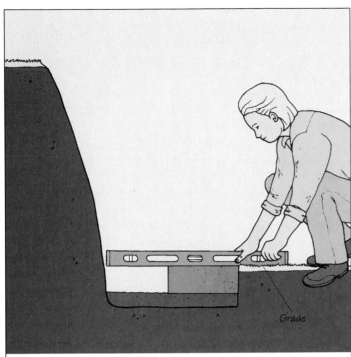

6 Set the first course of blocks in the trench, level with the grade of the tree well excavation.

7 Shovel compactable gravel or crushed stone behind the first course of block.

of blocks must be set with the tops of the blocks level with the grade. Level each unit on its own (back to front and side to side) and to adjacent units. Use the sand bed to correct minor irregularities in leveling by tapping the block down into the bed or building up the bed slightly. It is imperative that the base course be level, or the wall will not be stable. Complete the entire first course before starting the second course. Do not align the course according to the rough faces of the blocks; instead, align the pin holes or the machine-smooth backs of the blocks.

7 **Fill any voids and backfill.** Shovel ⅜- to ¾-inch gravel or crushed stone behind the first course of units and between the blocks in the curved section to secure them in place and to provide drainage for soil moisture. Some blocks have voids in them that must be filled with gravel. Gravel backfill is added after each course.

8 **Set the second course.** First clean off any excess backfill material from the tops of the first course of units. Set the second course of units on top of the first, offsetting each unit one-half the

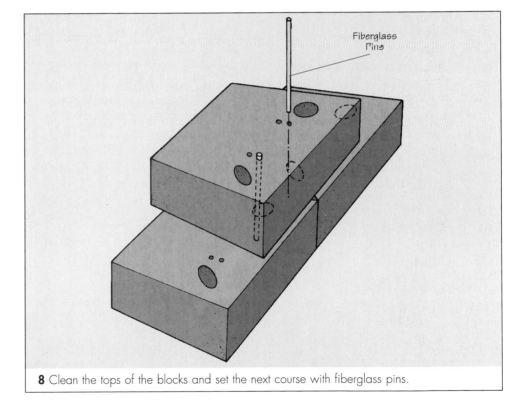

8 Clean the tops of the blocks and set the next course with fiberglass pins.

length of the block below to form a running-bond pattern. To secure the units to one another, insert the fiberglass pins in the holes on the top of the base course and lower a block onto the pins of two adjacent blocks.

Interlocking blocks may be set in a near vertical position or sloped back

into an embankment. The backward slope of the wall is dictated by the pin placement in the blocks. There are usually two or more pin holes on each side of the block. By placing the pins in the back holes every course or every other course (as suggested by the manufacturer), the wall will slope backward. Other kinds of retaining wall systems align the blocks with a lip on the back of the unit or by other means.

9 Set the remaining courses.
Set the remaining courses in the same manner as the first and second. Alternate the half- and three-quarter units in each course at the corner, insert the locking pins, and place the gravel backfill until you reach the 36-inch wall height.

10 Cap the wall. Retaining walls must be capped with a solid unit. Drainage voids and pin holes would obviously not be attractive in the final course. Manufacturers make cap units specific to their wall blocks and either make or recommend concrete adhesive that is applied with a caulking gun to secure cap blocks. An alternative to capping blocks is to adhere flat, natural stone, such as slate, on top of the final course. To place the cap course, clean off the top course and apply the adhesive. Lay the cap blocks next to one another and backfill with soil, not gravel. The backfill can then be planted with grass or other ground cover.

9 Continue assembling and backfilling until the wall reaches one course below final height.

10 Lay the cap course using concrete adhesive, then backfill with soil for planting grass or ground cover.

Stucco

Stucco is a versatile masonry material that can be formed into any shape and given many textures. In garden projects, it can transform an unattractive block wall into a lovely addition to the landscape. Stucco can also be applied to mesh that has been attached to plywood, for example when using stucco over the sheathing of a wood-framed house. In this section you will learn how to coat a brick or block wall with stucco. You'll also find instructions for building a stucco-coated driveway light, a project which will provide the information you need to apply stucco to any plywood surface.

Working with Stucco

Like mortar, stucco is made with portland cement, sand, and water. In exterior uses it is called stucco, but in interior uses it is called plaster. The term stucco applies to the entire thickness, from base to surface. Stucco is applied with a steel trowel, the same trowel used in finishing concrete. A plasterer's hawk may be used to carry convenient amounts of stucco to the wall.

Stucco on plywood. Applied over plywood, stucco is reinforced with steel mesh backed by two layers of building paper. The stucco is applied in two or three layers. The first layer is called the scratch coat. It is about ⅜-inch thick and its purpose is to embed the reinforcement in stucco. The scratch coat gets textured to help hold the second layer tightly to it. The second layer is called the brown coat. It too is about ⅜-inch thick. Not brown at all, the brown coat's purpose is to provide a uniformly smooth finished plane and provide uniform plaster suction over the entire surface. The brown coat may be painted any color or, more often, a ⅛-inch-thick third layer of colored stucco called the color coat can be applied over it instead of painting. The color coat presents both a colored and textured finished surface. If a color coat is not used, the scratch coat and brown coat are applied thicker to create a ⅞-inch total thickness.

Stucco on concrete block. Applied over concrete, concrete block, or brick, stuccoing is a little different. Then the stucco goes on in one ⅜-inch-thick scratch coat plus one ¼-inch finish coat. A color coat is

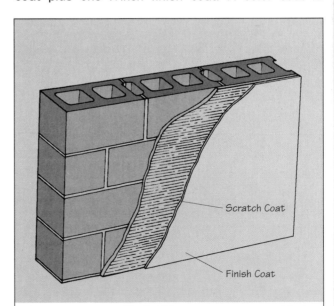

Stuccoing on plywood. Stucco applied to a plywood sheathed frame wall is a sandwich of two layers of building paper, mesh reinforcement, and three layers of applied stucco.

Labels: Building Paper; Fasteners; Metal Mesh; Stucco Scratch Coat; Stucco Brown Coat; Stucco Finish Coat; Foundation Drip Screed

Stucco on concrete block. When covering concrete block and cast-in-place concrete walls with stucco, two coats are usually applied—a scratch coat and a finish coat.

Labels: Scratch Coat; Finish Coat

sometimes applied, though the finish coat may simply be given a sand finish as the final treatment. No building paper or reinforcement is used. However, if the subsurface has been sealed or painted, the stucco won't bond well without additional surface preparation. You can improve the bond mechanically by chipping the surface in a 4- to 6-inch grid pattern with a rock hammer. Or you can paint on a concrete bonder. The bonder looks and acts much like white glue and is much easier to use than chipping.

Stucco moldings. Moldings are used at the bottom, sides, and top of stucco panels for a variety of purposes. They not only help to gauge the ⅞-inch thickness, used at the bottom, they allow any wayward water entering the wall through cracks to escape, to drip clear of the structure. What's more, moldings separate dissimilar materials on the structure. Moreover, they permit the stucco to expand and contract independent of the structure. Moldings include screeds, beads, corners, and control-joints. Casing beads are used to provide a finished edge around the perimeter of a stuc-

co panel. Screeds are used to establish the thickness of the stucco. Some screeds such as the foundation drip screed used in the driveway light project are used to prevent water from seeping under the stucco.

Control joints. Just like any masonry, stucco will crack. And just like any masonry project, large areas of stucco need control joints to control the cracking. Control joint strips are added to make panels no more than

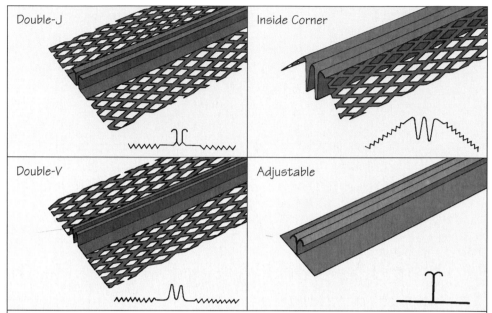

Control joints. Control joints control cracking in stucco. Double-J and double-V joints are designed to be used at regular intervals across flat expanses of stucco. Another type of joint is for inside corners. Adjustable control joints allow two-dimensional movement across the joint and is often used when stucco is joined to a different material.

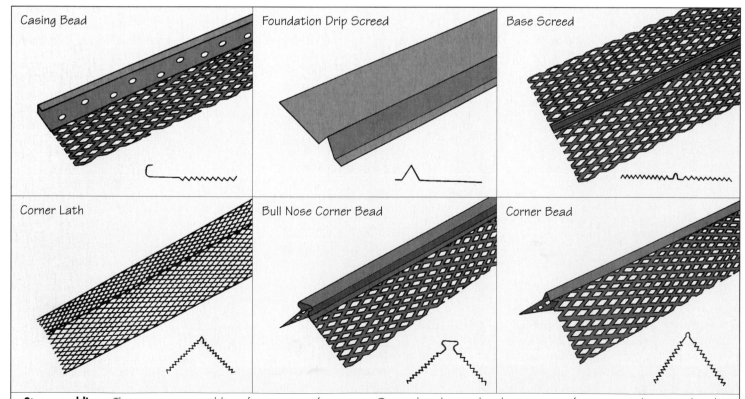

Stucco moldings. There are stucco moldings for a variety of purposes. Casing bead is used at the perimeter of stucco panels, corner beads establish straight corners, and screeds establish the thickness of stucco. Corner lath is used for rounded stucco corners.

144 square feet in area (when placed at approximately 12-foot intervals). In addition, control joints in stucco should be placed directly over control joints in masonry below. For example, block walls with control joints every 16 feet should have stucco control joints in the same places.

Control joints are usually located at doors and windows to relieve the concentrated stresses there. The length-to-width ratio of stucco panels created by control joints should be no more than 2½ to 1.

Most stucco moldings, including control joints, are available in 8- or 10-foot lengths in metal, mesh, or plastic.

Moist-curing stucco. No matter what the backing or finish, stucco is moist-cured for 48 hours to attain maximum strength and durability. In most climates, moist curing can be done by spraying the stucco at the beginning and end of each day with a fine mist from a garden hose. In dry climates you should spray more often.

Fresh stucco needs protection from rain and freezing—avoid working in cold weather. Fully cured stucco is hard like concrete, weather-resistant, and fire-resistant. It stands up to repeated wetting and drying, freezing and thawing. What's more, it will not rust, rot, or corrode, or become a meal for termites. Stucco materials are inexpensive and once the stucco is cured, it requires little maintenance. Stucco is used worldwide. Cracking, stucco's chief drawback, is caused by shrinkage or by movement of the underlying structure. Proper construction minimizes cracking.

Fiber-Reinforced Stucco

A fiber-reinforced cement—usually containing glass fibers—applied to masonry adds strength, waterproofing, and durability. Fiber-reinforced cements and mortars are mixed with water, then allowed to slack for a couple of minutes before a final mixing, following instructions on the package. Troweled over the face of a dry-laid concrete block and brick wall to a depth of ⅛-inch to ¼-inch, the coating takes the place of mortar

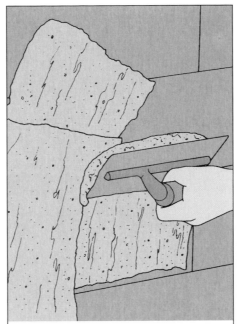

Fiber-reinforced stucco. A dry-laid concrete block wall is reinforced and weather-sealed by troweling a ⅛-in. layer of fiber-reinforced cement plaster over its surface.

bedding. The surface can be troweled smooth or textured, used as a final coat or as a base coat for other stucco. The material is available in 50-pound bags, covering about one square foot per pound to a ⅛-inch depth. If an admixture similar to concrete bonder is used, the single-layer coating need not be cured. Otherwise, it should be cured with a fine mist from a garden hose two or three times a day for several days.

Outside of earthquake country, reinforced cement plaster is often used as a surface-bonding agent for mortarless concrete block construction. Surface-bonded reinforced cement plaster does not, however, take the place of the engineered reinforcement and grouting of the block cores required by some building codes.

Stucco Mixes

The easiest way to make stucco is with a commercially prepared stucco mix. The mix usually comes in 60-pound bags; all you need to do is add water. You can mix the stucco in a wheelbarrow with a hoe or shovel. Mixing is much easier, though, in a rented plaster-mortar

mixer. A good stucco mix is easy to spread and trowel, sticking to the base it's applied to.

To proportion your own stucco mix, add three to five parts mortar sand to one part portland cement. (The exact proportions depend on the grade of the sand used.) To make home-proportioned stucco more workable, Type S hydrated lime—up to 25 percent by volume of the cement—may be added. Masonry cement may be substituted for portland cement, with the same proportions. In this case, hydrated lime is not added because these cements already contain plasticizers.

Tools for stucco. Stucco work requires the same tools as concrete work. The only additional tool you'll need is a pair of tin snips. You might need a rubber float if you want to create a sand texture finish.

Applying Stucco to Concrete Block

Stucco makes a great finished surface for concrete and concrete block. Because it is made with portland cement, stucco has a strong affinity for concrete, bonding firmly without reinforcement. Stucco not only hides mortar joints in the blocks, it helps to

Applying stucco to concrete block. When building a concrete block wall that is to be covered with stucco, slice the mortar joints off flush with the wall. Do not tool them.

weatherproof the wall. The concrete block garden wall shown on page 111 could well be plastered with stucco, adding color and texture at the same time. If you are building a wall to be covered with stucco, don't tool the joints. Strike them flush with the blocks instead.

For a typical garden wall you won't need any stucco molding except for control joints placed over the control joints in the block. Attach the joints to the wall with beads of outdoor construction adhesive to hold it in place until the stucco is applied.

Creating a good bond. Not necessary on a new concrete block wall, concrete bonder should be painted onto any wall that has questionable bonding properties.

Creating a good bond. Surface bond is important to hold the stucco to the block. Therefore, the surface for stuccoing must be clean and free of things like dust, efflorescence, grease, and paint. A new block wall should present no problems, but other walls need to be checked for what is called suction. Good suction makes for a good bond. To check suction, spray water on the surface and watch to see whether the water is absorbed—sucked in—by the surface. If it is, the wall has suction. But if the water beads up in droplets, as on a window pane, the suction is poor. On the other hand, suction is too great if the surface absorbs water immediately. This may be the case if you are stuccoing over brick. This condition can be controlled by spraying—but not soaking—the wall several times just before stuccoing it. If a good bond is doubtful, apply a concrete bonding agent to the wall.

1 **Mix the stucco.** As mentioned, the easiest way to make good stucco is to buy bags of stucco mix and just add water. Use Number 3 or Number 4 stucco mix. Or you can make your own mix as described in "Stucco Mixes," page 133. In either case, a good mix will be workable, easy to trowel, and will stick to the concrete block wall. It will not sag after application. Don't mix more stucco than you can use before it begins to set—one 60 pound bag at a time is about right.

First mix the ingredients dry, then add water to produce a good troweling consistency. Too little water will make it harsh and difficult to trowel. Too much water will make it runny and difficult to maintain the desired thickness without sagging. As with mortar, the stucco is the right consistency when you can slice it into sharp ridges that don't crumble. Mix for at least three to five minutes after adding the water. The stucco mix can be used immediately.

2 **Apply the scratch coat.** Apply layers of stucco with a 4x12- or 4x14-inch cement-finisher's steel trowel. Place the stucco mix on a 30x30-inch plywood mortarboard and either scoop the mix onto a plasterer's hawk or pick up a trowelful. (Some think a plasterer's hawk gets in the way.) Starting at the bottom of the wall, trowel stucco in a swath up the wall until the trowel runs out. Spread another swath slightly overlapping the first. Try to get the stucco about ⅜ inch thick. Use enough pressure to compact the stucco onto the concrete block surface, helping to create a firm bond. When several swaths have been applied, smooth over them with the trowel, as in finishing concrete. Smooth the thicker portions into the thinner ones for a uniform ⅜-inch thickness.

3 **Scratch the surface.** You need to help the next coat mechanically bond to the scratch coat. There are

1 The stucco is the right consistency if you can slice it into sharp ridges that don't crumble.

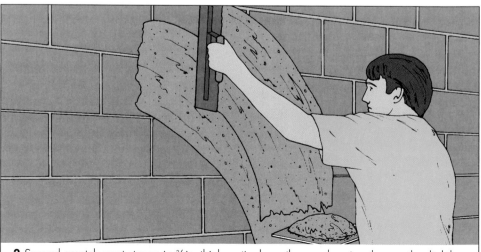

2 Spread scratch coat stucco in ⅜-in.-thick vertical swaths, overlapping the swaths slightly.

two ways to do this. If you have a trowel with ½-inch V-shaped notches, you can run that over the fresh scratch coat to create ridges. Or, you can let the stucco cure until it is hardened a little and then scratch it with a piece of ⅛-inch hardware cloth (a stiff wire mesh) or a piece of metal lath. Trowel or scratch horizontally, overlapping to cover the entire surface.

4 **Apply the second coat.** On concrete block the second coat is the finish coat. If a third coat will be applied, the second coat is called the brown coat. The second coat can be applied to the scratch coat as soon as the scratch coat has set enough to support the added weight. In hot, dry, windy weather, this may be as soon as four or five hours. More commonly, the second coat is applied one to three days later. If application of the second coat is delayed, keep the scratch coat moist by water-spraying it periodically for 48 hours. After that,

you can let it dry out, as long as you dampen it just before applying the finish coat.

The second layer is mixed and applied in the same way as the first, except thinner—¼ inch. Plan your work so that you stop only at a joint or pilaster, not in the middle of a field of stucco. Make the wall as smooth as you can get it. Even if you will be adding a color coat, try not to leave any deep scratches or other surface defects, since they will likely show through the final coat.

Moist-curing. Moist cure the second coat for at least 48 hours and let it dry one or two days before applying a color coat or painting, if that is to be done. Moist-curing can be done by water-spraying the stucco periodically or by covering the stucco with a plastic sheet to keep the moisture in. If desired, apply the color coat and texture it as described in Step 7, "Applying a Color Coat" on page 140.

Building a Stucco Driveway Light

A combination driveway light and house number display can be built of stucco-covered plywood to grace the front of your home. Typical of stucco-over-framed-wall construction,

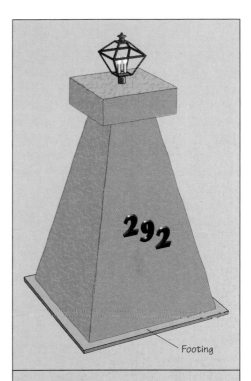

Footing

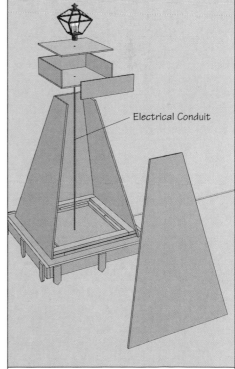

Electrical Conduit

Stucco driveway light. This driveway light is an excellent project for learning how to apply stucco to plywood.

3 As soon as the scratch coat has stiffened, score it horizontally. A scrap of metal lath or hardware cloth works well.

4 Spread stucco for the second coat about ¼ in. thick. Trowel finish-coat stucco out as smoothly as you can.

Imparting a Sand Finish

A popular surface treatment for stucco over a block wall is the sand finish. After the finish coat has set up enough to be firm, float the entire surface with a sponge float. Move the float in overlapping arcs. This will roll sand particles to the top of the surface. If the float digs in during floating, give the stucco more time to harden. Don't try to use this technique in a color coat—the sand particles are too small.

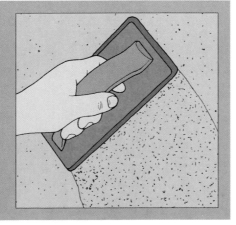

the stuccoing steps could be used to build almost anything, including exterior and interior house walls. Using reinforcing mesh with V-ribs designed to help hold stucco mix up against gravity, stucco can even be applied to ceilings. If used on a structure, building codes pertaining to stucco must be followed.

While we show building what could be called a truncated pyramid made from two 4x8 sheets of ¾-inch exterior-grade plywood, any shape you can build in wood can be stuccoed. Because the finished driveway light will be too heavy to move, it should be stuccoed on its permanent footing. All fasteners should be hot-dip-galvanized for long life. You can top the structure with any outdoor lighting fixture you choose. The project assumes you will provide electricity to the light with electrical cable encased in ¾-inch diameter conduit buried in the ground. Consult an electrician or a wiring book before doing the electrical work.

Making a Footing

The footing for the driveway light is a 51-inch-square concrete slab. Lay out the perimeter of the square as described in "Making Square Corners," page 24." Excavate the area to a depth of 7 inches. Run electrical conduit through the ground and into the bottom of the excavation. Install 2x6 form boards, keeping the tops of the boards level and about 1 inch above grade. See "Formwork," page 25. Place and tamp gravel to a depth of 4 inches.

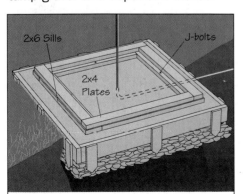

Making a footing. The driveway light will sit on a square slab. Sills and plates provide attachment for the plywood form.

Add reinforcing mesh as described in "Steel Reinforcement," page 26. Pour the concrete and screed it level with a 2x4. Since only the edges of the slab will be exposed in the finished project there is no need to finish the surface of the slab any further. Install four J-bolts, positioning them as illustrated. When the concrete has hardened enough to hold a shape, run an edging tool around the perimeter. See "Edging Joints," page 29. Remove the forms. When the concrete is cured, install the 2x6 sills and 2x4 plates as shown.

Building the Plywood Form.

The base over which you will apply stucco is built from two ¾-inch-thick 4x8-foot sheets of exterior plywood. To prepare the plywood for cutting out the four side panels, you'll need a chalkline and a measuring tape, plus a pair of sawhorses. The saw cuts are most easily made with a circular saw, but you can use a saber saw, or even a hand saw. The parts don't have to fit together exactly because stucco covers a multitude of discrepancies.

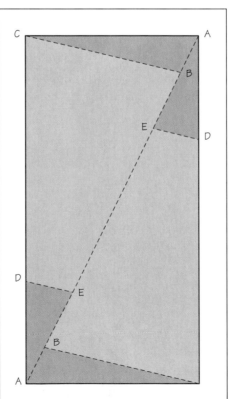

1 Mark two sheets of ¾-in. plywood as shown and cut them to make the four sides of the base for the driveway light.

1 Lay out and cut the base form pieces. The driveway light makes very efficient use of a 4x8 sheet of plywood. After cutting, only a few small triangles will be left over. Lay out the cuts as shown in the drawing. Start by snapping a diagonal chalk line from A to A. Then measure 96 inches along the diagonal from each A corner and make marks at B. Next measure 67½ inches along the plywood edges from each C corner and make marks at D. Measure 28½ inches along the diagonal from each A corner and place marks at E. Now snap chalk lines between each pair of B and C marks and each pair of D and E marks.

Now cut along the diagonal. Cut lines B to C and D to E to complete the sides.

2 Assemble the base form. Assemble the sides of the driveway light base around the sills. Join the sides with 2-inch galvanized drywall screws placed every couple of feet along the edges. Alternate the overlaps in panel ends. Also screw the sides into the sills and plates.

2 Assemble the sides by driving 2-in. drywall screws through the edge of one panel into the end of the next panel.

3 The form top is a simple box of ½-inch plywood. Top and bottom holes allow electrical conduit to pass through.

Make the top form.
3 Make the top from ½-inch exterior plywood. The top is a simple closed box with holes drilled through the top and bottom for the electrical conduit. Cut the parts, then sandwich the top and bottom panels together to drill the hole for the conduit. Assemble the sides to the bottom with 1½-inch galvanized drywall screws. Then use 2-inch screws to fasten the top to the base. Finally, screw the top panel in place.

Preparing the Form

When stuccoing on plywood, two layers of building paper separate the base from the stucco layers and wire mesh reinforcement is embedded in stucco to strengthen it and hold it in place.

There are two ways to install the paper and mesh. The easiest way, shown in this project, is to cover the plywood with a layer of Grade D building paper and then apply self-furring stucco lath. This material has an attached backing of Grade D building paper, a layer of soft kraft paper, along with a layer of hexagonal-mesh with 1-inch openings of 18-gauge wire. Fastened to the form, self-furring lath provides the required second layer of building paper as well as the necessary mesh reinforcement held slightly out from the backing so it will embed completely in the stucco.

The driveway light requires about 37 feet of self-furring lath. For a small project such as this you might not want to pay for an entire roll of self-furring lath. Instead, you can apply a second layer of Grade D building paper to the form, then fasten galvanized expanded-metal, diamond-mesh or rib lath, hexagonal woven-wire mesh, or 16-gauge (minimum) galvanized welded-wire lath with squares not larger than 2x2 inches. Use furring nails to attach the reinforcement to the plywood. These have thick fiberboard washers that slip behind the reinforcement to support it out from the wall.

Install foundation screed.
1 Use foundation screed around the bottom edges of the driveway light form and also around the bottom edge of the upper box portion. The driveway light is small so control joints are not necessary. Fasten the foundation screed with 1-inch roofing nails, 1-inch galvanized drywall screws, or power staples placed about a foot apart to firmly hold the screed to its base. (Moldings may be spliced by over-lapping them four inches, though that is not necessary for this project.) Don't attach the foundation screed to the foundation.

Install the building paper.
2 Cut 12-inch-wide strips of Grade D building paper and fasten them along the corners of the form, from top to bottom. Fasten the strips with roofing nails or ¼-inch staples every 12 inches or so. Then cover the side panels with four cut-to-fit sheets of building paper, with the upper sheets overlapping the lower ones by about 4 inches. When you finish, all plywood should be covered with at least one layer of building paper.

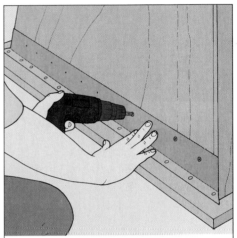

1 Attach mitered foundation screed moldings around the bottom of the form with 1-in. nails or drywall screws.

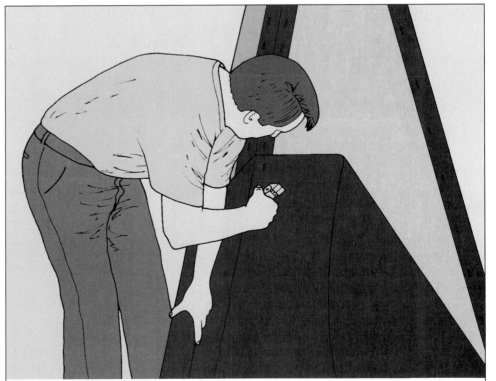

2 Staple Grade D building paper to the form, making sure the four corners are well covered with paper. Place ¼-in. staples about a foot apart.

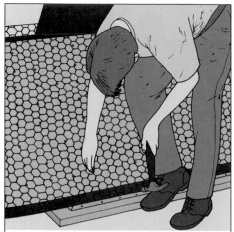

3 Install self-furring stucco lath from the foundation screed upward. Place fasteners as indicated by marks on the paper so they hold the mesh tightly to the backing.

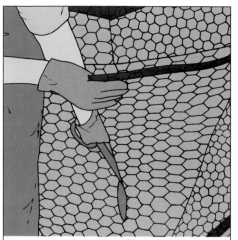

4 Use tin snips to cut the lath along the corners of the form.

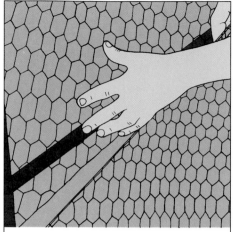

5 Do not nail stucco lath at the top until you fit the upper course of stucco lath behind the mesh of the course below, but in front of its building-paper backing.

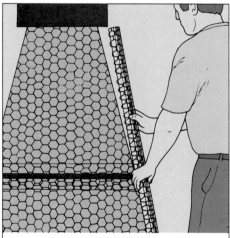

6 Install stucco corner bead, nailing them firmly along the outer edges with 1½-in. roofing nails. The corners also form screeds for use during finishing.

3 **Install a bottom course of self-furring lath.** Starting at the bottom, lap the reinforcement over the foundation screed. Attach the lath to the plywood with 1½-inch roofing nails, power staples, or galvanized drywall screws with large washers. Self-furring lath usually has nailing indicators; otherwise, fasten the lath every 6 inches, both horizontally and vertically. The fasteners should hold the lath wires firmly to the backing. Don't nail the top six inches of the bottom course yet.

4 **Cut the lath.** For a structure, such as a house that has plumb sides, you can just wrap the lath around the corners. But the lath won't

fit that way on the sloping sides of the driveway light. So use tin snips to trim the lath along the corners.

5 **Install the remaining lath.** At the top of the bottom course, pull the mesh away from its backing paper. Slip the bottom of the upper course—mesh and paper—between the lower course paper and mesh. Then nail. In larger projects, when lath must be joined vertically, you would overlap sections of lath four inches or more, weaving the mesh together exactly as described here for horizontal joints.

Cut pieces of lath to fit on the bottom, top, and sides of the top form and fasten these in place. Make the bottom pieces wide enough to fold over the base form and weave into the second course.

6 **Install the corner bead.** Cut lengths of corner bead to fit up the sides of the base form, butting under the top form. Fasten these with 1½-inch roofing nails. Cut pieces of corner bead to cover the corners of the top form, including the horizontal corners where the top and bottom meet the sides. Nail these pieces in place.

Stuccoing the Form

1 **Mix the stucco.** The desirable properties of good stucco mix are built in during proportioning and mixing. To save much time and effort,

use No. 3 or No. 4 ready-mixed stucco. Or mix your own as described in "Stucco Mixes," page 133. Add clean water, enough to make the stucco workable yet not so much water that it sags when applied. Don't mix more stucco than can be applied before the mix starts to stiffen. One 60-pound bag should be enough. Use of a power mixer is recommended, especially a bladed mixer designed for mixing plaster or mortar. A rotating-drum concrete mixer will work. First mix the dry materials to a uniform color, then add water and mix for three to five minutes more.

1 The easiest way to make a good stucco mix is to use ready-mixed stucco in 60 pound bags.

2 Apply swaths of scratch-coat stucco up the wall, compressing it in and around the reinforcement. It should go on about ⅜-in. thick to cover the mesh.

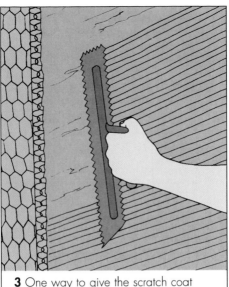

3 One way to give the scratch coat "tooth" is to tool it with a ½-in. V-notched trowel to form grooves.

4 As soon as the scratch coat has hardened, usually the following day, the brown coat can be applied. Trowel it on about ⅜-in. thick, and smooth it with the trowel.

2 **Place the scratch coat.** The first layer of stucco over plywood and lath is the ⅜-inch-thick scratch coat. Using a 4x12- or 4x14-inch steel trowel, scoop up mixed stucco and bring it to the bottom of the form. Sweep the trowel up with enough pressure to force the stucco into and all around the reinforcement. Get another trowelful of mix and place a second vertical swath slightly overlapping the first. Keep adding more swaths of stucco until the surface is entirely covered. Give special attention to forcing stucco mix into the mesh corner moldings. Stucco should completely embed all reinforcement. You can trowel in other directions to smooth and compact the stucco into place around the reinforcement. Cover the lath completely.

3 **Scratch the surface.** Immediately after placing the scratch coat, run a ½-inch V-notched trowel over the surface to form grooves. If you don't have a notched trowel, wait until the first scratch coat has stiffened a bit, then scratch the surface horizontally to create good "tooth" for bonding to the next coat. You can do this with a piece of hardware cloth or wire mesh.

4 **Apply the brown coat.** In a day or two, or when the scratch coat has set enough to hold the second

5 A length of angle iron makes a good tool for rodding. This process produces a flat, even plane between corner beads.

layer, you can apply the brown coat. It's made of the same mix as the scratch coat.

Evenly dampen the scratch coat, then apply the brown coat ⅜-inch thick, starting from the bottom and troweling upward across the scratched texture. Use the same steel trowel used for the scratch coat. The brown coat should end up at close to the proper thickness.

5 **Rod the stucco.** Give the stucco a little time to stiffen, then use a straightedge—a metal channel or angle is recommended—across the corner beads to strike off or "rod"

the stucco. Rodding makes the stucco a flat plane without high or low spots between corners. Rod the stucco much like striking off a concrete slab, cutting off the high spots and filling in low spots with more stucco mix and rodding over them again. If the stucco sags while rodding, let it stiffen more before rodding.

Make vertical stops in stuccoing at corners or where a change in appearance between applications will not be apparent. Horizontal stops, if any, should be cut square and should overlap any horizontal joints in the scratch coat by 6 inches or more.

6 **Float the stucco.** When the brown coat has stiffened somewhat, float it with the steel trowel, a wood float, or a texturing float, such as a sponge-rubber one, to produce an even finish all over. You can tell when to float by pressing the float against the stucco. Released, it should not stick. If it sticks, wait for further setting. Floating not only applies an even overall texture, it helps to compress the stucco against the wall, increasing its strength. If floated too early, the stucco surface will not be properly compressed.

Moist-cure the brown coat for 48 hours by covering with plastic sheet or by periodic spraying. The wall can either be painted or color-coated when it is completely dry.

7 **Applying a color coat.** Color coat mix in a wide variety of earth colors and others are available from your dealer to protect and color the stucco surface. Choose the color you wish and purchase a pre-packaged mix in that color. Add water to it and mix as for scratch-coat and brown-coat stucco. Whether the color coat is pigmented or plain white, be sure the tools and mixer are clean, as the color coat is based on white portland cement, which is discolored by even small amounts of gray stucco mix.

Dampen the brown coat, both for adhesion and to provide moisture for curing, then apply the color coat like other mixes, with a steel trowel. Spread it about ⅛ inch thick, smoothing it in varying directions with the trowel. Finally, impart the texture you like. While the color coat needs curing, hold off on that until the following day. Cured too early, stucco color variations may appear. The first curing spray should be a light fogging, without saturating the surface. Continue moistening the color coat periodically throughout the second day.

If you want to attach house numbers to your driveway light, use outdoor epoxy or polyurethane glue, holding them in place with tape until the glue sets.

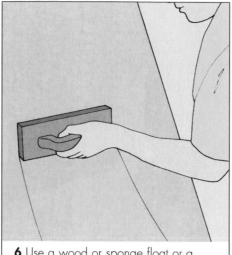

6 Use a wood or sponge float or a metal trowel to float the the stucco to the desired texture.

7 Spread the color coat ⅛-in. thick over the dampened brown coat.

Texturing Stucco

You can give stucco virtually any texture you like. Simply by experimenting with a float or trowel or other texturing tool, you can test different textures. Do it in the still-plastic color coat. Harsh-tooled textures that would be tough to clean or paint can be softened by "knocking down" with a light pass of the steel trowel. Here are two popular textures that are easy to create:

To make the popular skip-troweled texture, dip the trowel flat-faced into fresh color-coat mix and pull it away to leave sharp peaks and valleys on the surface of the trowel. Then lightly skip the loaded trowel over the surface, leaving behind high and low spots. Keep trying until it produces exactly the effect you like.

To make the star-track texture, simply press a short edge of the trowel in three or four directions to produce a "star" imprint. Space the stars however you like.

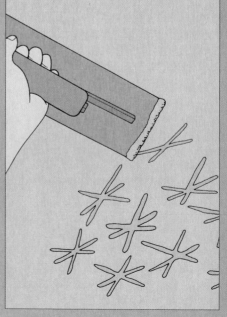

Stone

Because it is already a natural part of the landscape, stone blends effortlessly into any landscaping plan. Some of the most beautiful stone walls are made by artfully stacking stone without mortar. Alternately, stone can be bonded with mortar and topped with concrete as in the elegant wall shown above.

In addition to enhancing and defining the landscape, stone is the most popular choice for retaining walls used to re-shape the landscape.

Stone Techniques

Building with stone is likely the hardest, most satisfying project a homeowner can undertake. It's hard, obviously, because stones are heavy. You need to be in good physical condition, and you need to lift stones carefully to protect your back. Pace yourself. There's no hurry. After all, you are building something that will stand as a testament to your skill long after you are gone.

Knowing that you are using a basic element of the earth to build something of beauty that will survive you is what makes stonework so satisfying. Stone masonry can be relaxing, too. In our hectic, high-tech lives in which computer keys are the closest many of us come to actually touching our work, stonemasonry is refreshingly visceral. Sure, you'll do some layout measuring and run some guide strings, but stone is an irregular masonry unit that won't cooperate with precise measuring. Ultimately, the key to a sturdy and beautiful stone project lies in the judgments you make with your eyes and your hands. So enjoy the sun on your back, the sweat on your brow, and the dirt beneath your fingernails.

Since stone comes from the landscape, no other building material looks as beautiful or as natural for projects in your yard. In this chapter, you'll learn how to build stone walls (both dry stacked and mortared), including retaining walls. You'll also learn to pave with stone.

Choosing Stone

Although many types of stone are available throughout the country, only a few are suitable for building. Besides being accessible, suitable stones must satisfy certain requirements of strength, hardness, workability, and durability.

There are many ways to describe stone. It can be identified by the form in which it is used—rubble, ashlar, or flagstone. It can be identified by its type or mineral composition—granite, limestone, sandstone, slate, etc. And it can be described by the way in which it is obtained—fieldstone that is gathered from fields in its natural state and cut stone that is quarried with heavy equipment from large stone deposits. Stone can also be described in tech-

nical or scientific terms by its chemical composition or by its method of geological formation.

The familiar New England dry-stacked stone walls are made of fieldstone gathered from the fields by farmers as they clear the land for planting. The stones are most often a type of granite or sandstone, and they are laid in rubble form with little or no cutting.

Rubble stone. Rubble stone is irregular in size and shape. Fieldstone collected in its natural form is a type of rubble, naturally rough and angular. Quarried rubble comes from the fragments of stone left over from the cutting and removal of large stone slabs. The difference between the two is that fieldstone rubble is weathered on all its surfaces, while quarried rubble has some freshly broken faces. Rubble stone can be laid in a number of different ways, depending on its size and shape and how you want it to look. Rubble can also be roughly squared with a brick hammer to make it fit together more easily. Rounded fieldstone or river stone is hard to work with because the curved surfaces make it difficult to stack the stone with the necessary stability.

Ashlar. Ashlar is stone that has been cut at the quarry to produce relatively smooth, flat bedding surfaces that stack easily. It is generally cut into small squares or rectangles and has sawed or dressed faces, but the face of ashlar may also be left slightly rough. The free-form look of a rubble wall is quite different from the formal appearance of an ashlar wall.

Flagstone. Designed to be used for paving, flagstone is usually a quarried material that has been cut into flat slabs. (It is possible in some areas, though, to find fieldstone that is naturally flat enough for paving.) Cut flagstone ranges from ½ to 2 inches thick and may be shaped in either rough mosaic form or geometric patterns.

Common Types of Stone

The most common stones that satisfy the requirements of building construction are granite, limestone, sandstone, and slate. While many others, such as quartzite, bluestone, and serpentine, are available in some parts of the country, they are used less frequently.

Granite. Granite is an extremely hard, strong stone noted for its durability. Its color may be red, pink, brown, buff, green, gray, or black, depending on where it was quarried. The same hardness that makes granite so durable also makes sawing or cutting it very difficult. Granite that is cut and dressed is expensive because the stone is so hard to work with, thus it is usually used only on luxury commercial projects. For outdoor garden and landscape applications, granite is usually available as quarried or fieldstone rubble.

Limestone. Limestone is relatively durable, easily worked, and widely available in many parts of the country. It's an attractive stone and is sometimes characterized by embedded shells and fossilized animals and plants. Although soft when first quarried, limestone becomes hard with age and exposure to the weather. Because it's much more porous than granite, limestone is not as durable in cold, rainy, or snowy areas where it is exposed to repeated cycles of freezing and thawing.

Limestone is most often cream or buff colored but may be reddish or yellowish or have a gray tint. When quarried, limestone contains ground water (commonly called quarry sap), which includes varying amounts of organic and chemical matter. Gray-colored stone generally contains more natural moisture than buff-colored stone. As the quarry sap dries and stabilizes, the stone lightens in color and is said to "season." Buff stone will season in about 60 to 90 days, but gray stone may require seasoning for as long as six months. If unseasoned stone is placed in a wall, it may be very uneven in color for several months, or even as long as a year. There is no way to improve the appearance of the structure during the seasoning period. Left alone to weather, the stone eventually will attain its characteristic light neutral color.

Limestone is available as fieldstone and quarried rubble, as ashlar, and sometimes as flagstone. Because it is softer and more porous than granite, limestone is also easier to work with. It is easy to shape with simple tools.

Sandstone. You'll find sandstone in a variety of colors, ranging from buff, pink, and crimson to greenish brown, cream, and blue-gray. Light-colored sandstone is usually strong and durable. Reddish or brown sandstone is typically softer and more easily cut. Sandstone is available as fieldstone, quarried rubble, ashlar, and as flagstone split into thin slabs for paving. Sandstone is easier to cut and work with than granite but more difficult than limestone.

Slate. Most often thought of as a premier roofing material, slate is usually split into thin slabs at least ¼ inch thick. It's also used for flagstone and flooring. Small quantities of various mineral ingredients give color to different slates; the colors include black, blue, gray, red, purple, and green. "Select" slate is uniform in color and more costly than "ribbon" slate, which contains stripes of two colors. Slate is extremely durable as a paving material because it has low porosity and high resistance to the abrasion of repeated foot traffic. It is moderately easy to cut and shape but has a tendency to break in layers.

Buying Stone

Stone is sold by the cubic yard at quarries and stone suppliers. Cut stone will naturally be more expensive than fieldstone or quarried rubble stone, because of the labor required to produce it. Since availability and cost can vary by region, it is best to visit suppliers before you plan your project, so you can base your design on materials that are readily available in your area and within your budget.

Estimating Quantities

To estimate how many cubic yards of stone you will need, multiply the length times the height times the width of your wall in feet to get cubic feet, then divide by 27 to get cubic yards. If you are using ashlar stone, add about 10 percent to your order for breakage and waste. If you are

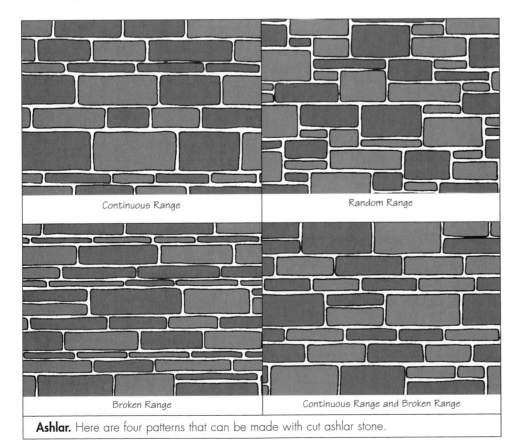

Continuous Range

Random Range

Broken Range

Continuous Range and Broken Range

Ashlar. Here are four patterns that can be made with cut ashlar stone.

using rubble stone, add at least 25 percent.

For flagstone to build a patio or walk, figure the square footage by multiplying the length times the width. The stone supplier will be able to tell you how much stone you will need based on this figure.

Tools for stonemasonry. Working with stone requires few tools. For cutting and shaping stone you'll need a small sledgehammer (sometimes called a hand drilling hammer or a baby sledge), which is tempered to strike metal tools safely. A brick hammer is helpful for chipping off small pieces of rock. A stonemason's hammer is similar to a brick hammer, but heavier with a broader edge. A rubber mallet is used to seat flagstones in sand. A point chisel and a pitching chisel are used to split stones. For laying out stone walls, patios, or walks you'll need wood stakes and mason's twine. Excavation work will require a shovel and spade. For any stone project, you'll need a tape measure and a

4-foot level. For walls, you'll need a line level. If you build a mortared wall or use mortar to cap a dry-stacked stone wall, you'll also need a bucket for measuring the mortar ingredients, a mason's trowel, and a wheelbarrow or mortar mixing box and mason's hoe for mixing. See "Tools for Working with Stone," page 9, for details on using these tools.

Cutting and Shaping Stone

When you are laying stone in mortar, you often can hide slightly irregular shapes by burying them in the mortar joints. When you are dry-laying stones without mortar, the fit of the stones usually must be more precise both for aesthetics and stability. For both types of stonework though, you will often have to cut and shape individual stones to make them fit better. Be sure to wear heavy leather gloves and safety goggles whenever you are cutting stone.

1 **Score the line.** While granite is difficult to cut, limestone, sandstone, and slate are relatively easy to work with once you get the knack. First, position the stone on solid ground for firm, even support. Do not lay the stone on concrete because the hard concrete surface may cause the stone to break in the wrong place. If you like, you can mark the cutting line with chalk, crayon or pencil. Then use a pitching chisel to score the cut by positioning the flat edge of the chisel along the intended line and tapping lightly with the hammer.

2 **Split the stone.** Often, the stone will break along the line before you have scored it all the way around. If not, strike one sharp blow to split the stone after scoring it. Remove any small bumps or protrusions with a point chisel, placing the point at the base of the bump and tapping with the hammer.

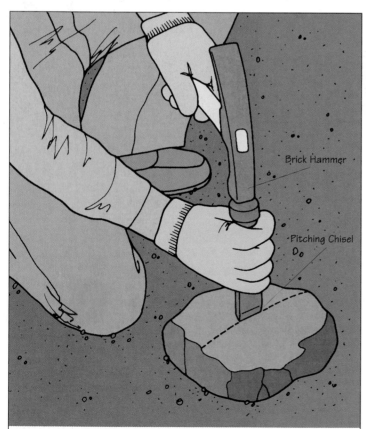

1 Lay the stone on flat earth. Use a pitching chisel and a hammer to score a line where the stone is to be split.

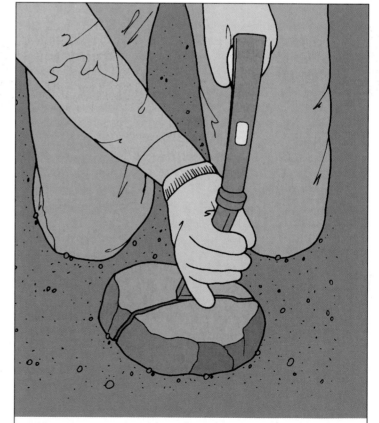

2 Place the chisel in the center of the scored line and strike it with a hammer to split the stone. Remove any bumps or protrusions with the chisel.

Stone Projects

Stone is rugged and durable, so projects made with stone provide a sense of strength and permanence. Whether you choose a dry-stacked or mortared wall, a patio or walk, or a stone retaining wall, the color and texture of stone will add character and rustic charm.

Dry-Stacked Stone Wall

Dry-stacked stone walls are built without mortar. Friction, gravity, and the interlocking of the individual stones hold the wall together. Although the work is physically hard, the techniques involved are simple. A dry-stacked wall is a bit flexible; it can absorb some frost heave within the ground. As a result, a concrete footing is not usually required for dry-stacked walls up to 3 feet high. You'll probably want to build no higher than 3 feet anyway, since it's tough to lift stones to that height. Also, most municipalities don't require a permit for a dry-stacked wall up to 4 feet high. But be sure to check with your local building department before building any wall. Even if no permit is required, there may be local zoning or planning regulations that will affect the construction and placement of your wall.

While construction techniques are straightforward, the stones may require some cutting and shaping to create good interlocking fits. Sandstone and limestone rubble usually are among the easiest to cut. If you are gathering rather than buying fieldstone, look for angular shapes, not rounded shapes. Save the largest stones for the base course, the squarest ones for the ends and corners, and the flattest ones for the cap. A dry-stacked stone wall consists of two "wythes," or vertical stacks. Space between the wythes is filled with small rubble, and the wythes are tied together every several feet with a bond stone that spans the entire thickness of the wall. Walls up to 3 feet high should have a base that's at least 2 feet thick. If you do build a higher wall, add at least 8 inches of thickness at the base for each foot of height. Each end and face of a dry-stacked wall must be "battered," or sloped inward ½ inch for every foot of height. The wall should sit in a 6-inch-deep trenched excavation. If necessary, 2 inches of sand can be placed in the bottom of the trench to improve drainage. If the ground slopes, dig the trench in a series of flat terraces.

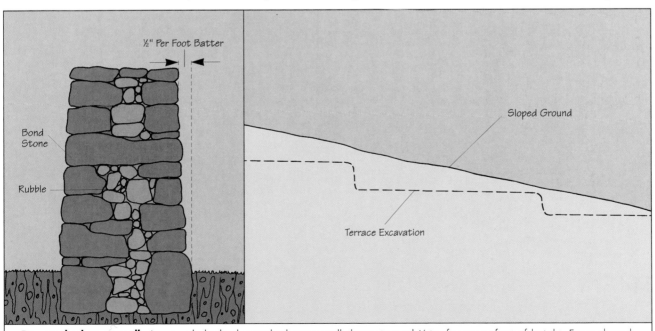

½" Per Foot Batter

Bond Stone

Rubble

Sloped Ground

Terrace Excavation

Dry-stacked stone wall. A properly built, dry-stacked stone wall slopes inward ½ in. for every foot of height. For a sloped site, use a terraced footing of several levels.

Making a Slope Gauge

This easily constructed slope gauge is designed to help ensure that the faces of your stone wall slope in at a rate of ½ inch per foot. Because this means that a wall face should slope a total of 1½ inches in 3 feet, it's simple to construct a 3-foot-long gauge from standard 1x2 lumber. (The actual dimensions of 1x2 lumber are ¾ by 1½ inches.)

The gauge has four parts; a slope board, a plumb board, a cross block, and a spacer block. Cut these parts from 1x2 stock to the lengths shown in the drawing. Assemble the gauge with 1¼-inch drywall screws. Predrill to prevent splitting the little spacer block; then attach it to the plumb board with a single screw. Fasten the slope board to the opposite end of the plumb board with one screw. Then screw the cross block to the spacer block and to the slope board.

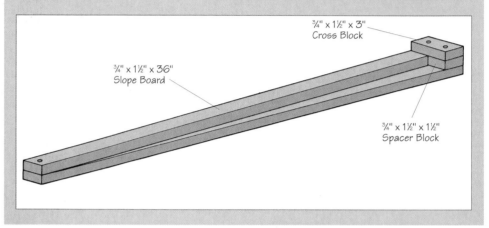

2 Lay the first course.

Lay two wythes of large stones with their top surfaces tilted slightly down toward the center of the wall, so that they are lower in the middle than at the outside edges. Use your largest stones for the first course, not only to create a good base but also to avoid lifting and adjusting these heavy pieces higher up. The corners and ends of walls are particularly vulnerable to damage, so choose stones for these locations that fit well together to add stability. Position the stones so that their most attractive faces are exposed. Dig out under the stones or fill in spaces with soil to get the stones to sit firmly without rocking. Fill the area in between the wythes with smaller stones. Pack the spaces between stones in this first course with soil to give the wall a stable base.

3 Lay the second course.

Lay the next course, setting the stones on the face of the wall slightly in from the face of the stones below. Carefully select each stone for the best fit with its neighbors. The less you have to shim the stones with small pieces of rubble, the better. Trim and cut the stones to fit as necessary. If a stone rocks on a point or sharp corner, shape it to sit down more squarely. Check your work periodically with a 4-foot level to keep

1 Excavate the trench.

Set four wood stakes just beyond the ends of the proposed wall site and stretch mason's twine between the stakes to mark the sides of the wall. Excavate a trench 6 inches deep and as wide as you need for the base (usually 24 inches). If the soil contains a lot of clay or drains poorly for some other reason, you can improve drainage and stability by digging deeper and adding 2 inches of sand in the bottom of the trench. Once the trench is dug, remove the stakes and twine.

1 Excavate a 6-in.-deep by 2-ft.-wide trench. If drainage is a problem, allow for a 2-in. sand bed at the bottom of the excavation.

2 Use the largest stones for the first course. Place them firmly in the trench, but lean them inward to the wall's center. Fill the area between wythes with small stones.

each course approximately level. Using a level to make sure the plumb board is plumb, hold the slope gauge against the wall to make sure that it tapers correctly from bottom to top. As before, set the large outside stones first, then fill in the middle with smaller stones.

4 Lay the bond stones. In each course, lay a bond stone that is the full width of the wall every

3 or 4 feet to tie the two halves of the wall together.

5 Set the level string. It's always a good idea to set a goal. Cut two stakes long enough to drive firmly into the ground while leaving enough to extend about 6 inches above your final wall height. Set the stakes so they are approximately centered across each end of the wall. Extend a mason's line between the stakes at

the final wall height. Place a line level on the twine and adjust the twine until it is level. Throughout the building process, sight down the line to make sure your wall is running in a straight line. As you get to the last few courses of stone, the level string will help you adjust your work so that the top of the wall will be level.

6 Shim as needed. If a stone does not sit firmly in place, break

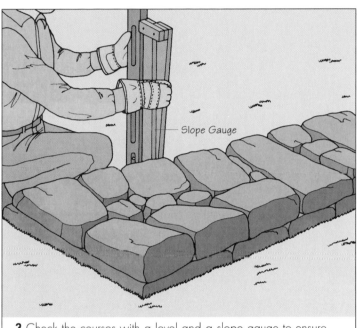

3 Check the courses with a level and a slope gauge to ensure the proper taper.

4 Lay a bond stone every 3 to 4 ft. to tie the wythes together.

5 A level string set between two stakes will help you to maintain a straight wall and keep the top course level.

another stone into small pieces and use the pieces as shims. All the stones should be slightly inclined toward the center of the wall so that the weight leans in on itself.

7 **Fill the wall.** After laying several courses of stone, fill in the small spaces along the face of the wall by driving in small stones with your hammer. This is called chinking and helps interlock the wall and tilt the stones inward.

8 **Lay successive courses.** The key to a stable wall is to avoid long uninterrupted vertical joints. To achieve this, always overlap the stones in successive courses. Stonemasons call this the "one over two, two over one rule."

9 **Interlock the ends and corners.** Interlock the ends and corners of the wall to provide stability. This is like dovetailing a carpentry joint, in which the two adjacent pieces are overlapped to form a strong connection. Use the stones that have the squarest sides and corners for these areas. Take your time and be patient with this part of the wall. If you can't find stones that fit well enough, try cutting and shaping some to form a strong, stable interlock.

10 **Cap the top of the wall.** Flat stones of roughly rectangular shape make the best caps. The top course should be as level as possible for the full length of the wall; in cold climates, many masons like to set the cap stones in mortar to protect the wall from moisture penetration and to prevent them from being knocked off. Mix the mortar in a wheelbarrow or mortar mixing box as described in "Mortar for Stone Walls," page 154. Trowel on a 1- to 2-inch-thick mortar bed, covering about 2 feet of the wall at a time. Fill in the joints between the cap stones with mortar, too,

6 Place small rocks as shims to set the stones snug and leaning in toward the center of the wall.

7 Chinking rocks into the gaps and holes will make a stronger structure.

8 Use the "one over two, two over one rule" to avoid long vertical joints in the wall.

9 Overlap the stones with the squarest sides and corners at the wall's corners and ends.

10 Lay a rounded mortar cap on top of the final course to prevent water penetration and to bolster the strength of the wall.

Stone Projects **151**

packing it firmly and using enough mortar so the surface joints are flat or slightly rounded and will not collect water.

Another attractive alternative is to use a cap of mortar on top of the last course to help tie the top of the wall together. You put the top course in a bed of mortar as described above and then add a mortar cap. Or you can use the mortar cap alone. In any case, make the mortar cap rounded to help shed water.

Stone Retaining Wall

A dry-stacked stone retaining wall relies on gravity, friction, and the interlock of the stones to resist the overturning motion of an earth embankment. Like the previous stone wall project, a dry-stacked retaining wall consists of two "wythes" or vertical stacks. A well-built dry-stacked retaining wall is superior to a mortared retaining wall because dry stacking leaves spaces for ground water to drain through. However, the stones may require considerable cutting and shaping to create the interlocking fits that are key to a good dry-stacked wall. See "Cutting and Shaping Stone," on page 146. Easily workable stone like sandstone or limestone rubble will usually be best.

Dry-stacked stone retaining walls up to 3 feet high do not require a concrete footing. They may be laid directly onto the soil in a 6-inch-deep trench. For stability, the inside of the wall must tilt toward the embankment at least 2 inches for every foot of wall height. If you don't mind looking at a sloped outer face, you can simply tilt the entire wall back. If you prefer a plumb outer face, make the wall gradually thicker as you build up.

Terraced walls. In addition to requiring a concrete footing, retaining walls more than 3 feet high get tricky to build, and in many municipalities, you'll need a building permit if the wall is more than 4 feet tall. Often, a better alternative to a single high wall is to build two shorter walls stepped back against the slope. At the base, a 3-foot wall should be 18 inches thick.

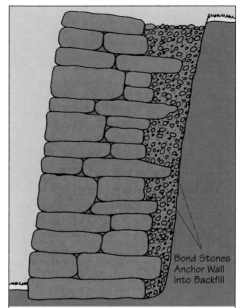

Stone retaining wall. A dry-stacked stone retaining wall will either tilt backward to the embankment or be thicker at the top. Use gravel as backfill behind the wall.

Terraced walls. Rather than build a retaining wall more than 3 ft. high, build sections of shorter, terraced walls

Building the Wall

1 **Excavate the trench.** Cut the angle of the embankment back 30 to 45 degrees from plumb to give you room to place the stones and the gravel for drainage behind the stones. Loose or sandy soils tend to collapse, so cut the angle more sharply.

In soil that drains well, excavate a 6-inch-deep by 18-inch-wide trench along the length of the wall. Remove all grass, sod, roots, and large rocks. The first course of stones can be laid directly in the excavation.

In dense or clay soils or in areas that do not drain well, excavate 10 or

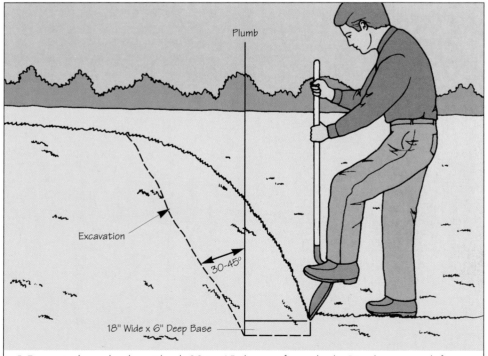

1 Excavate the embankment back 30 to 45 degrees from plumb. Dig deep enough for a gravel drainage base if needed.

12 inches deep and add a 4- to 6-inch deep gravel or crushed-stone drainage bed. Level the drainage bed with a rake and tamp the gravel or stone to compact it. Then lay down a layer of landscape fabric, which will allow moisture and air to penetrate but will prevent the sand from settling into the gravel. Overlap adjoining sections of fabric by 4 inches. Place a 2-inch bed of sand in the trench for leveling the stones.

2 **Set a string line.** A level base course is important to the stability of the wall. Drive wood stakes just beyond the ends of the excavation near the front face of the wall. Tie mason's twine between the stakes. Hang a line level on the twine and adjust the twine until it is level.

3 **Lay the first course of stones.** Starting at one end of the wall, carefully fit each stone, seating it firmly in the soil or sand bed and following the string line for level. Use your largest stones for the first course, not only to create a good base but to avoid having to lift and adjust these heavy pieces at higher levels. Dig out under the stones or fill in spaces with soil, if necessary, to get the stones to sit firmly without wobbling. Pack the spaces between stones in this first course with soil to give the wall a stable base.

4 **Set the next courses.** Set the next few courses of stone on top of the first, keeping in mind that you want the inside of the wall to slant back at least 2 inches for every foot of height. As mentioned, the front of the wall can be plumb or it can follow the slope. Lay stones in successive courses so that they overlap the stones above and below. Avoid creating continuous, straight vertical joints. The overlapping pattern will produce a stronger wall, giving it the stability it needs to resist pressure from the soil. Install long stones that stick back into the backfill about every 4 feet horizontally in each course. These are called bond stones or deadmen, and they help tie the wall into the hillside. Offset these bond stones in each course.

2 Set a mason's line to the level of the first course at the front of the excavation.

3 Lay the first course of stones. Either add or remove soil to ensure a level course. Fill any gaps between the stones with soil.

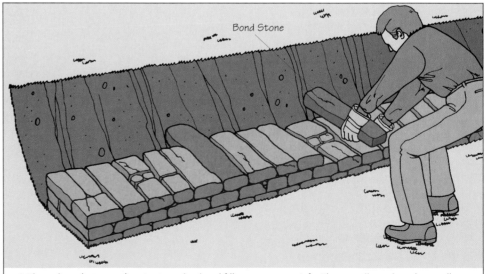

4 Place bond stones that jut into the backfill area every 4 ft. These will anchor the wall.

5 **Add drainage backfill.** After the first few courses of stone are laid, begin adding gravel as drainage backfill behind the wall. Try to keep the gravel layer at least 6 inches thick.

6 **Add the remaining courses.** Set the remaining courses of stone in the same manner. Remember to let each course of the inside wythe jut an inch or so farther toward the embankment so that the inside face will slant about 2 inches per foot. When building up the wall, carefully select each stone for the best fit. Check the fit of each stone as you lay it. If a stone wobbles on a point or sharp corner, shape it to sit more securely. See "Cutting and Shaping Stone," on page 146. You also can use small pieces of stone as shims to make the stones fit more tightly together; although for the best-looking wall, you'll want to minimize shims. If you do use shims, insert them from the outside of the wall. All the stones should be slightly inclined toward the soil embankment so that the weight of the wall leans into the hill. While stones should fit snugly together in a retaining wall, don't worry about filling every little void between stones. You want to leave plenty of natural "weepholes" to allow groundwater to pass through. Check your work periodically with a mason's level to keep each course approximately level. Continue backfilling with gravel every two or three courses.

7 **Cap the top of the wall.** You have some design options here. One approach is to stop building 6 or 8 inches before you get to the top of the slope. Pack dirt between the top course of stones and then cover the top of the wall with soil to bring it up to the top grade. Then you can plant a ground cover on top of the wall. The plant's root network will help prevent erosion and help hold the top of the wall together. This approach looks great in a casual country garden. Another approach is to leave the top of the wall exposed as you would for any freestanding stone wall. You can mortar the top course in place or cap the top course with mortar. See Step 10 "Cap the Top of the Wall," on page 150.

5 Add at least 6 in. of gravel backfill between the wall and the slope for drainage.

6 Place small stones as shims to lock the wall tightly together. Do not fill every gap in the wall; water must be allowed to pass through.

Mortared Stone Wall

A well-built dry-stacked wall will last for centuries, so why build a mortared wall? In most informal country or garden settings, there is no reason to use mortar except, perhaps, for the cap; dry stacking is the way to go. Use mortar if you want a more formal look or if the wall is in a place where people are likely to walk on it, sit on it, or otherwise disturb the stones. Mortared walls require less maintenance; you won't have to worry about stones occasionally becoming dislodged.

Filling the spaces with mortar allows you to use more irregularly shaped stones. You still want to select stones carefully so you won't have an ugly wall with huge mortar joints, but indi-

7 As a design option, lay 6 to 8 in. of dirt on the last course to bring the wall to top grade. Ground cover or grass can be planted in this soil.

vidual stones needn't fit together quite so well as is necessary for a dry-stacked wall. As you would for any stone wall, save the largest stones for the base course, the squarest ones for the ends and corners, and the flattest ones for the cap. Rubble stone that is at least roughly squared on all sides will work best for mortared walls.

Mortar also helps prevent water from passing through a wall. This was more important when stone was commonly used for basement walls or solid stone house walls.

Like dry-stacked walls, most mortared stone walls are constructed with two vertical stacks, called wythes. Unlike dry-stacked walls that must be tapered as they rise, mortared walls are built straight up with plumb faces on both sides.

Construction is similar, but mortared walls are a lot more work than dry-stacked walls, not only because of the mortar but because they require a steel-reinforced concrete footing below the frost line. This footing is required because mortar makes the wall into a stiff monolith that will crack if subjected to frost heave. A dry-stacked wall can absorb some frost heave movement with no damage.

Designing the Footing

Design and build a steel-reinforced footing as described in "Concrete Footings," page 63. As a general rule,

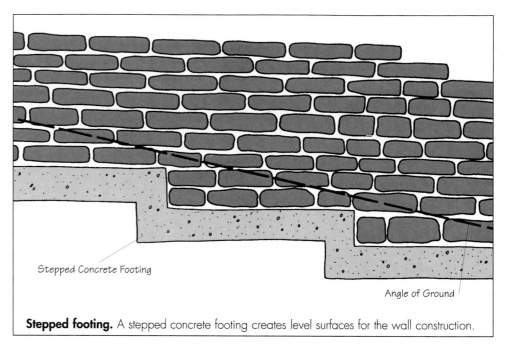

Stepped footing. A stepped concrete footing creates level surfaces for the wall construction.

Stepped Concrete Footing

Angle of Ground

make the footing thickness equal to the wall thickness. Make the footing twice as wide as the wall thickness. Check with your local building department for requirements about footings in your area. If the footings must be set very deep, it may be more economical to build a concrete wall to within a few inches of grade rather than building several courses of stone below ground level.

Stepped footing. If your wall travels down a hill, build your footings as a series of level steps. Stepped footings are also described in "Concrete Footings," page 63. For flatter slopes, build a footing that is deep enough so that its bottom is below the frost line and its top is level for the full length of the wall.

Mortar for Stone Walls

Masonry mortar is made with the same types of portland cements typically used in concrete. See "Mortar," page 79. The most common is a Type I general-purpose cement. Mortar for stone walls should be a mixture of one part lime, two parts portland cement, and nine parts sand. The lime should be a hydrated mason's lime; the sand should be a well-graded masonry sand with a range of fine to coarse grains. Some manufacturers produce factory-blended masonry cements that are combi-

nations of either portland cement and lime or portland cement and other natural or chemical agents. For small projects, masonry cements are more convenient because all that is required is the addition of sand and water. Naturally, you'll pay more for this convenience. Mix one part of the masonry cement with three parts sand.

Mortar must be consistent from batch to batch or the color and texture will vary. Mortar usually is mixed by volume proportions using a container of convenient size for consistent proportioning. Always use a container for measuring ingredients so that the proportional volume of materials is the same each time. A 1- or 2-gallon plastic bucket is a good choice and is not too heavy when full. Don't pack the materials in the bucket and don't mix more than you can use in about two hours because mortar is useless once it begins to harden.

If your materials cannot be stored close to where you'll be working, mix your mortar in a wheelbarrow so you can move it easily. If you are using a mortar box, make sure it's level so water won't collect in one end or a corner.

Mixing mortar. First, measure all the dry ingredients and mix them thoroughly with a mason's hoe. Blending will go more easily if you put half the sand in first, then the cement and

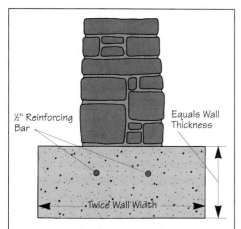

½" Reinforcing Bar

Equals Wall Thickness

Twice Wall Width

Designing the footing. Reinforce the footing with rebar. Make the footing twice as wide as the wall thickness. Make the footing thickness equal to the wall thickness.

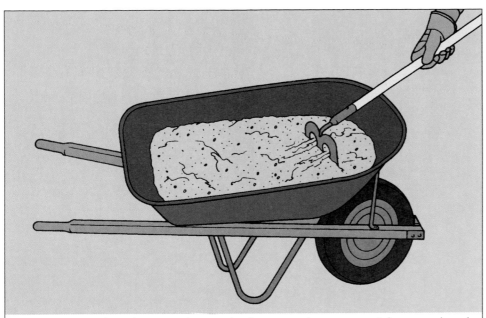

Mixing Mortar. Place the materials in a wheelbarrow and use a mason's hoe to push and pull the mortar ingredients together.

lime mixture, and then add the rest of the sand. Alternately pull and push the materials back and forth until the color is even. Then push the mix to one end of the mortar box or wheelbarrow, or make a hole in the middle, and pour 2 gallons of water in the hole or the empty end of the mixing box to start. Measure the water. Don't use a garden hose because it's too easy to get too much water. Using a chopping motion with the hoe, mix the dry ingredients into the water, pushing and pulling the mix back and forth until the consistency is uniform.

The amount of moisture in the sand will influence how much water is needed in a mortar mix to get the right consistency. If you buy bags of sand for small projects, it will be dry. If you buy sand in bulk by the ton for larger projects, it will be damp or wet. You should keep your sand pile covered so that the moisture content will not change drastically in wet or dry weather.

Masonry mortar for brick and block work should be the consistency of soft mud. But because stone is so heavy, a relatively stiff mix is better here, even though it is a little more difficult to work with. If the mix is still too dry after you add the initial 2 gallons of water, add more water in small quantities until the consistency is right. To check for proper consisten-

cy, make a series of sharp ridges in the mortar with the hoe or trowel. If the ridges appear dry and crumbly, more water is needed. Ridges that stay sharp without slumping indicate the right consistency. If you add too much water, add proportional amounts of cement, lime, and sand to bring the mortar back to the proper consistency.

Within the first two hours after mixing, mortar can be retempered once with a little water to replace evaporated moisture and restore proper consistency. In hot, dry, or windy weather, the time limits on retempering may be shorter. Do not retemper more than once; mortar that has begun to harden must be discarded because it will not develop a good bond with the stone.

Building a Mortared Stone Wall

1 **Snap a chalk line.** After the footing has cured for a few days, brush any dirt and debris from the surface. Measure and mark the location of the outside face of the wall, being careful to center the masonry in the middle of the footing. Square your corners and snap a chalk line along the length of the footing. Then snap another line to define the back of the wall. If your footing will form one or more corners, use the 3-4-5 triangle method described in "Making Square Corners," page 24, to make sure the corners are square.

2 **Lay stone in a test run.** First lay the stone on the footing in

1 Snap chalk lines to mark the front and back of the wall on the footing. The wall must be centered on the concrete footing. Square any corners.

a test course without mortar, laying the outside row of stones along the chalk line. Carefully select and fit the stones, turning them back and forth to get a secure, stable fit. Lay larger stones along the two outside faces of the wall; fill in the middle with smaller stones.

Mortared stone walls must have bond stones that extend through the full thickness of the wall. These will help hold the front and back wythes together. Space the bond stones every 3 feet or so horizontally and vertically. When you build the wall, stagger the bond stone positions in successive courses rather than putting the bond stones directly above each other.

3 **Begin spreading mortar.** Mix a batch of mortar as described in "Mortar for Stone Walls," on page 154, using one part lime, two parts portland cement, and nine parts sand, or simply use one part type N masonry cement to three parts sand.

After laying out the first course in a test run, remove a few stones at one end of the wall and begin to spread the mortar in a bed joint about 2 inches thick. Keep the mortar about ½ inch inside your guidelines, because it will spread when you lay the stone. This first course is very important—you want to lay enough mortar so that the bed joint doesn't develop voids when you lay the stones on it. Spread only enough mortar at one time to keep just ahead of your stone laying.

4 **Begin laying stone.** Brush or wash off any dirt or sand on the stones that would prevent the mortar from sticking. Start at one end of the wall or at a corner; lay the corner or end stone first, pressing it firmly down into the mortar and tapping it lightly with the trowel handle if necessary. To help keep the front of the wall straight, lay each outside face stone before you lay the stone behind it. To keep the stones clean as you work, have a bucket of water and a sponge handy to immediately wipe off spilled mortar.

Bond Stone

2 Lay a test course without mortar to get an idea of placement. Stagger the bond stones so they don't overlap one another in successive courses.

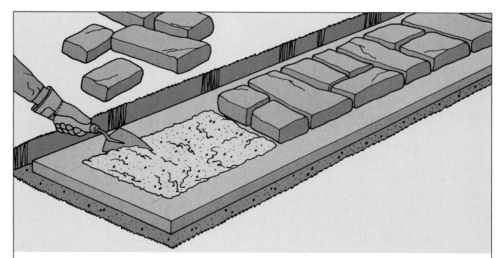

3 Remove some stones at the end and lay 2 in. of mortar, ½ in. from the chalk lines. Don't spread more mortar than you can quickly lay the stones into.

4 Lay the outside stones first. Place them into the mortar and tap the top with the trowel handle. Make sure the stones are clean before laying them.

5 Fill in between outside stones. Fill in the center of the wall with smaller, odd-size rubble stones. Add mortar on top of the fill stones as needed to make the course level. Use the trowel to throw mortar in between these stones and the larger ones which form the outside faces of the wall. Finish the entire first course before beginning the second course.

6 Rake the mortar joints. As you lay the wall, rake the mortar joints to accent the shape of the stones. If the stones have sharp edges, rake the joints out about ½ inch. If the edges are slightly rounded or broken, rake the joints out about 1 inch. Use the rounded end of a broom handle or a ⅜-inch round-headed bolt to do the raking. Remove excess mortar with a whisk broom. If you prefer the look of a joint that is flush with the face of the stones, just use the whisk broom without raking.

7 Tool the mortar joints. After the mortar begins to cure, you need to tool the surfaces of the joints to compress the mortar. It is important that the joints be tooled at a consistent moisture content, so they don't appear light in some areas and dark in others. The joints are ready for tooling when the mortar is "thumbprint" hard, meaning you can press your thumb against the mortar and leave a print impression without mortar sticking to your thumb. Don't wait until you have finished a large section of wall before you tool the joints—check the mortar frequently, and tool the joints a few at a time. As you tool the joints, small pieces of mortar called tailings will squeeze out—remove them with a soft-bristled brush.

8 Set the level line. Set wood stakes at the front corners of the wall and stretch mason's twine

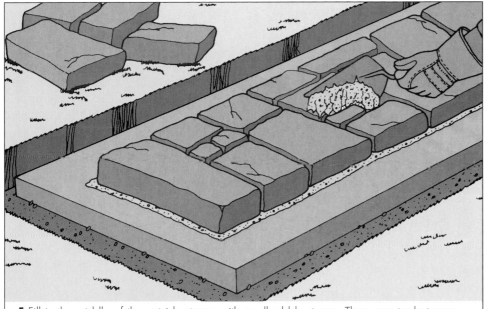

5 Fill in the middle of the outside stones with small rubble stones. Throw mortar between all the stones.

6 Use a whisk broom to remove excess mortar from the raked joints.

7 When the mortar is thumbprint hard, use a jointing tool to smooth and compress the joints.

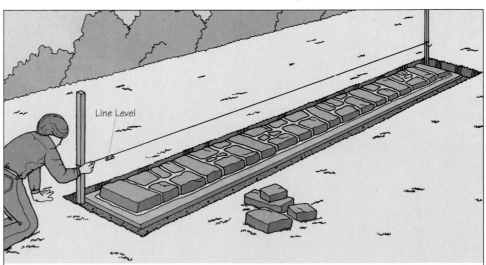

Line Level

8 At the outside corners of the wall, set a level line 3 to 4 in. above the top of the course being laid. This will keep the wall straight and level.

between them. Level the line with a line level. Tie the line about 3 or 4 inches above the top of the next course. This will help you keep the courses of stone approximately level and the wall straight.

9 **Build the leads.** After setting the line, build leading sections, or "leads," at the ends or corners. Masonry walls are always laid from the outside ends or corners toward the middle; the leads help establish the correct spacing and coursing heights for the rest of the wall.

Select your squarest, most regular stones for the leads. Before the mortar sets, use a 4-foot level to check that your leads are plumb on the ends and on both faces.

10 **Lay the middle courses.** Test fit several stones at a time. Follow the "one over two, two over one rule" that was described for dry-stacked walls. That is, try to make every stone cover a joint between two stones below so that you don't create continuous vertical joints. After test fitting, remove the stones, apply mor-

tar, and fit the stones back into place to fill in the middle courses of the wall. When fitting stones against one another, spread mortar only on the stone already in place. Be generous with the amount and work it in so you don't have voids. Move the mason's twine up as you work to keep the courses roughly level. After setting each stone, tap it lightly with the trowel handle to eliminate air bubbles in the mortar. Be careful not to get mortar on the face of the stones. If you do, remove it with a wet sponge before it dries. Don't let mortar droppings build up at the base of the wall—remove them as you go. When you finish each course, fill in between the wythes with small rubble stones.

11 **Insert wedges.** Because they are so heavy, it is sometimes necessary to temporarily support large stones with wood wedges to keep the mortar from squeezing out of the joints. Wet the wedges before you use them, so they won't wick water out of the mortar. Once the mortar has set, remove the wedges and fill the holes with more mortar.

12 **Lay the bond stones.** Remember to lay bond stones across both wythes about every 3 feet horizontally. Remember to stagger the bond stones so the joints do not all align vertically. Don't lay

9 Select the squarest stones to build the leads at the corners and ends of the wall. Check for plumb on the ends and on both faces.

10 After test fitting, apply mortar and lay stones in courses to fill in between the leads. Tap the stones in place with the trowel. Do not create long uninterrupted vertical joints.

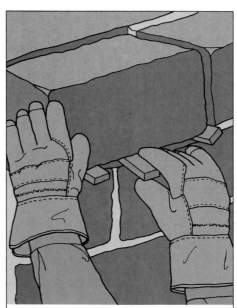

11 Insert wood wedges to support stones until the mortar sets. Wet the wedges before using them.

more than two courses of stone in a day—the mortar needs time to set up enough to support the weight.

13 **Cap the wall.** The top of a masonry wall requires special care and attention because it must protect the rest of the wall from rain and snow. The stones in the top course should be flat or slightly rounded on the top. Ideally, you want flat stones that are wide enough to span the full thickness of the wall. Even for a rubble wall, you may want to purchase cut stones for the cap course. Place a thick bed of mortar and set the cap stones on top of the wall. Make sure the joints between stones are completely filled with mortar; tool them to compress the surface of the mortar. Don't rake out the top joints as you did with those on the sides of the wall or they will collect water. If you like, you can top the wall with a layer of mortar. Make the mortar cap rounded to help shed water.

14 **Clean the wall.** After the wall has set for about a week, you can clean excess mortar off the face of the stones using a solution of 10 parts water to 1 part muriatic acid. Mix the solution in a plastic, not metal, bucket. Pour the water in first, then add the acid to it. Wet the wall with a garden hose, apply the cleaning solution, then immediately rinse the wall again with the hose to stop the etching action of the acid. Be sure to wear rubber gloves and goggles when working with acid.

Stone Paving

The simplest form of stone paving consists of laying flat stones directly in the earth; you dig under the stones just enough to make sure each one sits firmly without rocking. Grass or ground cover will grow between the stones; you can mow right over them if you like. This method is appropriate for a rustic, natural setting such as a garden path.

For a look that is a bit more formal, you can lay a flagstone walk or patio in a bed of compacted sand. This is a bit more work but still makes a simple project. You'll have flatter, more regular paving and sand joints between the stones instead of growing vegetation. The sand bed acts as a cushion and compensates for minor irregularities in the ground. For patios and walks, a 2-inch sand bed is usually adequate. If your soil has a large percentage of clay or doesn't drain well for other reasons, excavate an extra 4 inches deep and add 4 inches of compacted gravel. Once the bed is in place, laying the stones is a lot like doing a puzzle; you try stones in different combinations looking for the best fit that will give you small joints between stones.

12 Lay bond stones in the courses at a distance of about every 3 ft.

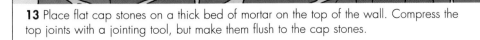

13 Place flat cap stones on a thick bed of mortar on the top of the wall. Compress the top joints with a jointing tool, but make them flush to the cap stones.

14 After cleaning the wall with a muriatic acid and water mixture, spray it clean with a garden hose.

Laying a Patio or Walk in Sand

1 Lay out the perimeter. Measure and lay out the size and shape of the area with wood stakes and string using the 3-4-5 method described in "Making Square Corners," page 24, to create square corners. Set stakes adjacent to any existing construction to mark where the edge of the paving will be, and set stakes for the outside corners a little beyond the proposed paving edge. For free-form shapes, lay out the curves with a garden hose. Then go around the outline, sinking a spade in the earth to score the perimeter of the paving. When this is done, remove the stakes and string, as well as any hose.

2 Excavate the soil. When you set the stones they should be about 1 inch above ground. So, allowing for the 2-inch sand bed, you want to excavate to a depth equal to the thickness of the stone plus 1 inch. If you'll be using a 4-inch gravel base, add 5 inches to the thickness of the stone. Remove all grass, sod, roots, and large rocks. Set the sod aside because you will need it to fill in around the edges of the stone paving. Place the gravel now, if you are using it, and tamp it down with a hand tamper or mechanical tamper.

3 Install a weed barrier. Install a layer of landscaping fabric on the excavation or on top of the gravel.

Lap adjoining sections by at least 4 inches. Landscaping fabric is designed to prevent weeds from growing in the cracks while still allowing water and air to pass through.

4 Spread and screed the sand bed. Top the landscaping fabric with ordinary construction sand. Use a straight length of 2x4 to "screed" the sand level.

5 Install paving stones. Starting in one corner, place the stones on the sand and tamp them into place with a rubber mallet. Make sure that the stones are solidly bedded and do not wobble. If necessary, dig out a little sand to make the bedding more solid. Arrange the straight stone edges

1 After marking the perimeter of the walk with stakes and string, use a spade to score the outline of the excavation.

2 Excavate to a depth that will set the stones 1 in. above ground. Allow for the thickness of the stone, 2 in. of sand, and if needed, a 4-in. gravel base.

Landscaping Fabric

3 Install a layer of landscaping fabric on the excavation or on top of the gravel.

Tamper

4 Top the landscaping fabric with sand. Tamp, then screed it level with a straight 2x4.

5 Use a rubber mallet to seat the flagstone in the sand base. Leave ½ to ¾ in. between stones. Check the stones periodically for level.

6 Sweep sand into the joints between the stones. Wet the walk down to compact the sand and repeat the process in a few days, if necessary.

toward the outside perimeter and fit the irregular edges together, leaving about ½ to ¾ inch between the stones. If you have to kneel on the sand bed at first to lay the stone, use a piece of plywood as a cushion to keep from creating depressions in the sand. After you have laid a few courses, you should be able to move around and kneel on the stone instead. Use a 4-foot level to maintain the paving roughly level.

6 **Fill the joints with sand.** When all the flagstones are in place, sweep the joints full of sand to stabilize the stone. Dampen the sand with a garden sprayer to compact it and then sweep more sand into the joints. Fill the joints again in a few days if the sand settles a little.

Cutting and Shaping Flat Stone

Use a pencil or crayon to mark pieces of stone that need to be trimmed for a better fit. For small sections, trim the pieces off with a brick hammer. Cut larger pieces to fit by drawing a line with a pencil or crayon, placing the stone on the ground, and scoring along the line with a pitching chisel. Prop the scored flagstone on a board or pipe, and tap off the unwanted piece with a hammer.

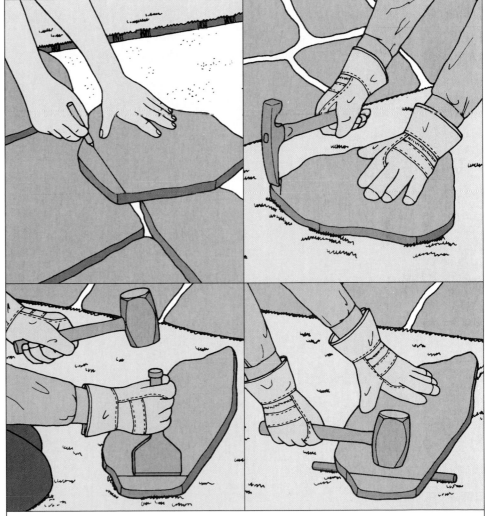

Cutting and shaping flat stone. (Top left) Hold the stone to be cut over those in place and approximate the cutting line. Mark the stone with a crayon or chalk. (Top right) Small sections of stone can be nicked off with a mason's hammer. (Lower left) Large cuts are scored with a pitching chisel along the marked line. (Bottom right) Split the stone along the scored line by placing it over a section of pipe and gently striking it with a hammer.

Maintenance & Repair

Although concrete, brick, and stone are extremely durable, sometimes they do need maintenance or repair. Concrete, brick, and stone structures and surfaces are not easily demolished and replaced, which makes proper maintenance and repair the only solution. The time for this maintenance is pretty clear-cut: When you notice damage of any type, fix it as soon as you can to prevent the damage from worsening. This chapter explains a few common repairs for concrete, brick, and stone.

Water-Repellent Coatings

Materials that absorb moisture can be damaged by repeated freezing and thawing. Concrete and masonry surfaces are absorbent, although some materials absorb moisture more readily than others. A troweled concrete surface, for instance, is denser and, therefore less absorbent, than a concrete-block surface. Clear water-repellent coatings, available in many proprietary formulations, can help decrease water absorption and keep surfaces looking good.

Although new brick construction does not usually require such treatment, new concrete block is often treated with a water repellent, particularly in cold, rainy climates. Concrete slabs and light-colored stonework are often treated to help reduce staining from dirt and other substances.

Water repellents are available in both water- and solvent-based formulations. The water-based mixes may need to be applied more often, but they have less odor and are safer both for you and the environment. Both types of coatings are thin and nonelastic, so they will not seal any cracks in the surface. Always test a coating on a small, inconspicuous area before beginning work to make sure that you will be happy with the results. (Some water repellents are designed to be applied to specific materials only—read the product label before you buy.) Don't use heavy-duty commercial coatings, because they leave an undesirable glossy finish.

If you use a water-repellent coating, plan to reapply it every three, five, or seven years, depending on the specific product and the manufacturer's recom-

mendations. The application of water-repellent coatings doesn't require any special skills or equipment. Always follow the manufacturer's instructions concerning handling, application, cleanup, and disposal.

Tools for application. Water-repellent coatings can be brushed, rolled, or sprayed on, depending on the size of the surface to be treated. For either water- or solvent-based coating, you will definitely need a paintbrush for painting around the edges (called cutting-in). If you're rolling the coating on, use a synthetic roller cover (use a long-napped one for rough surfaces) and a roller pan. Spraying requires low-pressure (20 psi) spray equipment with a stainless-steel, fan-tip nozzle. You will also need plastic dropcloths to protect adjacent surfaces and landscaping. Be sure to wear eye protection and rubber gloves when applying the product.

Applying the Coating

Allow the mortar in new masonry walls or freshly placed concrete to cure fully—for at least 28 days—before applying water repellent. Make sure the surface to be coated is clean and free of any dirt and oils, which would prohibit absorption of the coating. If general or spot cleaning is necessary, allow the surface to dry thoroughly before applying the coating. If there is a nearby air-conditioning unit, turn it off while applying the coating so that the fumes aren't drawn into the air intake.

1 **Protect adjacent surfaces.** Cover windows, doors, and any surfaces you don't want coated with plastic sheeting. Also cover grass, bushes, and any plants in the work area.

2 **Paint around the edges.** Be sure to prepare the water-repellent product according to the manufacturer's instructions. Use a brush to paint around the edges of the surface you're protecting. Apply long, even strokes that do not overlap too much.

3 **Start at the bottom of the wall.** Apply the coating from the bottom upward. Dip the roller in the pan and roll upward in a long continuous vertical line. Saturate the wall—there should be a 6- to 8-inch rundown below the contact point. If you'll be spraying on the coating, spray only when there is lit-

1 Use plastic sheeting to protect areas of the house and ground that you don't want coated with water repellent.

2 Paint with a brush around the edges of the surface you're protecting. Apply long, even strokes.

3 Apply the coating from the bottom upward by dipping the roller in the pan and rolling upward in a long continuous vertical line.

Repairing Cracks in Concrete

When concrete is exposed to repeated cycles of freezing and thawing, it can crack or spall (flake). Uneven settlement of the soil beneath the concrete is another cause of cracking. To repair a small cracked area of concrete, you need to remove the damage and patch it with a cement-based patching compound.

When a larger section of concrete has been damaged, such as an entire panel of a sidewalk or patio, more aggressive demolition and repair is required—most often complete removal and replacement of the section. You need to break up the existing concrete with a sledge hammer, remove the pieces, level the ground, install formwork, pour and then finish the concrete as described in "Concrete Techniques," page 17.

Here are instructions for repairing a small area of damaged concrete. In addition to the patching materials, you will need a cold chisel, a small sledge hammer, a whisk broom, a bucket or other mixing container, a putty knife or trowel, and a concrete-finishing trowel.

tle or no wind, to keep overspray from drifting onto other surfaces. Allow the coating to penetrate the surface for two or three minutes and then apply more, again saturating the surface. When the first coat is dry to the touch, apply a second saturating coat in the same way.

1 Remove cracked or crumbling concrete to 1 inch below the surface using the cold chisel. Wear heavy gloves and safety goggles to protect your eyes from flying chips.

Commercial Patching Compounds

Instead of mixing your own, you can buy concrete patching compounds at most home centers and building-supply stores. Some are epoxy- or latex-enhanced mixtures, others are merely premixed cement and sand. Some patching compounds are packaged in a cartridge for application with a caulking gun. These can be particularly handy for patching narrow cracks. Other compounds are packaged for application with a putty knife. Follow the manufacturer's instructions for placement and curing—often it's not necessary to cut a key before applying the product.

2 Form a "key" between the patch and the existing concrete by holding the chisel at an angle and undercutting the edges of the area to be patched.

3 Remove debris with a whisk broom and clean the patch area with a hose.

1 **Remove the damaged concrete.** Using the cold chisel, remove all cracked or crumbling concrete to a depth of about 1 inch below the surface. Wear heavy gloves and safety goggles to protect your eyes from flying chips.

2 **Undercut the edge of the patch.** To form a key between the patch and the existing concrete, hold the chisel at an angle and undercut the edges of the area to be patched.

3 **Remove the debris.** Remove debris with a whisk broom and hose the patch area clean. Keep it moist for several hours or overnight. Sponge out any standing water before proceeding.

4 **Mix the patching cement.** In a small bucket or other container, mix one part portland cement and three parts sand with enough water to make a stiff paste. In a separate container, mix a small amount of portland cement with enough water to make a cement "paint." Coat the edges of the patch area with the

4 Coat the edges of the patch area with cement paint. Then pack cement paste firmly into the patch with a putty knife or trowel.

5 Level the mixture with a straight-edged, concrete-finishing trowel.

6 After troweling, allow the patch to sit for a few hours, then cover it with a sheet of plastic held down by bricks or rocks.

cement paint to serve as a primer. After the cement paint, pack the cement paste firmly into the patch with a putty knife or trowel. Cut deeply into the mixture to remove any air pockets.

5 **Fill and smooth the patch.** Level the mixture with a straight-edged concrete-finishing trowel. Let the patch sit for about one hour, then float or trowel to match the surrounding surface.

6 **Cure the patch.** After troweling, let the patch sit for a couple of hours, then cover it with a sheet of plastic. Hold down the edges with bricks or rocks. For the next week, lift the plastic cover daily and sprinkle water on the patch.

Repairing Concrete Steps

Concrete steps receive a lot of wear and tear during normal use. But heavy use, such as being subjected to loaded-dolly and hand-truck traffic, can sometimes damage the edge or corner of a step. Here's how to fix it:

To repair a concrete step, the tools you need are a cold chisel, a small sledge hammer, a trowel, a concrete-finishing trowel, an edging tool, a paintbrush, and a whisk broom. A section of ¾-inch-thick plywood, as wide as the height of the stair riser and as long as the stair width, is used as a form board. A few bricks

or a couple of concrete blocks hold the form upright. Also have on hand a bucket or other mixing container, portland cement, and sand.

Edge Repairs

1 **Chip away the damaged concrete.** Using a small sledge-hammer and cold chisel, remove all loose or damaged concrete at the edge of the step. Hold the chisel horizontally—parallel to the stair tread. This method will control chipping better. Wear heavy gloves and eye protection.

2 **Undercut the edge.** Holding the chisel at a sharp angle, undercut the edge of the damaged area to form

1 Use a small sledgehammer and cold chisel to remove all loose or damaged concrete at the edge of the step.

2 Holding the chisel at a sharp angle, undercut the edge of the damaged area to form a V-shaped interlocking groove with the new concrete.

a V-shaped interlocking groove with the new concrete. This is called a key. With a whisk broom and spray of water from a garden hose, remove all debris from the damaged area. Keep it moist overnight.

3 Set the form board in place. Cut the plywood to the height of the step riser and brace it firmly against the riser with bricks or concrete blocks. You may need to reinforce the board with a 2x4 attached to a stake at the bottom of the steps and butted up against the riser.

4 Mix the patching cement. In a bucket, mix one part portland cement and three parts sand with enough water to make a stiff paste for the repair. In a separate container, mix a small amount of portland cement with water to make a watery cement "paint." Now, coat the edge with the cement paint.

5 Fill and smooth the patch. Pack the cement paste firmly behind the plywood form board with a trowel, cutting deep into the mixture to remove air pockets. Then level the mixture with a straight-edge concrete-finishing trowel. Make sure the surface is level with the rest of the step. Let the patch sit for about one hour, then float or trowel to match the surrounding surface.

6 Edge the patch. Use an edging trowel to apply a rounded shape to the edge of the new patch. Carefully remove the form board after a few hours, and smooth the surface if necessary with the finishing trowel. For the next week, keep the patch moist by sprinkling it with water daily, and avoid heavy use for another week.

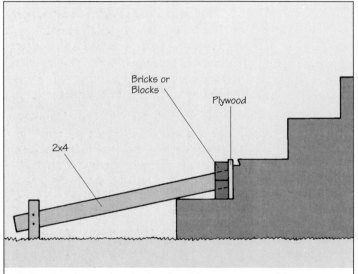

3 Cut the plywood to the height of the step riser and brace it firmly against the riser with bricks or concrete blocks. A 2x4 may be needed to reinforce the board.

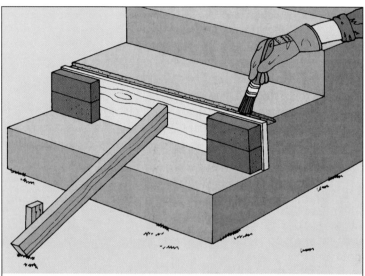

4 In one bucket, mix a stiff paste for the repair. In a separate container, make a watery cement "paint." Coat the edge with the cement paint.

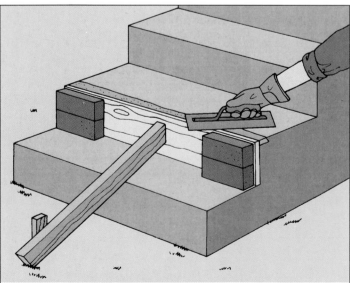

5 Pack the cement paste behind the plywood form board with a trowel. Level the mixture with a straight-edge concrete-finishing trowel, making sure the surface is level with the rest of the step. Let the patch sit for an hour, then trowel or float the surface smooth.

6 Round the edge of the new patch with an edging trowel. Remove the form board after a few hours and smooth the surface with the finishing trowel.

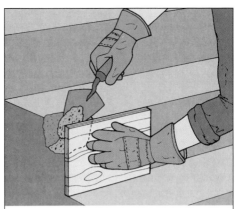

1 Use a trowel to construct a new corner with the stiff cement paste. Hold a piece of plywood on the step against the riser of the damaged step when working.

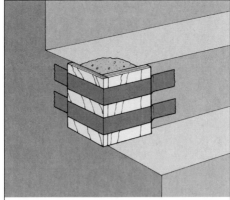

2 Use scrap plywood secured with duct tape to hold the repair in place.

Corner Repairs

Prepare a damaged corner for patching the same way you would a damaged step edge. Remove loose concrete with a chisel, and clean away all debris. Then mix one part portland cement with three parts sand and enough water to create a stiff paste for the patch. In another container, combine a small amount of portland cement with enough water to make a cement paint for applying before the patching material.

1 Build up the corner. Paint the damaged area with the cement "paint," then use a trowel to construct a new corner with the stiff cement paste. Hold a piece of plywood on the step against the riser of the damaged step so you're working only one side of the patch. Smooth the cement so that it's level with the rest of the step.

2 Secure the repair. Hold the repair in place with scrap plywood secured with duct tape. Remove the form after about one hour, smooth the surface if necessary with a floator trowel, and allow the repair to cure for a week, sprinkling it with water daily. Don't subject the repair to heavy use for about three weeks.

Replacing a Single Brick

It's fairly easy to replace a loose or broken brick. Finding a brick to match the existing units may be the most difficult part of this job. When searching for the right brick, bear in mind

that it's more important to match the color of the original brick than it is to match either the exact size or the texture. Bricks can be cut to smaller sizes or made "larger" with large mortar joints. Texture is not noticed at a distance. If an exact match is not possible, choose a brick that is slightly darker than the existing bricks, rather than slightly lighter—it will be less conspicuous.

To replace a loose or broken brick, you'll need a brickset, brick hammer, whisk broom, trowel, jointing tool, stiff-bristle brush, Type N masonry cement or mortar mix, and a wheelbarrow, bucket, or other mixing container.

1 Remove the existing brick. Use a brick hammer and a brickset held at a steep angle to remove the mortar surrounding the damaged brick. Make sure not to chip undamaged bricks. Remove the damaged brick, breaking it into pieces with the chisel if necessary. (Protect your hands with heavy gloves, and your eyes with safety goggles when doing this repair.) When you are done, sweep the mortar debris and dust it out of the cavity with a whisk broom. Save at least one piece of the damaged brick to use for color matching.

2 Wet the cavity. Before you insert a new brick, thoroughly wet the new brick and the bricks surrounding the cavity. This keeps moisture from being drawn out of the mortar. Let the surfaces of the bricks dry to the touch while you mix a small batch of

1 Remove the mortar surrounding the damaged brick using a small sledgehammer and a brickset held at a steep angle.

mortar as described in "Mortar," on page 79. Make the consistency of the mortar slightly stiffer than a typical mix by using less water.

3 **Spread the mortar.** Using a mason's trowel, spread mortar on the bottom and sides of the cavity and on the ends and top of the replacement brick.

4 **Push the brick in place.** Insert the brick into the cavity, allowing excess mortar to squeeze from the

joints. Make sure the joints are completely filled with mortar—there must be no gaps or voids. Remove this mortar with the edge of the trowel. If necessary, force extra mortar into the joints with a trowel.

5 **Tool the joints.** When the mortar has become hard enough that you can leave a thumbprint impression without any mortar sticking to your thumb, use a jointing tool to tool the surface of the mortar to

match the adjacent joints. In hot, dry weather, keep the repaired area moist for several days by spraying it lightly with a garden hose two or three times a day.

6 **Brush the joints.** If any mortar is squeezed out at the edges of the joints when they are tooled, remove it with the edge of the trowel. After the mortar has set up, remove mortar crumbs with a stiff-bristle brush.

2 Wet the new brick and the area surrounding the cavity where the damaged brick was before inserting a new brick.

3 Spread mortar on the bottom and sides of the cavity and on the ends and top of the replacement brick using a mason's trowel.

4 Insert the brick into the cavity, allowing excess mortar to squeeze from the joints. Remove excess mortar with the edge of a trowel.

5 When the mortar is thumbprint hard, tool the surface of the mortar to match the adjacent joints.

6 Remove mortar crumbs with a stiff-bristle brush after the mortar has set up.

Repointing Masonry Joints

Masonry mortar that is properly mixed and installed will usually last for decades before it requires maintenance. However, mortar that is not well made and mortar in a wall that is damaged by repeated freezing and thawing may require repair. The repair of masonry mortar joints is called repointing. You should inspect masonry joints periodically and repair any damage as soon as possible to prevent it from worsening.

To repoint mortar joints, you will need a narrow point chisel, brick hammer, whisk broom, mortar hawk, pointing trowel (a narrow trowel designed for repointing), stiff-bristle brush, and a jointer to match the profile of the existing joints. You will also need a Type N masonry cement or mortar mix, and a bucket or other mixing container.

1 Remove the loose mortar. Hold the point chisel at a sharp angle and tap it with the brick hammer to remove loose or damaged mortar to a depth of about 1 inch. Be careful not to damage the masonry units. Wear safety goggles to protect your eyes from flying chips.

2 Clean out the joints. Sweep debris from the joints with a whisk broom. Moisten the joints with water from a garden hose. This is important, to prevent the wall from wicking moisture from the new mortar.

3 Mix the mortar. Mix mortar according to the instructions given in "Mortar," on page 79, making small batches that can be used in two hours or less. Use a little less water than you normally would so that the mix is slightly stiff. It will be easier to handle with the pointing trowel and less runny.

The new mortar should match the old mortar closely. If necessary, mix sample batches, varying the proportion of ingredients, and apply some of each batch to the least conspicuous joint. Keep a record of the exact proportions of each mix, and allow each test batch to cure for several days before judging the color match—the mortar will lighten as it cures.

1 Hold the point chisel at a a sharp angle and tap it with a brick hammer to remove loose or damaged mortar to a depth of 1 inch.

2 Sweep debris from the joints with a whisk broom.

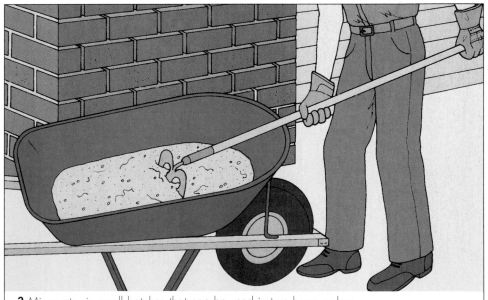

3 Mix mortar in small batches that can be used in two hours or less.

4 Push mortar into the joints using a pointing trowel filling the head joints first and then the bed joints.

5 Tool the joints to match the profile of the existing joints. Tool the head joints first and then the bed joints.

6 After the mortar has set up, brush the surface with a stiff-bristle brush to remove dried mortar crumbs.

4 Place mortar in the joints. Using the pointing trowel, push mortar into the joints, filling the head (vertical) joints first and then the bed (horizontal) joints. Don't try to fill the entire joint at once—instead, build up the mortar in two or three thin layers, allowing each layer to stiffen slightly. With a damp sponge, remove excess mortar on the face of the brick immediately.

5 Tool the joints. Tool the joints as described in "Tooling Mortar Joints," on page 92, matching the profile of the existing joints. Don't wait until you have finished a large section of wall before you tool the joints. It's important that the joints be tooled at a consistent moisture content so that they do not appear light in some areas and dark in others. The joints are ready for tooling when the mortar is "thumbprint" hard, meaning that you can press your thumb against the mortar and leave a print impression without mortar sticking to your skin. Tool the head joints first and then the bed joints. Check the mortar frequently, and tool the joints a few at a time when the mortar is just the right consistency.

6 Brush the joints. If any mortar is squeezed out at the edges of the joints, remove it with the edge of the trowel. After the mortar has set up (which takes one-half to two hours, depending on weather conditions), brush the surface with a stiff-bristled brush to remove dried mortar crumbs.

Maintaining and Repairing Stucco

Stucco can be cleaned with a garden hose equipped with a pressure nozzle or you can use a pressure washer. But before you hit the stucco with pressurized water, wash it down gently with clean water from bottom to top. This keeps any soil washed from upper portions of the wall from soaking into lower portions. Wash the dirt to the bottom and off the wall. Spray the wall a second time to rinse off still more soil. Power-spraying with a rented pressure-washer will remove even more dirt. Be sure to avoid blasting the surface directly with high pressure. Instead, hit the wall with a glancing stream from a fan nozzle.

Fixing Damaged Stucco

Holes, crumbling, and chipped corners in stucco can be repaired easily. The only difficult part is matching the color and texture of the old stucco.

1 Prepare the damaged area. Start by scraping out any loose, crumbly stucco to a solid edge with an old screwdriver. (You'll probably damage the screwdriver blade.) Snip out any damaged or corroded mesh. Then dampen the area with water.

2 **Reinforce the hole.** You need to reinforce the hole only if you are repairing stucco on plywood. (Most repairs will be to stucco on plywood. Holes in stucco over masonry are rare because the stucco bonds so well to block or brick). If the hole is large or contains no reinforcement, use tin snips to cut a piece of diamond-mesh stucco lath cut to fit the opening. Fasten the lath with 1-inch galvanized deck screws. Apply concrete bonder to the edges of the patch using a brush or roller. If the repair is over brick or block, apply bonder to the bottom of the hole as well.

3 **Fill the hole.** Wait for the bonder to become tacky but not dry. Mix standard stucco using less water to make it thicker, or purchase a stucco patching compound with texturizer. Trowel the mix into the area in a layer about ¼ inch thick. (The patching compound works like putty; follow the directions that come with it.) Let this layer set until firm. Build up layers of stucco or patching compound until the patch is about ⅛ inch below the surrounding surface.

4 **Scratch the patch.** After the stucco has set a bit, scratch the patch with a piece of hardware cloth or wire mesh.

5 **Apply the finish coat.** Mix finish-coat stucco to match the color of the existing stucco or use more patching compound and apply it to level the patch with the wall. Texture the patch with a trowel, float, sponge, or other tool to match the adjoining stucco as closely as you can. If you are successful, the patch will scarcely show. More than likely though, you will notice some difference. Don't blame yourself; even professionals pale at having to match new stucco to old.

6 **Cure the patch.** Finally, cure the patch by taping plastic over it. Wait at least two days before removing the plastic.

1 Rake out any crumbling stucco with an old screwdriver to create a firm base for the repair.

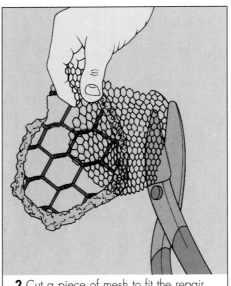

2 Cut a piece of mesh to fit the repair.

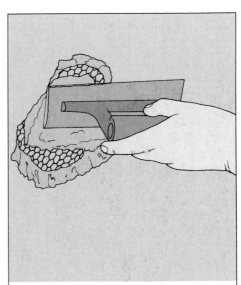

3 Fill the hole with extra-thick stucco or stucco patching compound in ¼-inch-thick layers, forcing it around the mesh.

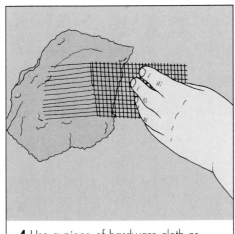

4 Use a piece of hardware cloth or wire mesh to scratch the patch.

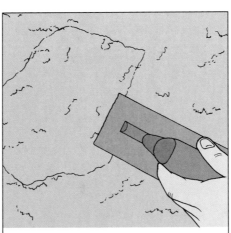

5 Fill the hole to the top with color-matched stucco mix and texture it with the trowel or other tool to match the surrounding area.

6 Cure the patch by taping plastic over it. Leave the plastic in place for at least two days.

GLOSSARY

Actual Dimensions The measured dimensions of a masonry unit.

Aggregate Crushed stone, gravel, or other material added to cement to make concrete or mortar. Gravel and crushed stone are considered course aggregate; sand is considered fine aggregate.

Bat A brick that is cut in half lengthwise.

Brick Clay that is molded to shape and fired at very high temperatures in a large kiln or oven. The color of the natural clay determines the color of the brick.

Broom Finish The texture created when a concrete surface is stroked with a stiff broom while the concrete is still curing.

Building Bricks These bricks, also called common bricks, are rough in appearance but structurally sound. Building bricks have chips, cracks, and slight deformations.

Buttering Placing mortar on a masonry unit using a trowel.

Collar Joint The vertical joint between wythes.

Concave Joint A masonry joint that is recessed and formed in mortar. A curved steel jointing tool is used to make a concave joint.

Concrete Fresh concrete is a semifluid mixture of portland cement, sand (fine aggregate), gravel or crushed stone (course aggregate), and water.

Concrete Block A masonry unit which consists of an outside shell with a hollow center that is divided by two or three vertical webs. The ends of the unit may have flanges that accept mortar and join with adjacent blocks, or they may have smooth ends for corners and the ends of walls.

Concrete Pavers Commonly used for driveways, patios, and sidewalks, concrete pavers come in a number of shapes and colors and are designed to be laid in a sand base without mortar; some interlock to form repeating patterns.

Construction Joints A joint that is installed wherever a concrete pour is interrupted for more than 30 minutes or stopped at the end of the day. The section being poured is closed off with a temporary stop board.

Control Joints Special joints, also called contraction joints, which are tooled into the surface and make concrete crack in straight lines at planned locations.

Curing Providing proper moisture to a slab to reduce cracking and shrinkage and to develop strength.

Darby A long tool used for smoothing the surface of a concrete slab.

Edging Joints The rounded edges of a pour that are resistant to cracking.

Excavation To dig out earth or soil so that a slab will be supported by a sub-grade that is hard, uniformly graded, and well drained.

Face Brick A type of brick used when consistency in appearance is required. A batch of face brick will be quite uniform in color, size, texture, and face structure.

Fire Brick A brick made of a special clay and baked at an extremely high temperature to make the unit resistant to heat.

Flagstone Pattern "Carving" a design into concrete to a create a pattern.

Flashing Masonry flashing can be made of metal, rubberized asphalt sheet membranes, or other materials. It is used to control moisture in masonry walls either by keeping the top of a wall dry or by collecting water inside a wall so that it can be drained out through weep holes.

Floating The process of smoothing the surface of a pour with a float made of steel, aluminum, magnesium, or wood. This action drives large aggregate below the surface.

Footing Concrete footings are used to support garden walls of brick, block, or stone. Footings are also used for stairs and are usually located below the local frost line to avoid damage from frost heave.

Formwork The forms, or molds, that contain and shape wet concrete. Forms are usually built from lumber; plywood is used for curved sections.

Frost Heave Shifting or upheaval of the ground resulting from alternate freezing and thawing of water in the soil.

Frost Line The maximum depth to which soil freezes in the winter. The local building department can provide information on the frost line depth in your area.

Header The brick position in a wall in which the brick is rotated 90 degrees from the stretcher position so that the ending is facing out.

Hydration The process of cement particles chemically reacting with water. When this happens the concrete hardens into a durable material.

Isolation Joints Strips in formwork that separate new concrete from existing adjacent construction and other concrete slabs that might expand and contract differently or experience different soil settlement or other movement.

Mortar A mixture of cementitious materials, fine aggregate, and water. Mortar is used to bond bricks or blocks.

Nominal Dimensions The measured dimensions of a masonry unit plus one mortar joint.

Pitted Surface The process of scattering ordinary rock salt evenly over the concrete surface after troweling or brooming the concrete. This creates a pitted texture that resembles travertine marble.

Portland Cement A mixture of burned lime, iron, silica, and alumina. This mixture is put through a kiln and then ground into a fine powder and packaged for sale. The cement is the same color as the gray limestone quarried near Portland, England.

Prepackaged Concrete Mix A mix that combines cement, sand, and gravel in the correct proportions and requires only the addition of water to create fresh concrete.

Ready-Mix Concrete Wet concrete that is transported from a concrete supplier. The concrete is ready to pour.

Rebar Reinforcing bar (called rebar for short) is used for concrete that will carry a heavy load, such as footings, foundation walls, columns, and pilasters.

Reinforcing Mesh Steel wires woven or welded into a grid of 6- or 10-inch squares. The mesh is primarily used in flatwork, such as sidewalks, patios, and driveways.

Rowlock A brick laid on its face edge so that the end is visible in the wall.

Sailor A brick standing upright with the face positioned out.

Screeding Using a straight 2x4 moved from one end of a concrete pour to the other to strike off excess concrete.

Segregation A condition that results when the concrete is overworked—such as when trying to remove air bubbles—and the water separates and rises to the top.

Soap A brick that is halved in width.

Soldier A brick standing upright with the edge facing out.

Split A brick that is halved in height.

Steel Reinforcement Reinforcing mesh or rebar that is used to strengthen concrete.

Stretcher A brick that is laid lengthwise in the course.

Troweling Finishing the concrete after it has been screeded. This finishing step is for interior concrete applications and concrete without air-entrainment.

Wall Coping The final course of material or masonry units on a brick wall. Coping a brick wall ties the masonry units together and helps retard water penetration.

Weep Hole A hole in a retaining wall that allows water to seep through and thus relieve pressure against the wall.

Wythe The vertical section of a wall that is equal to the width of the masonry unit.

INDEX

METRIC CONVERSION CHARTS

Lumber

Sizes: Metric cross sections are so close to their nearest U.S. sizes, as noted at right, that for most purposes they may be considered equivalents.

Lengths: Metric lengths are based on a 300mm module, which is slightly shorter in length than an U.S. foot. It will, therefore, be important to check your requirements accurately to the nearest inch and consult the table below to find the metric length required.

Areas: The metric area is a square meter. Use the following conversion factor when converting from U.S. data: 100 sq. feet = 9.29 sq. meters.

Metric Lengths

Lengths Meters	Equivalent Feet and Inches
1.8m	5' 10⅞"
2.1m	6' 10⅝"
2.4m	7' 10½"
2.7m	8' 10¼"
3.0m	9' 10⅛"
3.3m	10' 9⅞"
3.6m	11' 9¾"
3.9m	12' 9½"
4.2m	13' 9⅜"
4.5m	14' 9⅓"
4.8m	15' 9"
5.1m	16' 8¾"
5.4m	17' 8⅝"
5.7m	18' 8⅜"
6.0m	19' 8¼"
6.3m	20' 8"
6.6m	21' 7⅞"
6.9m	22' 7⅝"
7.2m	23' 7½"
7.5m	24' 7¼"
7.8m	25' 7⅛"

Metric Sizes (Shown Before Nearest U.S. Equivalent)

Millimeters	Inches	Millimeters	Inches
16 x 75	⅝ x 3	44 x 150	1¾ x 6
16 x 100	⅝ x 4	44 x 175	1¾ x 7
16 x 125	⅝ x 5	44 x 200	1¾ x 8
16 x 150	⅝ x 6	44 x 225	1¾ x 9
19 x 75	¾ x 3	44 x 250	1¾ x 10
19 x 100	¾ x 4	44 x 300	1¾ x 12
19 x 125	¾ x 5	50 x 75	2 x 3
19 x 150	¾ x 6	50 x 100	2 x 4
22 x 75	⅞ x 3	50 x 125	2 x 5
22 x 100	⅞ x 4	50 x 150	2 x 6
22 x 125	⅞ x 5	50 x 175	2 x 7
22 x 150	⅞ x 6	50 x 200	2 x 8
25 x 75	1 x 3	50 x 225	2 x 9
25 x 100	1 x 4	50 x 250	2 x 10
25 x 125	1 x 5	50 x 300	2 x 12
25 x 150	1 x 6	63 x 100	2½ x 4
25 x 175	1 x 7	63 x 125	2½ x 5
25 x 200	1 x 8	63 x 150	2½ x 6
25 x 225	1 x 9	63 x 175	2½ x 7
25 x 250	1 x 10	63 x 200	2½ x 8
25 x 300	1 x 12	63 x 225	2½ x 9
32 x 75	1¼ x 3	75 x 100	3 x 4
32 x 100	1¼ x 4	75 x 125	3 x 5
32 x 125	1¼ x 5	75 x 150	3 x 6
32 x 150	1¼ x 6	75 x 175	3 x 7
32 x 175	1¼ x 7	75 x 200	3 x 8
32 x 200	1¼ x 8	75 x 225	3 x 9
32 x 225	1¼ x 9	75 x 250	3 x 10
32 x 250	1¼ x 10	75 x 300	3 x 12
32 x 300	1¼ x 12	100 x 100	4 x 4
38 x 75	1½ x 3	100 x 150	4 x 6
38 x 100	1½ x 4	100 x 200	4 x 8
38 x 125	1½ x 5	100 x 250	4 x 10
38 x 150	1½ x 6	100 x 300	4 x 12
38 x 175	1½ x 7	150 x 150	6 x 6
38 x 200	1½ x 8	150 x 200	6 x 8
38 x 225	1½ x 9	150 x 300	6 x 12
44 x 75	1¾ x 3	200 x 200	8 x 8
44 x 100	1¾ x 4	250 x 250	10 x 10
44 x 125	1¾ x 5	300 x 300	12 x 12

Dimensions are based on 1m = 3.28 feet, or 1 foot = 0.3048m

Dimensions are based on 1 inch = 25mm

For *all* of your home improvement and repair projects, look for these and other fine **Creative Homeowner Press books** at your local home center or bookstore...

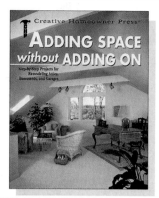

ADDING SPACE WITHOUT ADDING ON

Cramped for space? This book, which replaces our old book of the same title, shows you how to find space you may not know you had and convert it into useful living areas. 40 colorful photographs and 530 full-color drawings.

BOOK #: 277680   192pp., 8½"x10⅞"

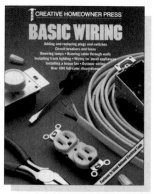

BASIC WIRING
(Third Edition, Conforms to latest National Electrical Code)

Included are 350 large, clear, full-color illustrations and no-nonsense step-by-step instructions. Shows how to replace receptacles and switches; repair a lamp; install ceiling and attic fans; and more.

BOOK #: 277048   160pp., 8½"x11"

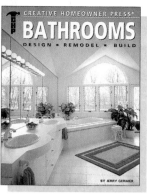

BATHROOMS

Shows how to plan, construct, and finish a bathroom. Remodel floors; rebuild walls and ceilings; and install windows, skylights and plumbing fixtures. Specific tools and materials are given for each project.

BOOK #: 277053   192pp., 8½"x10⅞"

DECKS: Plan, Design, Build

With this book, even the novice builder can build a deck that perfectly fits his yard. The step-by-step instructions lead the reader from laying out footings to adding railings. A bonus section includes three deck designs. 500 drawings and photographs.

BOOK #: 277180   176pp., 8½"x10⅞"

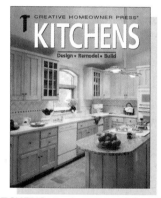

KITCHENS: Design, Remodel, Build

This is the reference book for modern kitchen design, with more than 100 full-color photos to help homeowners plan the layout. Step-by-step instructions illustrate basic plumbing and wiring techniques; how to finish walls and ceilings; and more.

BOOK #: 277065   192pp., 8½"x10⅞"

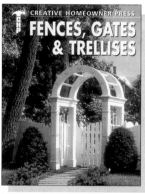

FENCES, GATES & TRELLISES

From wood to vinyl and chain link, this book tells you how to build fences and gates, as well as the trellises and arbors that complement them. Projects include privacy fences, picket fences, a grape arbor, a fan trellis, and more. 70 color photographs and 325 illustrations.

BOOK #: 277981   160pp., 8½"x10⅞"

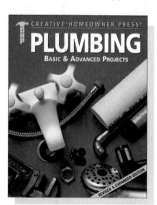

PLUMBING: Basic & Advanced Projects

Take the guesswork out of plumbing repair and installation for old and new systems. Projects include replacing faucets, unclogging drains, installing a tub, replacing a water heater, and much more. 500 illustrations and diagrams.

BOOK #: 277620   176pp., 8½"x10⅞"

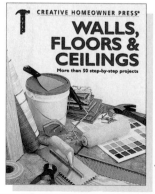

WALLS, FLOORS & CEILINGS

Here's the definitive guide to interiors. It shows you how to replace old surfaces with new professional-looking ones. Projects include installing molding, skylights, insulation, flooring, carpeting, and more. Over 500 color photographs and drawings.

BOOK #: 277697   176pp., 8½"x10⅞"

WORKING WITH TILE

Design and complete interior and exterior tile projects on walls, floors, countertops, patios, pools, and more. Included are ceramic, resilient, stone, and wood parquet tile. 425 color illustrations and over 80 photographs.

BOOK #: 277540   176 pp., 8½"x10⅞"